Forest Giants of the Pacific Coast

Forest Giants

▲ OF THE PACIFIC COAST ▲

Robert Van Pelt

GLOBAL FOREST SOCIETY

Vancouver and San Francisco

in association with

UNIVERSITY OF WASHINGTON PRESS

Seattle and London

GLOBAL FOREST

Pure Science.

www.GlobalForestScience.org

This publication was supported
by Global Forest Society grant #GF-18-2000-141.

Library of Congress Cataloging-in-Publication Data
Van Pelt, Robert.
Forest giants of the Pacific Coast / Robert Van Pelt.
p. cm.
Includes bibliographical references (p.).
ISBN 0-295-98140-7 (pbk.: alk. paper)
1. Conifers—Pacific Coast (U.S.) 2. Conifers—Pacific Coast (B.C.)
3. Trees—Pacific Coast (U.S.) 4. Trees—Pacific Coast (B.C.) I. Title

SD397.C7 V36 2001
585'.0979—dc21   2001027171

Canadian ISBN 0-9684143-1-1

The paper used in this publication is acid free and recycled from 10 percent
post-consumer and at least 50 percent pre-consumer waste. It meets the
minimum requirements of the American National Standard for Information
Sciences—Permanence of Paper for Printed Library Materials,
ANSI Z39.48–1984. ∞

Dedicated to Wendell Flint, whose lifetime passion

for measuring trees directly provided the template

and inspiration for this book

▲

Contents

Preface ix

Acknowledgments xi

Introduction xiii

The Trees 1

    Giant Sequoia 2

    Coast Redwood 16

    Western Red Cedar 30

    Douglas Fir 42

    Sitka Spruce 58

    Sugar Pine 72

    Incense Cedar 80

    Yellow Cedar 86

    Noble Fir 94

    Port Orford Cedar 100

    Jeffrey Pine 106

    Ponderosa Pine 114

    Western Hemlock 122

    California Red Fir 130

    California White Fir 136

    Western White Pine 142

    Western Larch 148

    Grand Fir 156

    Pacific Silver Fir 164

    Engelmann Spruce 172

Appendix 1: Tree Summaries—English Measures 180

Appendix 2: Tree Summaries—Metric Measures 186

Appendix 3: Predicting Volume from Diameter 192

Appendix 4: How to Nominate a Tree 193

Glossary 194

Sources of Information 197

Index 198

Preface

Going to the woods is going home....The sunshine falls in glory through the colossal spires and crowns, each a symbol of health and strength, the noble shafts faithfully upright like the pillars of temples, upholding a roof of infinite leafy interlacing arches and fretted skylights.
　　—*John Muir, 1901*

I have always loved the outdoors. When I was in the Boy Scouts in the 1960s, my troop went on many hikes through the glacial landscapes of the Midwest. One particular hike was during the winter, and our guide was showing us how to recognize different kinds of trees. I knew most of the common plants and trees by the shape of their leaves. But it was winter, and this man was showing us how to identify trees without using leaves: "This is a red oak—you can tell by the dark, furrowed bark and the flat, somewhat shiny ridges. This one here is a white oak—it has softer, flaky bark that's very light gray." I was amazed that he was able to do this without seeing the leaves, so I dug through the snow to the leaves on the ground to verify his identifications. This is my first recollection of what was to become a lifelong obsession.

Another lifelong interest of mine is facts and figures, and I nearly always have a copy of *The Guinness Book of World Records* and *The World Almanac* nearby to consult. Naturally (or inevitably), I eventually put the two passions together and began measuring trees. As a student at the University of Wisconsin in Madison, I came across a copy of *Wisconsin's Champion Trees,* by Bruce Allison, which lists trees both native and exotic to Wisconsin, along with the largest individuals for each species. Some of the trees were in Madison, so I began to search them out. These trees were special—older, bigger, more eccentric, and with a longer history, and hence more extreme—and they stood out from the average tree. I became involved in the state program for Wisconsin, and began to remeasure some of the trees that had not been measured for many years. Eventually I nominated a few newly discovered giant trees myself.

After visiting the great forests on the Pacific Coast, I knew that I had to move out West. During the summer of 1985, while working at Lake Crescent Lodge in Olympic National Park, I discovered that the national champion grand fir was located nearby. That was a treat. At that time Wisconsin had only one national champion, and most of their state champions were much smaller than the nation's largest. But in Washington, right under my nose was the world's largest known grand fir—nearly 7 feet in diameter and 231 feet tall. There was just one problem: when I finally located the tree, I was astounded to realize that it was dead, and, to judge by the amount of moss on the log, had been so for sev-

eral years. Since my information about the tree was obviously dated, I contacted the American Forestry Association (AFA), the keepers of the National Register of Big Trees, to see where the new champion was located. To their surprise (and mine), they did not know the tree was dead. That's how I found out that although Washington has some of the largest trees in the world, it was one of only two states that did not have a state coordinator to check the trees and attempt to keep the records current for the National Big Tree Program. Shortly thereafter I became Washington's state coordinator, bought some tree-measuring equipment, and nominated a grand fir I found elsewhere in the Olympics (officially, it was the same size as the dead champion). Since then I have nominated dozens of trees and, in 1987, I began the Washington State Big Tree Program. In 1985, when I first arrived, Washington had 13 national champion trees. Today, we have nearly 50!

My interest in writing this book has been building over several years. Part of the incentive was to refine the way record size is determined. The AFA (now AF—American Forests) uses a point system to determine how big a tree is; a tree gets AF "points" based on its girth, height, and crown diameter. This is a useful system for many species, but it has drawbacks. For instance, it is biased in favor of trees that have multiple trunks that diverge near the ground. Moreover, I have always been interested in how tall trees can get and what the tallest of each one of the various giant conifers in the Pacific Northwest was. The AF's National Register did not help me with this. With few exceptions, a national champion is not the tallest known individual tree. When I began the Washington State Program, I decided to use the point system, but also to list the dimensions of the tallest and stoutest known individuals, and often the tree with the widest crown. So for any given species several trees may be listed, whether for a particular dimension or for total points. Doing this requires a great deal more work, as two to three times as many trees are under consideration. As far as I know, Washington is still the only state that does this—although Randy Stoltmann adopted this method for his program in British Columbia.

During the late 1980s, Oregon and California had no state big tree program, and so I began measuring trees everywhere I went. Eventually I developed a database that today covers more than 5,000 trees up and down the West Coast. With the help of friends, books, articles, and maps, I began to track down trees that were what we call "West Coast champs"—meaning the largest known on the West Coast for their particular dimension. The national champions automatically became West Coast champions by having the most points, but for my list the other dimensions needed to be filled in. There were also thousands of introduced trees to measure—no easy task, as the West Coast has possibly the world's greatest collection of exotic trees. Since then, both Oregon and California have rejuvenated their state Big Tree programs and each has begun listings of both native and introduced trees that are now accessible online.

This book is not about the largest trees on the Pacific Coast, just the largest *known* trees on the Pacific Coast. That's a big difference, as for most of the species the largest trees are as yet undiscovered. The chance of finding a new record for giant sequoia is nearly zip, likewise for coast redwood, but for the remaining species chances of replacing at least one tree currently listed as a record are good. The purpose of a book like this is not only to educate, but to stimulate interest in increasing the range of our knowledge, incidentally making the next edition even more complete. Therefore, I invite readers to document new discoveries so that they may be measured and included in future editions. Measurement of volume is not easy, and requires the use of expensive equipment, but a measurement of height and DBH along with some photos is usually enough to get a good estimate of size. For scale, it helps if the photos include either the tape wrapped around the tree at the point of measurement, or people standing near the tree. A nomination form has been placed in Appendix 4 of this book. Simply photocopy the page, fill it out completely, and send it along with the photos to the address shown on the form.

Hunting for giant trees is a great adventure, and I have had many while working on this book. One of the most recent took place late in November 1999. Rand Knight and I went up to Vancouver, British Columbia, to measure a western hemlock and Pacific silver fir, both discovered earlier by Randy Stoltmann in the mountains behind the city. We were joined by Ralf Kelman and Shaun Muc, two of Canada's up-and-coming big-tree hunters. We found both trees (Norvan's Castle and the Cabin Lake Tree) and made it safely back to town, but both trips turned out to be near-disasters. On the first day, a 5- to 7-mile jaunt to the giant western hemlock named Norvan's Castle and back became a 13-mile hike, and I learned the British Columbia definition of "rough trail"—a course straight up a slope following a

series of tree trunks and branches tied with pink flagging tape. Finding the tree was glorious, but we ended up hiking out the last 4 miles of trail by moonlight.

I thought the second day would be easier. We were looking for a Pacific silver fir near the top of Black Mountain in Cypress Provincial Park. The tree was located on the far side of Cabin Lake, over a ridge and down a steep scree-slope. No problem. We found the tree, the Cabin Lake Fir (again a glorious specimen), measured and photographed it. Then the rain began. In order to avoid the small but steep cliff we had descended to get to the tree, we thought we'd skirt the ridge and come up on the other side of the lake. Somehow we ended up going down too far, skirted the wrong ridge, and ended up a mile or more from where we wanted to be. After wandering around the subalpine forests and meadows of Black Mountain for a couple of hours, we finally made it back to a trail. We arrived at the parking lot at dusk soaked, freezing, and exhausted—but victorious.

That night, at a brew pub, we sat and marveled at the weekend's adventures. Two fantastic discoveries, each located in amazing, seldom-visited old-growth forests, yet both practically visible from where we were sitting. I also reflected with amazement on all the trees I have visited in preparing for this book. From south-central California to Vancouver Island, and from the oceanfront to the Rocky Mountains, these 117 trees are some of the earth's greatest creations. I feel incredibly fortunate that the tools, the time, and the means to attempt and complete this project were available to me. Although I'm confident that my passion for trees comes through readily in these pages, I truly feel that working on this book was perhaps the greatest experience of my life.

The earliest ideas for this book began when I first made the drawings of some of Washington's big red cedars for the 1991 Washington Big Tree Program I was managing. The concept fully jelled in 1994, when my forestry professor purchased the Criterion 400 survey laser that we were going to use for mapping forest stands. This was the tool that allowed me to accurately measure wood volume, rather than just height and diameter. The rest just fell into place. I don't even want to think about the time and money it took to visit, measure, and photograph all of these trees—not to mention all of the dead-ends, runners-up, and not-quites. I do know that I drove over 200,000 miles and hiked in excess of 700 miles just for these 117 trees. And that I would do it all over again in a second, if given the chance. My hope is that as others read these pages new trees will be discovered, and that this work will continue. For the motto of every big-tree hunter is "There is always a bigger one out there somewhere." ▲

Acknowledgments

Even though my name stands alone on the cover, this book would not have been possible without the abundant support I have received over the years from a great many people. First and foremost I am indebted to my wife, Kathy, who shares a love for trees and has been supportive of this project since its inception. Jerry Franklin, professor, mentor, friend, and employer for more than the last decade, has understood my obsessions and allowed me some extra freedom (and equipment) to pursue them. Pat Soden at the University of Washington Press expressed interest in publishing this book back when it was still in the formulative stage, which helped me keep plodding along amid many other ongoing projects. Reese Halter with Global Forest is an enthusiastic supporter who has supplied not only incentive but financial support for the printing of the book. My tree-measuring friends up and down the coast, who have helped me with various parts of this book and with tree discoveries, include Bill Beese, Ron Brightman, Frank Callahan, Al Carder, Adrian Dorst, Maynard Drawson, Chris Earle, Wendell Flint, Ron Hildebrant, Arthur Lee Jacobson, Ralf Kelman, Rand Knight, Shaun Muc, Erik Piikilla, Steve Sillett, Randy Stoltmann, Michael Taylor, Dwight Willard, and Robert Wood. Randy Stoltmann was the big tree coordinator for British Columbia, and his untimely death in 1994 was devastating to the British Columbia Big Tree Program, the BC conservation movement, and to a great many friends. His love of trees and wild areas will forever be an inspiration for me. Thanks to Wendell Flint for pioneering many of the ideas about stem volume, and for doing the first comprehensive work on giant sequoias. His book, *To Find the Biggest Tree,* was one of the main inspirations for this book. Thanks to Al Carder, whose book *Forest Giants of the World: Past and Present,* a monumental effort that was decades in the making, is the most authoritative account of giant trees of the past. Thanks to Michael Taylor for his love of coast redwoods and his undying efforts to find the largest and tallest specimens. Thanks to Steve Sillett for his contagious enthusiasm, which has led to several new discoveries. He has helped document redwood sizes through direct measurement, aiding my ground-based measurements. Our friendship has grown tremendously and now we explore many new areas together. Thanks to Arthur Lee Jacobson, who has accompanied me on several big tree treks and has also been a great source of inspiration. Thanks to the many friends and associates who have accompanied me on my countless journeys hunting down these big trees. Abundant praise goes to Chris Earle, Steve Sillett, Arthur Lee Jacobson, and Kathy Van Pelt for plodding through and editing several versions of the text and greatly improving the book. Finally, thanks to those who have discovered new record trees over the years, and to all the people who love trees. ▲

Introduction

The Big Tree Program

The National Big Tree Program was started in 1940 when the popular conservation magazine *American Forests* asked "Where are the largest trees in the United States?" Early in 1941 they published a list of 77 trees, a start on the more than 800 tree species native to the United States. A few trees on this list are still the largest known: the western red cedar at Quinault Lake (the largest tree in Washington), the General Sherman giant sequoia in California (the world's largest tree), and the Founder's tree coast redwood (still among the tallest trees), among others. Also prominent on this first list is the name of Elers Koch, forest supervisor for the Lolo National Forest in Montana, who nominated six of the trees.

The Big Tree Program struck a chord somewhere in the American psyche, and by 1945 the second Big Tree list was published, including 228 trees. Whether it was the appeal to our love of superlatives, or something about Americans and their obsession with facts and figures (of which I am more guilty than most), the Big Tree Program now seems inevitable. This second list saw the first nominations by Oliver Matthews from Salem, Oregon, who in the next 20 years would become a Northwest legend among tree-lovers, and it also described the giant ponderosa pine at La Pine, Oregon, and the Queets Douglas fir.

The AF point system (described below) was adopted in the 1950s as a way to settle disputes about similar-sized trees. Since then, the Big Tree Program has gradually grown to include nearly every tree species native to or naturalized in the United States. Today, coordinators in each of the 50 states are responsible for checking and updating information on the national champions, and many of the states now have similar state programs. The national champions automatically become state champions, but the lists include all native species from that state. Many state programs, including mine in Washington, also maintain lists of the biggest introduced trees.

How Trees Are Measured

To quantify the actual size of a tree, foresters typically measure two things: the DBH (diameter at breast height), and the height of the tree. To measure the diameter directly, one would need a caliper or some other sort of device that could measure the distance between the two sides of a tree. This is rarely done, as such a technique becomes impractical with large trees. A simpler method is to assume that the tree is round and to measure the circumference of the tree with a tape measure, and divide that number by π to get the diameter. A third measure, crown spread, is also used by many big-tree programs to aid in comparing trees. We will now look at each of these measures in greater detail.

Diameter and Circumference

The diameter is the distance straight through the tree, which is usually estimated from the circumference, or the distance around the tree. If the circumference is assumed to be a circle, then the diameter is the circumference divided by π (3.14159).

Formula 1
Diameter = Circumference/π

The diameter is the simplest measurement and the one most people think of when contemplating a tree's size. Ideally, a tree should be measured at "breast height," which is 4.5 feet or 1.37 meters above average ground level (fig. 1). In most ecological or silvicultural applications, the tree is measured at 4.5 feet above the

4.5′

Figure 1. Measuring a tree on flat ground.

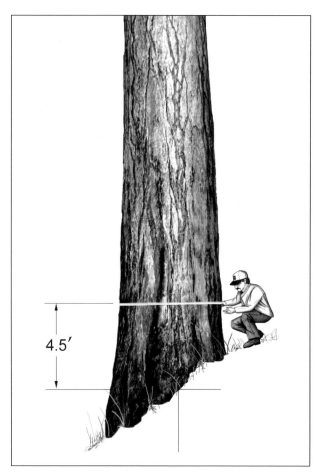

Figure 2. Measuring a tree on a slope.

Figure 3. Measuring on very steep slopes; here the tape is set at the lowest practical point.

high side of the ground. This is done to avoid adding the wider influence of the roots. Many of these scientific applications use this measure to make other predictions about the tree, such as its biomass or wood volume. These predictions become more accurate when the roots are not included. In the big-tree world, however, we are simply comparing trees, and for better or worse the measurement is made above the average ground level.

Problems arise with the phrase "above average ground level," as many trees grow on slopes or uneven ground. Here the rule is to measure 4.5 feet up from both the high side and the low side, find the midpoint between the two, and take the measurement there (fig. 2). If the slope is so steep that the average location is below the ground level on the high side—that is, if the distance between the two measurements is greater than 9 feet—then the lowest practical point is used (fig. 3). Further complications arise when branches obstruct or influence the appropriate location. A tree with low branches, for example an open-grown or city tree, might give a larger measure at 4.5 feet than at 3 feet. The

rule that the tree be measured at 4.5 feet or the smallest reading obtainable below that point ensures that the smallest possible reading is used (fig. 4). Burls or other irregularities often occur on the lower trunks of trees. If a burl occurs at the spot where the tape is to be stretched, then the tape is lifted to the spot just above the burl. For sprouting trees, such as hazels, which frequently have several stems at 4.5 feet, just the largest stem is measured (fig. 5).

Height

Tree heights are much more difficult to measure than diameters. Accurate measurements require the use of fairly sophisticated equipment, such as lasers. Hand-held devices such as clinometers also give good results when care is taken. To measure a tree's height requires finding a spot from which both the top and bottom of the tree are visible. Only three measurements are then needed to determine the height of a tree: (1) the angle to the top (a_t), (2) the angle to the bottom (a_b), and (3) the distance (d) to the tree. The height of the tree on flat ground is then:

Formula 2.
Height = $d \star [\tan (a_t) + \tan (a_b)]$

On slopes, because the distance measured to the tree is not the horizontal distance (d_h), a cosine correction must be added to compensate for the angle (fig. 6). The height formula then becomes:

Formula 3.
Height = $[\cos (a_b) \star d] \star [\tan (a_t) + \tan (a_b)]$

Leaning trees are especially difficult to measure. Almost every tree featured in this book leans to some extent, which means that the highest point of the tree is not directly over the trunk. If the tree is leaning only slightly, the problem can be avoided by measuring the height perpendicular to the lean. Strong leans, however, cannot be measured in this way, so the angle of the lean itself must be measured. The formulas presented above assume that the top of the tree is directly above the base of the tree. If they are used for a leaning tree, the tree will be calculated to be either taller or shorter than it really is, depending on the location of the observer. For example, consider the tree depicted in figure 7. If the observer were to measure the tree from location A and use Formula 2, the tree's height would be calculated to be equal to line segment Bc, a line much

Figure 4. Measuring low-branching trees.

shorter than the real height, segment Bb. Alternatively, an observer at D would see the top of the tree as being at a, and without correcting for the lean would thus calculate the tree's height as being greater than it really is, as segment Ba.

The way to accurately account for the lean is to measure two distances, one to the base of the tree (d_b), and the other to a point below the tip of the tree (d_t), at C. The formula for calculating the height of a leaning tree is then:

Formula 4.
Height = $[\cos (a_b)] \star \left([(d_b \star \tan (a_b)] + [(d_t \star \tan (a_t)]\right)$

Fortunately, modern laser-based height-measuring devices avoid all of these problems by taking the distance directly from the top of the tree. These devices have completely revolutionized the way we measure trees. It's now possible to obtain precise height measurements in a few seconds, so that dozens of trees can be measured in a single day. The big change that survey lasers have brought with respect to measuring tree height is in the calculation of distance to the tree. Because they take the distance directly off the location of the topmost sprig of the tree, they eliminate the need to find the spot on the ground directly below the top (which is almost never where the trunk is). Also eliminated is the time-consuming task of stretching a tape from the tree to the point where the top is visible, an adventure often involving dense brush, stream crossings, canyons, and other diversions.

Figure 5. Measuring multistemmed trees; only the largest stem is measured.

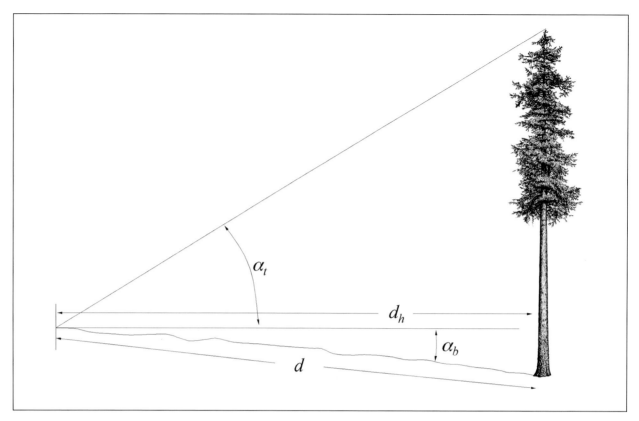

Figure 6. Measuring tree heights. Height measurement requires three variables: d_h, the distance to the tree; a_t, the angle to the top of the tree; and a_b, the angle to the bottom of the tree. If the horizontal distance cannot be measured directly, it must be calculated (see text).

To get a very accurate measurement on a 300-foot Douglas fir, for example, could take several hours using a tape and clinometer. The same tree can now be measured with greater accuracy in a few minutes. Just a few years ago I never left the house without a clinometer and tape—now I almost never carry them. In a comparison of methods, the Paradox Tree, one of the world's tallest trees, measured 366.7 feet tall by survey laser. The tree was later climbed and measured by direct tape-drop (the most accurate way) and found to be 367 feet, a difference well within the margin of error for either technique.

Crown Spread

This measurement gives the average spread of the tree's branches, and is the average between its widest spread and narrowest spread. This distance is found by standing under the farthest-reaching branch on one side and measuring to the farthest-reaching branch on the opposite side, and then repeating the measure with the narrowest spread (fig. 8). This is most easily done with an assistant and a 100-foot tape measure. The two measurements are then averaged, and so average crown spread is basically the average diameter of the crown of the tree. If the crown is assumed to be elliptical, the average crown spread can be obtained by measuring and averaging any two perpendicular crown diameters.

AF Points

When you are comparing a short, stout tree and a tall, thin tree, which is bigger? In 1951 the American Forestry Association (later changed to American Forests, or AF) came up with the point system to create a basis for resolving this sort of problem by quantitatively comparing differently shaped trees. A tree's AF point total is derived by adding together three measurements: (1) the trunk circumference, in inches at breast height; (2) the height of the tree, in feet; and (3) the average diameter of the live crown (with one point for every 4 feet of crown spread). Obtaining both the circumference and height measures requires knowing what the ground level is. For a tree growing on a lawn that's easy, but for forest giants on uneven ground it can be difficult. That difficulty explains why what may seem like a fairly easy determination is, in fact, the main source of discrepancy between tree measurements.

The Brummitt Fir, for example (the tallest known Douglas fir), is on a steep slope. The tree is 319 feet tall from the high point of the ground, yet it is 339 feet tall measured from the top to where the tree enters the

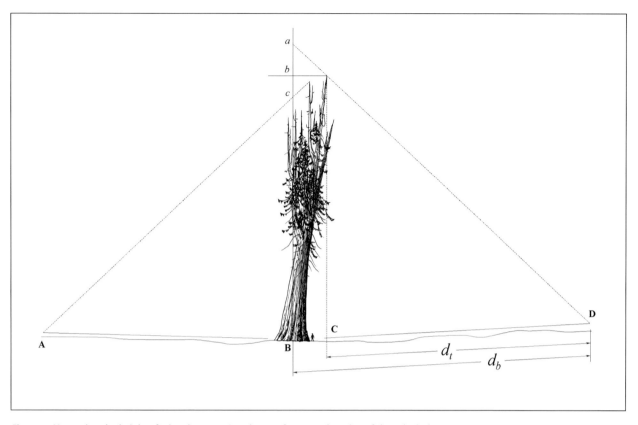

Figure 7. Measuring the height of a leaning tree. See the text for an explanation of the calculations.

ground on the downhill side: there is a full 20 feet between the high and low sides of the tree. Because this distance is greater than 9 feet (twice breast height) we cannot take a breast-height measurement. In cases like this, a ground-level measurement is made on the high point of ground (called the lowest practical point—see fig. 3 above). Because of this we take the average and call the tree 329 feet tall. My measurements will differ slightly from others in this regard, as many foresters and ecologists measure DBH from the high point of ground only.

By the nature of the way the AF point total is calculated, the point champion is often a tree that has a huge trunk but is not necessarily tall. Nearly everyone, though, admires especially tall trees, and while the tallest trees in the world are on the Pacific Coast, they are poorly represented in the National Register. When I began the Washington State Big Tree Program in 1987, I kept records not only on the point champion, but also on the trees with the thickest trunk, tallest height, and occasionally greatest crown spread. This means that several trees are listed for each species, but it also allows the interested person to know what the tallest known individual of a given species is. British Columbia adopted this protocol shortly after I did, and Great Britain has maintained a list of the tallest known specimens for decades.

How Wood Volume Is Measured

Another shortcoming of the AF point system shows up when really big trees are being measured. The criterion that trunk diameter must be measured at breast height is a necessary one for standardization, but it means measuring the roots of our largest trees. In addition, many trees have very different trunk shapes. Because of these circumstances, the stem volume of a tree is the best indicator of its size. Although this is a more difficult element to measure, it is a far more accurate one than DBH when you are trying to compare the sizes of really large trees. Our really large trees are conifers, most of which have a single stem. These trees have 85 to 95 percent of their wood volume in the stem, so that a relatively simple measurement of the stem volume should be sufficient to compare trees. Wendell Flint, in his book *To Find the Biggest Tree,* describes how a team of engineers used volume measurements to compare the present-day size of giant sequoias with measures dating back to the 1930s. Volume has also been the standard for comparing the giant kauri trees in New Zealand.

The volume measurements listed in this book were all collected by the author, using the Criterion 400 survey laser (Laser Technologies, Inc.). Survey lasers provide the extremely accurate distance measures that are essential in accurately mapping tree trunks or measuring

Figure 8. Measuring crown spread. The maximum reach of branches is measured and then averaged with the minimum branch spread to determine the average crown spread.

tree heights. Most lasers also have built-in clinometers, used to measure vertical angles, and these have revolutionized the way we measure tree heights. For volume, the distance and vertical angle information can be combined with a horizontal angle measurement to determine the diameter of a tree at any given height. Multiple diameter measurements are then used to construct a

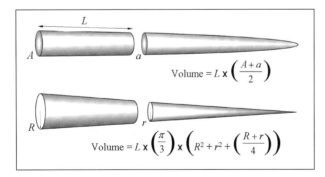

$$\text{Volume} = L \times \left(\frac{A+a}{2} \right)$$

$$\text{Volume} = L \times \left(\frac{\pi}{3} \right) \times \left(R^2 + r^2 + \left(\frac{R+r}{4} \right) \right)$$

Figure 9. The parabolic frustum (top) and the conic frustum (bottom) are the most common shapes of sections of tree trunks. Lower trunks are often parabolic, while a conic shape is more common within the crown of the tree. The A and a represent cross-sectional areas, the R and r are radii, and L represents the length of the segment. All units must be of the same type (all in feet, or all in meters).

series of parabolic or conic frustums (depending on the tree shape at that point—if enough data is collected, the two formulas are nearly identical), which are estimated individually and then combined to yield the volume of the stem. A frustum is a section of a conic shape where the two ends are perpendicular to the axis. The parabolic and conic frustum shapes and their associated formulas are shown in figure 9. For each tree, at least two locations were used to get clear shots of the tree trunk for measurements, and three or four locations are usually needed to get the required information. The aptly named Adventure Tree (a coast redwood) required seven separate station locations to collect the needed data.

Further complications arise when the stem is not circular in cross-section. Some of our simpler trees, such as the true firs or pines, have stems that are fairly circular in cross-section. Western red cedars and coast redwoods, however, are usually far from circular, a situation that calls for a great many more measurements and calculations in order to accurately assess the volume. The equation for an elliptical cross-section is often sufficient for use with many trees, but even this is too simple for some of the really gnarly trees.

Trees with reiterations (multiple tops) require separate measurements on each reiteration. In this book, all reiterated trunks are used in volume calculations, but no branches are used. This distinction may seem an arbitrary one to some, but I feel this method best represents tree size for the great variety of trees that are being compared. For many species, measuring only the main stem would be sufficient and adding the reiterations would not change things much. Several species, however, nearly always have multiple reiterations when they reach great size—western red cedars being the best example. Many of these trees have several trunks of roughly equal size, as with the Kalaloch Cedar. Any arbitrary judgment as to which one of these trunks is the main trunk would clearly misrepresent the size of this tree.

The most difficult part about measuring volume is measuring the base of the tree. The base of the tree is not only concave, it is usually not on level ground, and can also contain bulging roots. Nevertheless the base can contain a substantial fraction of the total volume. Wendell Flint pioneered the techniques of accurately measuring trees for volume, and he carefully maps out the base of each tree with a transit to measure its irregular "footprint." He then calculates the volume of the part of the tree between the high and low points of ground by taking into account the area of the footprint, the vertical distance between high and low sides of the tree base, and the ground perimeter. I have adopted a variation of this method and was kindly allowed to use his footprint maps for some of the giant sequoias in developing my own volumes for these trees.

Tree Drawings

Painting and drawing have, from time to time, occupied much of my life. Once I became interested in trees my artistic passions met my scientific ones, and the drawings in this book are the result. Combining art and science has long been a goal in my life and I take pride in creating botanically accurate drawings. My first "modern" tree drawings, which accurately depicted specific trees rather than generalized ones, were of the western red cedar champions I created for the 1991 edition of the book I prepared for the Washington Big Tree Program. These illustrated the great differences between the trees, despite the fact that their dimensions and point totals were very similar. Because trees usually grow in forests, it is often not possible to take a clear photo of the individual tree. Thus the drawings allow people to see the tree—the whole tree—as they never can in person. After that book was released, many of the comments I received were about the drawings. I added still more drawings in *Champion Trees of Washington State,* published by the University of Washington Press, and I was overjoyed when they showed an interest in the book you are now holding.

I call the drawings "architecturally correct" because I use laser measurements to ensure proper proportions. The laser is used not only to collect data on the size of the trunk and the height of the tree, but also for the heights of various branches, reiterations, breaks, kinks, or any other eccentricity—details that will aid me in doing an accurate drawing. Sketches are made in the field and photographs are used to capture the specifics of each tree. In dense forests, a dozen or more photos are needed to capture all parts of the tree, while trees in clearcuts require very few. The drawings are obviously of only one view. Sometimes this view is chosen out of necessity, as the trees are often located in dense forests where a single view is all I can clearly see. If there was a choice, however, I tried to pick a view that shows some of the tree's unique character. Still, a two-dimensional portrayal of these magnificent trees is often an injustice: their supreme character must be fully appreciated first-hand. The drawings may also have a different aspect even for those trees that allow a clear view of the entire stem, such as the General Sherman or the General Grant. This is because when you are at the tree, you are looking up at it, and in both these cases branches coming out toward you appear taller than their true tops, even though they are not. By correcting for this, the drawings are more accurate than even a photograph would be—in terms of proportions.

Distribution Maps

For each of the 20 species featured in this book I have provided a map depicting its geographical distribution. Maps showing the major forest types, distribution of Pacific rain forest, and the scope of the book—the six forest types of the Pacific Coast—have also been provided. These maps were all produced by the author and are being published here for the first time. They were generated using a great number and variety of source materials, both digital and printed. These were then combined in a geographic information system to show the individual coverages for each species, as well as to create the backgrounds and forest-type maps. Much of the detail contained in these maps cannot be shown at the scale of this book, as they are perhaps the most detailed species distribution maps ever produced for these tree species.

The maps are intended to show the distribution of each species relative to the Pacific Coast. On each map the featured trees of this book are shown in relation to the overall range of the species and to the Pacific Coast in general. On each species map, small stars represent the locations of the featured trees, and on the forest-type map in figure 10, all 117 tree locations are shown.

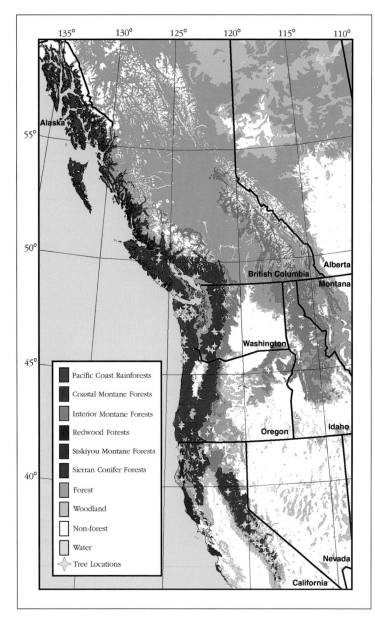

Figure 10. The six major productive forest zones of the Pacific Coast, showing locations of the 117 trees featured in this book.

Forests of the Pacific Coast

The forests of the Pacific Coast are among the tallest and densest forests on earth. What I here call Pacific Coast forests represent three major biomes, those of the Pacific Northwest, the Northern Rocky Mountains, and the Sierra Nevada. While they differ in many aspects of climate and species composition, they share many similarities. Obviously, the Northern Rockies are not on the coast, but the vegetation there is strongly influenced by coastal weather patterns. This factor allows many of our coastal tree species to thrive there, and a few of them reach their largest size in this inland forest zone. Within these major biomes, by ignoring the

less-productive forests near both upper and lower timberlines, I have delineated six major forest types: Pacific Coast Rain Forests, Redwood Forests, Coastal Montane Forests, Interior Montane Forests, Siskiyou Montane Forests, and Sierran Conifer Forests. These six, along with the 117 featured trees, are depicted in figure 10.

The entire Pacific Coast of North America has a winter wet–summer dry environment. Even the rain forests of the Olympic Mountains and Vancouver Island have a significant dry season during the summer. Worldwide, the temperate rain forests of the west coast of North America are well known, although definitions of what exactly constitutes a temperate rain forest vary—one strictly based on precipitation is shown in figure 11. Much of the area depicted gets the bulk of its precipitation in the form of snow, making it functionally different than areas at lower elevations. The very mild winter temperatures throughout the region extend the growing season past what many temperate areas throughout the world receive; indeed, the area is dominated by conifers partly because they are able to continue photosynthesis through the winter months. While in most temperate forests throughout the world (as in those of eastern Asia, eastern North America, and Europe) evergreen conifers assume a successional role or are restricted to severe habitats, the reverse is true along the Pacific Coast. Here evergreen conifers completely dominate the main upland forest, with nearly all forest area covered by conifers; the deciduous broadleaf trees are the ones restricted to early successional roles (alders, cottonwoods, willows) or stressed habitats (oaks).

There are several exceptions to this basic rule. In the Siskiyou and Klamath Mountains of southwestern Oregon and northwestern California, several broadleaf evergreen trees often make up a significant part of the forest. Tanoak *(Lithocarpus densiflorus),* Pacific madrona *(Arbutus menziesii),* and golden chinkapin *(Chrysolepis chrysophylla)* are the primary broadleaf evergreens that assume this role. Also, in the interior forests of eastern Washington, northeastern Oregon, northern Idaho, and northwestern Montana, one of the primary forest trees, although a conifer, is deciduous. This is the western larch. On those crisp October days when the larch needles have turned a brilliant gold, I am thankful that we have this additional feature in our forests.

Pacific Coast Rain Forests

Perhaps the most famous of our western forest types is the temperate rain forest. These forests support huge, moss-covered trees that were formerly seen as a vast timber reserve. Now, reduced by logging to a few scattered remnants, they have become famous as a conservation battleground. The dominant trees in this forest type are Sitka spruce, western red cedar, and western hemlock. While Douglas fir is absent or uncommon throughout much of the rain forest, the few that are present can grow to gargantuan proportions. Nearly all of the largest Douglas firs now known are from coastal rain forests. Fire is a stranger to these forests, leaving wind and fungi as the primary causes of death among our old rain-forest trees. Trees like western hemlock have wood that is not adapted to resist decay and thus this species does not attain great size or age in this forest. Western red cedars, however, are quite resistant to both wind and fungi, and along the coast grow to proportions unimaginable to those familiar with this tree in the Cascades or northern Rocky Mountains. Sitka spruce, while only slightly more resistant to disturbance and decay than western hemlock, can grow at phenomenal rates for five centuries or more, which is more than enough to reach record proportions.

Trees in the Pacific Coast Rain Forests can support literally tons of *epiphytes* (plants growing on trees). These include mosses, lichens, ferns, shrubs, and even trees. Several ancient red cedars support epiphytic hemlocks that would be reckoned as impressive trees in the forests of Europe or the eastern United States. These epiphytic plants and trees are not parasitic in any way. They simply use the gnarly red cedar wood as a place to grow. There is ample moisture and organic matter to support a great many plants, and trees that do this are appropriately termed "hanging garden trees."

Most of the rain-forest trees listed in this book are located on the Olympic Peninsula or Vancouver Island. The remoteness of both areas delayed significant logging pressures until the latter part of the twentieth century, and thus many ancient forests in the area now have some protection. As I write this, though, virgin valleys of ancient rain forest on Vancouver Island are being logged. While the press is focused on a few, high-profile valleys, neighboring ones of similar character are being cut. Some of these forests probably contain trees comparable in size and character to those described in this book. Nearly all of the coastal rain forests of Oregon have been logged or burned at least once, and this is the main reason why only three trees from the Oregon coast make it into this book. Past logging has also razed nearly all the ancient forests of the Willapa Hills of southwestern Washington, an area that has only two trees represented

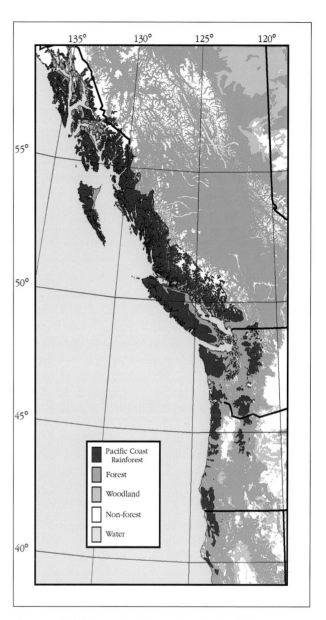

Figure 11. Distribution of rain forests along the Pacific Coast.

here. These two areas support some of the most productive forest lands in North America, so it is no wonder that they have been heavily logged. It is unfortunate, however, that these two areas have very little public land. Had there been more, the inventory of this book would be much different, as a good deal of evidence remains to show that larger trees than those listed here (particularly Sitka spruce and Douglas fir) once stood in these places.

Redwood Forests

Because the northern range of coast redwood is within a rain-forest environment, Redwood Forests partly overlap with Pacific Coast Rain Forests. The forests of Jedediah Smith and Prairie Creek Redwood State Parks, and the nearby Redwood National Park, receive from 80 to 120 inches of annual precipitation, and thus are rain forests. These forests also have a mixture of western hemlock and Sitka spruce, species characteristic of rain forests to the north. The competition supplied by the lofty redwoods must offer a strong incentive to grow tall, as we have measured several Douglas firs and Sitka spruces in these areas over 300 feet tall among the redwoods. Even the much smaller western hemlock has been measured at over 250 feet here—the tallest currently known for the species. The forest that grows along Prairie Creek, north of Orick, California, is the only place on earth known to me where three species that reach 300 feet tall grow side-by-side.

South of Eureka the redwood forests are considerably drier and lose much of the lush, drippy character of the northern forests. The alluvial forests of Humboldt Redwoods State Park and the adjacent Avenue of the Giants have canopies that are often dominated by a single species—coast redwood. Even the understories of these forests can be quite simple, dominated almost entirely by wood sorrel *(Oxalis oregana)*, and sword fern *(Polystichum munitum)*. The result is a fantasy scene of dense, giant columns of coast redwood above a green carpet of sorrel and fern. Many of our images of the cathedral groves of coast redwoods come from these or similar areas. In these drier redwood forests, the giant trees are restricted to alluvial habitats where an easily accessible water supply provides a haven from the long summer drought. The alluvial forests of Humboldt Redwoods State Park and similar areas have more live tree biomass per acre than any other place on earth. Farther from the coast and thus better protected from winter storm winds, these southern, inland forests are where the tallest trees are. Of the 26 tallest known trees, 22 are found on well-watered alluvial sites south of Eureka—only four are found in the rain forests to the north.

Conversely, all but one of the largest coast redwoods listed in this book are from the northern, rainforest section of the coast redwood belt. Even in these areas there is a strong summer drought, and most of the ancient ones have charcoal on their bark indicating former bouts with fire. Wind also plays an important role in these coastal rain forests. Very few of the old trees have their original tops. The coast redwood is exceptionally gifted in being able to resprout new foliage after damage, with the result that most of the giants have multiple tops. These tops give evidence of the trees' ability to rebuild new crowns after the original ones have snapped off, and of surviving countless fires and winter storms over the millennia.

Coastal Montane Forests

Douglas fir reigns in the mountain forests of the Pacific Northwest. Most of the commercial timberland in western Washington and Oregon is from this zone, so few big trees remain and the landscape now consists of Douglas fir plantations. Some of the early cutover areas are already growing their third rotation of trees. As a consequence, only one of the Douglas firs listed in this book is located in this zone. Historically, many of the largest Douglas firs known were recorded from this zone. Several trees 15 to 18 feet in diameter were recorded from the Cascades and lower mainland of British Columbia, and still others were recorded in the 380- to 415-foot-tall range. These trees grew taller than any living tree today.

While many sections of the Cascade forests are as wet as the coastal rain forests, their higher elevation causes much cooler summer temperatures, and much of the precipitation falls in the form of snow, producing a distinct species composition. Drought is less of a factor than at lower elevations, and some of these areas may go 2,000 to 4,000 years without a fire. These are the forests of Pacific silver fir, western and mountain hemlock, and yellow cedar that occur at mid elevations on the western slopes of the Olympics, North Cascades, Vancouver Island, and the adjacent mainland. In these forests, these species achieve their maximum ages, each having trees with recorded ages close to 1,000 years, and yellow cedar close to 2,000. A western hemlock from British Columbia was recently found to have reached the ripe old age of 1,238. Coastal Montane Forests are also where these trees reach their largest sizes. While the floodplain forests grow western hemlock to exceptional heights, the trees in the warmer lowlands are attacked by decay and do not live more than a few hundred years. The upper montane forests allow the trees to grow three or four times as long. Though not as tall, they achieve far greater wood volume.

Interior Montane Forests

A part of the interior west known as the Inland Empire, or the Northern Rocky Mountain region, is not on the coast, but is strongly influenced by storms that pass through the Pacific Northwest. This area includes eastern Washington, northeastern Oregon, northern Idaho, western Montana, and southeastern British Columbia. The Inland Empire contains some very productive forests and is the range of the great western white pine and western larch forests that helped fuel America's western expansion over the last 150 years. While drier than the coastal forests, the region is still moist enough to support western red cedar and western hemlock in places as far east as Glacier National Park in northern Montana. This area provided a transitional link for the timber industry between the forests of the Great Lakes and the forests of western Washington and Oregon. During the relatively brief period of the 1880s and '90s, the Inland Empire was the major wood producer for this country.

Many of the species found here (Douglas fir, western hemlock, western red cedar, grand fir) are also found in more coastal environments, where they grow to greater sizes. Others, like Engelmann spruce, are found throughout the Rocky Mountains but grow to their largest size here. Western larch grows only here. Western white pine grows throughout the coastal forests and Sierras but achieves its largest size here.

Siskiyou Montane Forests

The cross range that connects the Cascade Mountains to the north, the Sierras to the south, and the Coast Ranges to the west is the Siskiyou/Klamath Mountain complex. This area of ancient and complex geology is at the boundary of several biomes, and the result is very high species diversity with a high endemic population (species found only there), known to locals as the "Klamath Knot." Most of the Pacific Northwest species are found here, and many of them end their range here as small, isolated populations. Most sierran tree species are also found here. A single township in the middle of this notable jumble contains 21 species of native conifers. With the possible exception of New Caledonia (41 species of native conifer on a 200-mile-long island), this is, to my knowledge, the only place on earth that can make such a claim.

The Knot includes a wide range of climates and environments. Rain forests occur at the westernmost part of the range, where Kelsey Peak receives 180 inches of annual precipitation, while the eastern end is quite arid—Ashland receives only 19 inches per year. The unusual abundance of ultramafic rock outcrops (rocks with a high concentration of heavy metals) further adds strangeness and diversity to the plant communities.

Because the mountains here are lower than the Sierras, wild areas such as the Trinity Alps Wilderness or the Marble Mountains Wilderness include productive, mixed-conifer forests. This is in stark contrast to the sierran wilderness areas, which tend to occur in alpine or subalpine environments. Siskiyou species in this book include the Port Orford cedar, an endemic native, while the more widespread incense cedar achieves its greatest development here. Several other sierran species achieve dimensions in the Siskiyou/ Klamath complex that are comparable to their brethren in the Sierras.

Sierran Conifer Forests

The Sierras have some of the most beautiful forests on earth. The great forests of Yosemite, Sequoia/Kings Canyon, and Calaveras fall within this truly spectacular mountain range that John Muir aptly called the Range of Light. The Sierras are the destination of millions, who are drawn by the great expanses of granite and high waterfalls of Yosemite and other nearby areas. In terms of forests, the Sierras are most famous for their 66 groves of giant sequoia, but they also contain the world's finest pine forest. The 3 largest of the world's 112 pine species are native to the Sierras, and their largest individuals are found there. The Sierras are far enough south that they experience two timberlines (an upper and a lower). The lower timberline occurs where the forests of the mountains give way to nonforest vegetation as one descends from the mountains. This descent brings you into grasslands and woodlands on the west side, steppe on the north and northeast sides, desert to the southeast, and chaparral to the south and southwest.

The main forested belt of the Sierra occurs at an elevation between about 3,000 and 8,000 feet, and is frequently divided into three zones. The lowest of these, the Lower Transition Forest, is dominated by ponderosa pine and incense cedar, with Douglas fir common in the northern half of the Sierra. This zone is very hot and often contains a large component of hardwood shrubs and trees. The next zone up is the major forested belt of the Sierras, the Mixed Conifer zone. The major components of this zone are sugar pine and California white fir, although most of the trees present in either the zone below or above are commonly found here as well. Finally, the Upper Montane zone is dominated by California red fir, either alone or with western white pine, Jeffrey pine, and/or lodgepole pine.

While many of the mixed-conifer forests have been logged (at least partially), vast old-growth pine forests may still be found in the Yosemite, Calaveras, and Sequoia/Kings Canyon parks. In fact, over half of the 32 trees featured from the Sierras are from either Yosemite National Park (11 trees) or Sequoia/Kings Canyon National Park (6 trees).

Scope of Book

Although several broadleaf trees are locally important components of Pacific Coast forests, none attain the giant dimensions of the big conifers. And even though some oaks, maples, and cottonwoods can reach huge sizes, such big trees are usually in rural or even urban settings. Most of our national champion trees of these "forest" species are not located in forests. Partly because of this difference, I have limited the trees covered in this

book to the 20 largest conifer species found in our western forests. It is these species that really separate the
Pacific Coast forests from all others. However, a twen-
ty-first species was nearly included in this book—
mountain hemlock (*Tsuga mertensiana*). While mountain
hemlock forms an important part of the forests in the
Olympic and Vancouver Island rain forests, many of the
giants of this species occur farther south into Oregon
and California, where the species is largely subalpine,
growing in open parkland environments rather than
true forests. This growth pattern was the reason I decided to leave it out of the book.

For reasons already mentioned, I have problems
with the thought of one "champion" for each species,
and have therefore decided to list several trees for each
species. This will give the reader a good representation
of what constitutes a giant for that particular species, and
some of these may be easier to see or perhaps more
interesting than the champion. For the Big Five species
(giant sequoia, coast redwood, western red cedar,
Douglas fir, and Sitka spruce—all of which reach sizes
greater than 10,000 cubic feet) more specimens are
illustrated than for the other 15. With the giant kauri
from New Zealand the only proven exception, these are
the five largest species of trees in the world. Altogether,
this book describes 117 individuals from 20 species,
truly the elite from the greatest forests on earth. ▲

The Trees

▲

GIANT SEQUOIA *Sequoiadendron giganteum*

Walk in the sequoia woods at any time of year and you will say they are the most beautiful and majestic on earth.
—John Muir, 1878

Giant sequoias are the world's largest trees. With breast height diameters of up to 29 feet and heights to 307 feet, they reign supreme. They are found in the Sierra Nevada Mountains of California in 66 groves that range in size from six trees in the Placer County Grove to 5,000 acres of trees in the Mountain Home Grove. Most groves are located in or around the Sequoia and Kings Canyon National Parks, but a few groves are fur-

ther north beyond Yosemite National Park. All of the largest sequoias are south of the Kings River, although two very large trees were cut from the North Calaveras Grove, one of the northernmost groves, for exhibitions during the 1850s.

Research on the wood volume of giant sequoias began long ago. While there is still a remote possibility of finding a really large sequoia, this species has been very thoroughly explored. The credit for our current state of knowledge on large sequoias goes to Wendell Flint, author of *To Find the Biggest Tree*. Flint is a retired mathematics teacher who has spent much of the last 50 years researching and accurately measuring the volumes of the largest giant sequoias. His book summarizes both past and current records of giant sequoia sizes. Giant sequoia is unusual in that there has been much less logging pressure on this species than on most of the other species included in this book.

Early foresters did not have a standard technique for measuring these giants, and wild exaggerations appeared in nineteenth-century literature. Rivalries between local

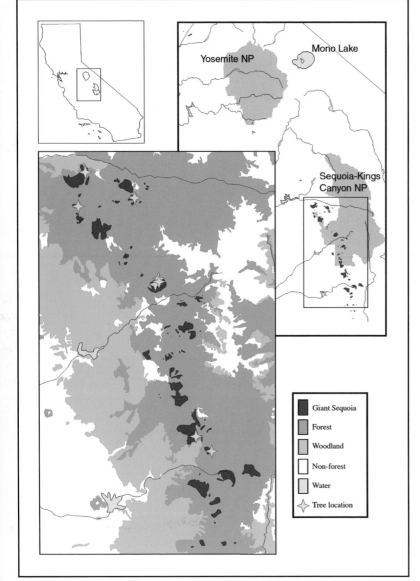

Giant Sequoia
Forest
Woodland
Non-forest
Water
Tree location

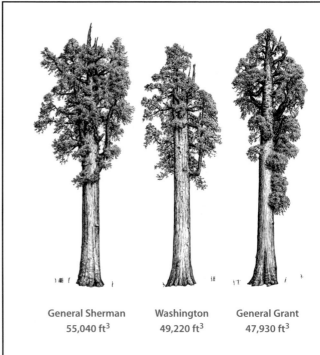

General Sherman	Washington	General Grant
55,040 ft^3	49,220 ft^3	47,930 ft^3

The narrow spires of young sequoias stand in stark contrast to the complex, broccoli-like crowns of old trees. These are growing among the huge stumps of the logged-over Converse Basin.

surveyor J. W. Jourdan was assembled to settle the dispute. Two trees from each county were selected for the contest. Fresno County nominated the General Grant, the namesake tree of General Grant National Park (changed to Kings Canyon National Park in 1921), and the Boole, the largest remaining tree in the heavily logged Converse Basin. Tulare County nominated the General Sherman from Giant Forest, and the Hart, a large tree in the Redwood Mountain Grove, which was then being considered for inclusion in the national park.

By 1931 the Jourdan team had made detailed measurements on the four trees. Their results, ranked in order of size, were: (1) General Sherman, (2) General Grant, (3) Boole, and (4) Hart. This much-publicized event cooled the fires to find big trees; the care and accuracy of the team's measurements were evidently too much to argue with. What is surprising now is that the choice of trees was not called into question for decades, as Giant Forest contains many giant trees, including several rivals to the two Generals that were measured. Today, we know that the Hart Tree, for example, barely makes a list of the top 20 largest sequoias. Incidentally, Flint's research indicates that only two historic trees might have been larger than the General Sherman. The Burnt Monarch in Big Stump Grove had a much larger base and could easily have been larger, and the Washington Tree might also have been larger before its top blew out. ▲

communities often revolved around their claims to the largest tree. In the 1920s, competition heated to a boiling point between the Chambers of Commerce of Tulare and Fresno Counties, and a team of engineers headed by

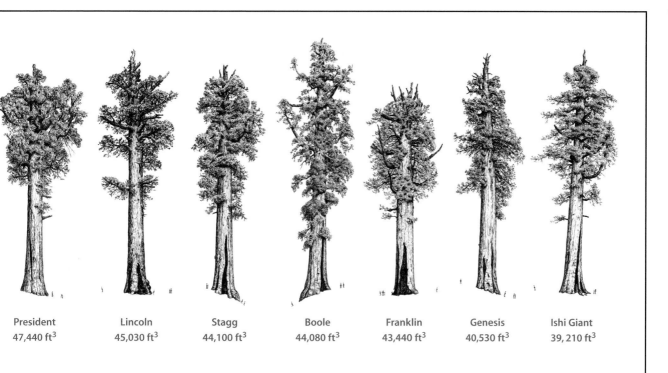

President 47,440 ft³ Lincoln 45,030 ft³ Stagg 44,100 ft³ Boole 44,080 ft³ Franklin 43,440 ft³ Genesis 40,530 ft³ Ishi Giant 39,210 ft³

General Sherman

Volume	55,040 ft³	1,489 m³
DBH	27.1 ft	825 cm
Height	274 ft	83.5 m
AF Points	1,321	

Giant sequoias were discovered right before the Civil War and their native range was extensively explored during and after the war, hence the preponderance of Civil War heroes in the naming of these trees (at least three trees were named after Robert E. Lee). The fact that the world's largest tree is named after a brutally savage yet brilliant general does not sit well with many people. The General Sherman was first noted and named in 1879 by James Wolverton. In the last part of the nineteenth century a group of socialists calling themselves the Kaweah Colony lived in the area and renamed the tree the Karl Marx. Upon formation of Sequoia National Park, the name General Sherman was restored and has remained. After the Jourdan team of engineers established in 1931 that the Sherman was the largest tree, the tree's fame was assured. From time to time, and even as recently as 1975, other trees have been called up to challenge the Sherman, but the General has never been outranked.

The General Sherman's DBH is not the largest (27 feet; at least five trees are larger), nor is it (at 274 feet) the tallest—more than a dozen trees are over 280 feet and at least two are over 300 feet. What

is remarkable about this tree is how it keeps its diameter. This is the world's only tree with a diameter greater than 20 feet at 35 feet off the ground. At 150 feet it is still nearly 16 feet thick. It is one of the most heavily visited trees in the world, towering with silent grace over throngs of awestruck tourists. Using the AF system, the tree is outpointed by four other giant sequoias; however, in this case the point system has yielded to accurate volume measurements.

To stand next to this tree and gaze at the debris on the ground at its base is to feel truly small. The debris includes the remnants of 3- to 6-foot diameter branches that broke off over the centuries. The appearance of the tree does not appreciably change when these breaks happen, as it has dozens of these enormous limbs. The sheer volume of branches and reiterations that this tree possesses is also very impressive when compared to its brethren. The President comes closest to

This view is from the early twentieth century, before any "official" measurements had been made. At the point shown at the top of the photo, the trunk is still nearly 18 feet thick.
(Photo courtesy U.S. National Archives)

having the size of crown and branches of the Sherman, but even that is a stretch. I include four reiterations in my volume calculation for the tree. Two of these are easily visible from the main views of the Sherman, and are equal to full-sized trees in their own right. The other two are closer to the trunk near the top of the tree, and are assuming the role of "leader" in place of the dead top. My drawing includes another reiteration (toward the lower right), which was there for most of this century until the 1970s, when it broke off in a winter storm. Amazingly, even though this trunk was over 4 feet thick and 140 feet tall, the classic view of the Sherman did not change much since an even larger trunk with a similar shape was hiding right behind it.

The main trunk has 52,599 cubic feet of wood, which is slightly more than the 50,100 measured in 1931. The difference could be explained by differences in measurement techniques and technological advances, but I consider the increase in volume real change. Consider that the surface area of the Sherman, which roughly corresponds to the amount of cambium in the tree (the living part of the tree that makes wood), is in excess of 17,000 square feet. Add to this, say, about a thirty-second of an inch of growth of wood a year, and in 70 years that adds up to over 3,000 additional cubic feet of wood. People don't realize it, probably because they cannot see the change, but these huge trees, just because of their sheer size, are among the fastest growing things on earth. ▲

The earth's largest living thing and the undisputed King of Trees, the General Sherman is estimated to weigh nearly ten times as much as the heaviest whale.

GENERAL SHERMAN

Washington

The Washington is a massive yet unassuming tree. Located in Sequoia National Park's Giant Forest along a spur trail, this is also a seldom-visited tree. On all of the occasions I have walked out to see this tree, which are many, I have yet to encounter a single person. Yet this tree has a trunk that is a near twin to the General Sherman. While the General Sherman and General Grant have large enclosures to protect the root systems from trampling, the lonely Washington is a giant that can be seen up close. The massiveness of the trunk is hard to capture in words or even photos—firsthand experience is required. When I take people to this tree, I make sure they walk all the way around. The view from opposite sides is so different not just because the wall of the trunk blocks one's field of view, but because of the differing appearance of the trunk itself.

What is odd is that while this tree is second in size after Sherman, it was never claimed to be the largest, as many other giants were. The Grant, Lincoln, President, Boole, Garfield, and the Bull Buck have all been declared the largest at one time or another over the past 14 decades. Here is a tree larger than all of those contenders, seemingly content in quietly knowing the truth. Perhaps

Volume	49,220 ft³	1,394 m³
DBH	27.9 ft	851 cm
Height	254 ft	77.4 m
AF Points	1,327	

the odd crown—three reiterated trunks emerge from the blasted-out top 185 feet above the ground—has contributed to this underestimation. In fact, the Washington is the only living tree that might have at one time been larger than the General Sherman, since its trunk is larger right below the break. In any case, today's upper crown is much smaller than one would expect given the trunk dimensions. Was that the reason for the oversight? Perhaps—yet 93 percent of the volume of this tree lies below the break, a point many people tend to overlook about these giant trees.

According to Wendell Flint, the tree also had a crown fire after the break, and the open trunk became hollowed into a large cave. Knowing this, Steve Sillett led an IMAX crew up the Washington for a film they were shooting on California. Later, he returned

The giant "arm" of the Washington is as big as many of the individual trees in this forest, yet is dwarfed by the massive trunk, still 17 feet thick at the point where the arm branches off.

and took detailed measurements of the trunk, the reiterated crown, and "The Pit," as they called it. I used these detailed measurements to calculate the upper trunk volume of the tree. The Pit is more than 100 feet deep, ending just 76 feet above the ground in a damp, musty chamber. What is unusual is that this huge cavern was apparently not completely created by fire, as there is little evidence of fire in the bottom—fungal decay seems the main culprit. Huge mycelial mats line parts of the chamber, indicating healthy fungal growth. This is surprising, as giant sequoias are one of the few trees that are rarely (and even then slowly) attacked by decay fungi.

Calculating the wood volume for the top of the main trunk was quite a challenge. The opening of The Pit is not flat-topped, and the highest piece of wood sticking up above the chamber at 226 feet gives no indication that the trunk at this point was anything but a round, normally formed trunk. The highest point at which a full trunk diameter can be measured is at 192 feet, where the tree is still an impressive 12.5 feet thick. My volume numbers are based on the part of the trunk that is still actually there, but it is easy to imagine a large, normally formed top above this point centuries ago—a time when this tree may very well have been the world's largest. ▲

The tape wrapped around the Washington Tree is at 7'4" above average ground level, and indicates that the circumference is 82'2".

General Grant

By presidential decree officially declared the National Christmas Tree in 1965, the General Grant is considered by many the most attractive giant sequoia. The famous view of this tree has been photographed many times. That view was slightly improved when a couple of fir trees that were in the way were cleared out (something many photographers occasionally wish they could do). While most of the largest giant sequoias have dead tops, from the main viewpoint the Grant appears to have an intact top. This is actually an upward-tending side branch that obscures the true top, which is dead. Even so, the crown has a very pleasing form, nicely offset by the interesting texture of the trunk. The upper trunk of the tree, easily visible through the crown, has a smooth texture, with light, almost silvery bark and horizontal bumps traversing the surface. This contrasts nicely with the typical deep, vertical furrows of bright orangy bark that make up the first 150 feet of the trunk.

The very large base of this tree has caused it to be proclaimed the world's largest since its discovery in 1862. Even though a good chunk of the base is missing owing to past fires, at over 31 feet this tree still is among the largest in basal diameter for any giant sequoia. This quickly drops to 25 feet at 10 feet up, where it is still larger than any other. From this huge base there is a smooth and pleasing taper to the trunk (not the almost grotesque lack of taper exhibited by the General Sherman or the Washington), which tops out at 266 feet. The total trunk volume is 47,930 cubic feet, thus placing it third in size among the world's trees.

My drawings, because they consist of only one view, sometimes miss much of the character of ancient trees. The General Grant is such a tree. Fortunately, from up near the old Gamlin Cabin in Kings Canyon National Park's Grant Grove, there is a sweet view of the tree from a direction perpendicular to that of the drawing. Seen from that angle, the

Volume	47,930 ft³	1,357 m³
DBH	29.0 ft	885 cm
Height	266 ft	81.1 m
AF Points	1,380	

The wonderfully colored and textured upper trunk of the General Grant contrasts nicely with the deep orange fluting of the base. The upper trunk is the largest of any known sequoia, with a volume of 4,000 cubic feet in the top 75 feet.

Grant presents quite a different appearance, and you may at first think you are gazing at another tree when the massive upper trunk becomes apparent. Above 200 feet, this tree has a much larger trunk than any other giant sequoia. ▲

President

Volume	47,440 ft^3	1,318 m^3
DBH	25.5 ft	779 cm
Height	245 ft	74.7 m
AF Points	1,234	

The President is one of those trees that produces an exclamation from most people who see it. Growing along the Congress Trail in Giant Forest of Sequoia National Park, it's a tree millions of people have walked by over the years. Perhaps its location, looming over a trail intersection, makes it impressive. Or perhaps it is because the ground surrounding the tree is bare and no trees obscure the view. Or perhaps it is because the Chief Sequoyah Tree is right behind it, and the two trees together make one of the more spectacular sights in Giant Forest. Or perhaps it is because from 105 to 140 feet the trunk is thicker than that of the General Sherman.

Visitors barely block a small portion of the President, one of my favorite sequoias. The massive crown is held aloft by the ample base. The Chief Sequoyah Tree is visible in the right background.

Or possibly it may be because the President is 27 feet thick at the base, the fourth-largest tree on earth.

Whatever the reason, the President is a spectacular sight. The crown probably holds more foliage than any other sequoia I have seen. Not only does the crown consist of over a dozen huge branches, some of which stretch out for over 70 feet from the trunk, but the foliage is very dense. A few of these giant branches have lost their ends, having broken off through the millennia. Even so, the luxurious crown of the President shades one-fifth of an acre.

As Steve Sillett and I were measuring this tree, which stands along one of the busiest sections of trail in Giant Forest, our equipment naturally drew a crowd. Several people inquired "How big is it?" while others wanted to know its name. At least one person asked if we were going to cut it down. I think many people (myself included), have a difficult time estimating the size of something so large. It's easy to tell that an 8-foot-thick sugar pine is larger than a 6-foot-thick white fir nearby, simply because these dimensions are familiar to us— they are things our size. But with huge sequoia trees you may be comparing 25 feet to 27 feet, and that's a different matter. ▲

Lincoln

Volume	45,030 ft³	1,275 m³
DBH	26.3 ft	800 cm
Height	250 ft	76.2 m
AF Points	1,262	

The Lincoln is one of many trees once thought to be the world's largest, but its size seemed to be discounted by its location in Giant Forest, home of the General Sherman. Located along the Alta Trail, not far from the President and McKinley Trees, this fifth-largest tree would be much more famous if located in any other grove. But because it is in Giant Forest with several other trees of similar size, most people see it as just another giant tree. Named "Lincoln" for the president at the time of its discovery, the name is well suited, as the tree is "rugged and adorned with lumps and bumps," to use Wendell Flint's appropriate description. The impressive trunk was once topped by a crown of very large, very long branches, and huge scars at the base reveal that this tree has been through some major fires. The crown is now much reduced in size and vigor, but the stubs of the giant branches attest to its former glory. The result is that this is one of the more gnarled and venerable-looking giant sequoias.

The DBH of this tree is over 26 feet and reduces to 21 feet at 15 feet above the ground. The bulk of the main trunk varies from over 18 feet down to 15 feet before reaching the crown. Within the crown the trunk gradually tapers, reducing itself after giving rise to several gigantic branches, each several feet in diameter. The craggy, dead tip of the tree tops out at 250 feet, but not until the tree has accumulated 45,030 cubic feet of wood. ▲

Winter is a great time to visit the huge trees in Giant Forest. The road is usually open and one can ski or snowshoe through the peaceful groves in isolation. On one trip there on Presidents Day, Kathy and I saw the Lincoln Tree (shown here), the Washington, and the President, and very few people.

Stagg

Volume	44,100 ft³	1,249 m³
DBH	25.5 ft *	777 cm *
Height	242 ft	73.8 m
AF Points	1,223	* Measured at 6'11

The Stagg Tree is the largest privately owned tree in the world. The southernmost tree found in this book, the Stagg is in the Alder Creek Grove near Camp Nelson, California. Although this tree was accurately measured in 1931 and has long been known to be one of the largest, it was not named until the 1960s when the Sequoia Crest development was put in. The development consists of a few dozen cabins scattered throughout the grove, although there is no development in the vicinity of the Stagg Tree. Wendell Flint explained about the naming of this tree: "Mr. Amos Alonzo Stagg was a famous coach and humanitarian at the University of the Pacific in Stockton, California."

The tree has an enormous base, adorned with deep cinnamon-colored bark. The section of the trunk below the high point of the ground bulges out instead of sloping in, and this convex lower side gives the Stagg a great deal more volume than its 25.5-foot diameter would suggest. In fact the much larger base of the Boole has only slightly more wood in its lower 10 feet than this tree. Above the bulge, the Stagg becomes columnar and has a trunk comparable to some of the larger trees. For just the section of the trunk between 20 and 35 feet, only the General Sherman has a thicker trunk, and it is not until 160 feet above the ground that the trunk finally drops below 14 feet in diameter. The tree has a dead top, as do all the sequoias featured in this book, perhaps related to fire damage visible near the base. Two of the fire scars have connected inside the tree, so now there is a "flying buttress" on the tree's uphill side. Other than this ostensible blemish, the tree is nearly perfect, with a luxuriously foliated crown. The tree does not have the huge, long-reaching branches of the President or the General Sherman, and in fact the moderate branches appear out of scale with its enormous trunk. This tree has been the subject of several film documentaries, including *Tickle the Sky*. Careful exploration of its crown using ropes to get access revealed a large chamber in the main trunk near the top. The floor of this chamber consists of a deep soil that supports a variety of herbs and shrubs normally found on the forest floor. ▲

Wendell Flint, author of *To Find the Biggest Tree,* stands beside the flying buttress of the Stagg. The huge fire scar is probably one reason for the tree's dead top, but its crown has a vigorous crop of foliage.

Boole

Volume	44,080 ft³	1,244 m³
DBH	29.5 ft *	898 cm *
Height	267 ft	81.4 m
AF Points	1,403	* Measured at 5'8

The very large and impressive Converse Basin Grove was one of the few giant sequoia groves to be almost completely logged. Legend has it that the man running the logging operation, Frank Boole, saved the largest tree in the grove and cut nearly all the others. This is one of the most imposing trees on earth. Now named the Boole Tree, it grows near the lip of Kings Canyon in Sequoia National Forest among small trees that have sprouted since the logging. In early photos the tree presented a stark contrast to the surrounding environment; since then many of these young trees have grown rapidly, transforming the logged-over landscape into a vigorous young forest. The Boole was long thought by many to be the largest giant sequoia of all, but the Jourdan team of engineers included it in their measurements from the 1930s, and dispelled this rumor. The basal dimensions of the Boole are very large and, like the General Grant, easily outpoint the General Sherman. However, while the basal diameter is impressive (29.5 feet) the main trunk tapers rapidly to diameters in the mid-teens, which are rather average values for large sequoias. Nevertheless, with its huge base and intact top it still manages to accumulate a little more than 44,000 cubic feet of wood, and currently ranks as seventh largest among the world's trees.

The short hike to see the Boole Tree is well worth the effort, though the sparse shade on the hike may mean you need to bring extra water. The impressive footprint of the tree covers over 900 square feet, more than any other tree on earth. The famous Montezuma cypress at Oaxaca, Mexico, is renowned for having a large base, but its footprint occupies only 743 square feet. The base of the Boole is on a gentle slope and the trunk has several catfaces

(large burn scars) at various points. The tree seems to have suffered from the exposure caused by logging the surrounding canopy, as early photos of the tree show a much fuller crown. My drawing of the upper and outer crown shows the tree as restored to its 1930s condition, based on photos taken at that time. Today most of the tree's large branches are dead or dying, although the lower and inner crown is still quite vigorous. ▲

The enormous base of the Boole Tree, complete with flying buttresses, is best appreciated from a small meadow below the tree. The tape visible in the photo is stretched level with the high point of ground on the opposite side of the tree.

Franklin

Volume	43,440 ft^3	1,223 m^3
DBH	24.4 ft	742 cm
Height	223 ft	68.0 m
AF Points	1,162	

The impressive fire scars at the base of the Franklin extend to 55 feet above the ground. A big chunk of the lower trunk is missing, resulting in two caves, one 13 feet and the other 8 feet deep.

Just like Ol' Ben, the Franklin Tree is stout, balding, and aged. For years known as the "Near Washington Tree," this giant remained unnamed until the 1990s. Like so many of the trees in Giant Forest, this tree would be world famous if it were located anywhere else. Giant Forest has an unfairly high proportion of giant trees, which causes some of the biggest to be overlooked, as this was for many years. Wendell Flint found and measured several unnamed giants when he was preparing his 1987 book, and this was the largest. The name Franklin was chosen as it fits in with the Founding Fathers theme already present in this section of the forest, as well as with the obvious physical similarities.

Calculations have been made to find giant sequoias with the maximum diameter for a given height. The names Sherman, Washington, Grant, and Boole dominate this list, yet between 60 and 90 feet above ground the Franklin is the diameter champion. Was the long oversight due to the tree's DBH of a mere 24.4 feet, or was it due to the shortness of the tree? In any case, Wendell Flint saw past these measures and discovered that this tree was one of the really large ones. The abundance of extremely large, dead branches, along with the very heavy trunk, leads me to think this tree may be very old. In addition, it is not growing on a rich site as are many of its larger brothers. The Sherman and the Boole, for example, are located adjacent to wet meadows. Instead, the Franklin grows next to an exposed granite outcrop, and has seen some major events during its lifetime, as witnessed by the massive fire scars disfiguring the base. One of these fires might have blown out the top centuries ago, allowing the multiple tops to develop. Now even these are long dead. ▲

Genesis

Volume	40,530 ft³	1,148 m³
DBH	23.6 ft	718 cm
Height	253 ft	77.1 m
AF Points	1,161	

The Mountain Home Grove is one of the few sequoia groves owned by the State of California. At over 5,000 acres, this is the largest of all the groves, and is located mostly within Mountain Home State Forest. The remainder is within the boundaries of Sequoia National Forest, with small portions held by Tulare County and private owners. The grove has an interesting and varied history—at its center are the remains of a mill in which many of the surrounding sequoias were made into lumber. Other sections of the grove, on both state and federal land, are pristine, with some areas spilling over into the Golden Trout Wilderness.

The Genesis Tree was found and first measured in 1985 by Wendell and his friend Mike Law. At the time, the Adam Tree (with a volume of 35,107 cubic feet) was the largest known tree in the grove. My first encounter with the Genesis Tree occurred in late 1998 when I spent a few days with Wendell at his Camp Nelson cabin. We visited several other trees, including the Great Bonsai, which gets my vote for the gnarliest giant sequoia. (It may even be the gnarliest tree on earth, but see El Viejo del Norte below.)

While the base of the tree does not have the massiveness of a Boole or a Grant, the upper trunk is very respectable, being close to the Grant or the Stagg in size. The lower 30 feet contain less wood than any of the other sequoias listed here, however, and this is what throws it out of the running. The Grant, for example, has over 3,000 cubic feet more wood than the Genesis in just the lower 30 feet, whereas for the next 100 feet, the two trees are nearly identical. ▲

Wendell Flint and I stand at the base of his discovery, the Genesis Tree, the most recent tree to be found to have a volume of more than 40,000 cubic feet. The base is adorned with some impressive fire scars, one of which nearly reaches the tree's center.

Ishi Giant

Volume	39,210 ft³	1,110 m³
DBH	28.2 ft	859 cm
Height	255 ft	77.7 m
AF Points	1,338	

Ishi was the last member of the Yahi tribe. He walked out of the Lassen wilderness near Oroville, California, in 1911, and lived the rest of his life in a museum at the University of California. Dwight Willard discovered this tree late in 1992 while working on his compendium called *Giant Sequoia Groves of the Sierra Nevada*. The fact that one of the largest known trees remained undiscovered until the 1990s is astonishing, considering how thoroughly this species has been explored.

I first saw this tree in July 1999 when Steve Sillett and I were in the southern Sierras tying up various loose ends for this book. Dwight was going to meet us and show us the tree, but somehow our signals crossed and we never hooked up. At two P.M. Steve and I decided to try to find the tree ourselves, using a map that Dwight had given me earlier. Eight hours later we stumbled back to the car, coming within minutes of having to spend a night in a clearcut with no warm clothes or food. Other than finding the tree (which we did), just about everything that could go wrong did. The original road we tried was washed out, so we had to come in from a different direction. We got lost at least three times, including hiking back a couple of miles on the wrong road and then backtracking to find where we were. We spent the last hour of waning light trying to find the trail we came in on, seconds away from giving up for the night.

The Ishi Giant has two flying buttresses, formed by the largest fire scar I have ever seen. The tree actually straddles an intermittent creek that flows through that part of the Kennedy Grove in Sequoia National Forest. It also leans. The fire scar, the supply of water, and the lean are all factors that can cause a tree to develop an enlarged base. In this case it worked, since the Ishi's lowest measurable diameter of 32'5" is larger than the Grant (31'4"), the Washington (29'10"), or the Boole (29'5"). Above this point, however, the trunk tapers quickly to average size. It has the smallest main trunk of the trees listed here. The intriguing character of the tree, the fire scar, and the adventure I had in seeing it all combine to make this one a favorite. ▲

The Ishi Giant, from this view, is 40 feet wide at the base; Steve Sillett's outstretched arms provide some idea of its size.

Redwood is unsurpassed in magnificence by any other conifer, and no coniferous forest of the continent equals in impressiveness, beauty, and luxuriance the redwood forests of northern California.
—*Charles Sprague Sargent, 1900*

While coast redwoods are currently the world's tallest trees, they probably were not always so. Historic records for redwoods are scanty, but research by Dr. A. C. Carder indicates that both the Australian mountain ash *(Eucalyptus regnans)* and Douglas fir at one time exceeded 400 feet, a number not known to have been reached by coast redwood. This is certainly a debatable issue, although it must be debated without the benefit of supporting facts. There is, however, fairly solid evidence that before logging began the world's largest trees were coast redwoods. While there is only weak evidence of giant sequoias with a volume larger than the General Sherman, at least two coast redwoods of the past were measured at larger than 55,000 cubic feet. The coast redwoods we have with us today are the mere table scraps of a great and fantastic race of trees. If it were not for the foresight shown by the Save-the-Redwoods League early in this century, there would likely be very few big redwoods left. Today, we have a few state parks and one national park that contain scattered, impressive remnants of what once was a vast and continuous coast redwood forest.

The now legendary 1963 *National Geographic* expedition under the leadership of Paul Zahl measured several trees to identify the world's tallest tree. At that time, Congress was considering establishing Redwood National Park in California, and the expedition found that four of the six tallest trees were located in the proposed park, along Redwood Creek. Some tall trees were left out of the competition, including the Dyerville Giant, but these were not measured, possibly on purpose. (The Dyerville Giant fell over in 1991.) For over 20 years, Zahl's results were considered gospel. Perhaps the expensive equipment and careful techniques the expedition used were enough to satisfy any potential measurer. After all, even with expensive equipment, measuring the height of a 365-foot tree is no simple task.

Map

124°   122°

42°

40°

38°

36°

- ■ Coast Redwood
- ■ Forest
- ■ Woodland
- □ Non-forest
- ■ Water
- ✦ Tree locations

Del Norte Titan
36,890 ft³

Iluvatar
36,470 ft³

The area at the confluence of the Eel River and Bull Creek within Humboldt Redwood State Park has the world record for standing biomass, as well as the world's tallest forest; it holds nearly 90 percent of all of the world's known trees over 350 feet tall.

While Wendell Flint was documenting the largest giant sequoias, from the 1950s to the 1980s, no one was measuring giant coast redwoods. When Michael Taylor and Ron Hildebrant entered the scene during the mid-1980s, they were amazed at the relative ease with which they could find new record trees. One factor here is that height records are more transient than volume records due to tops dying back, siltation around the roots, rapid top growth of other trees, and similar circumstances. Michael and Ron found that what was the world's tallest tree in 1963 had shrunk, and that several other very tall trees had been ignored during the 1963 survey.

Although Michael's primary interest was in tall trees, which he has an uncanny gift for locating, his keen eye led him to the discovery of most of the redwoods listed here. He and Ron established a set of records for the largest coast redwoods (which had never been done), while also revising and updating the list of tallest trees. Michael walked roads and trails and bushwhacked in all of the parks to find the potential champions. When I first used the survey laser in 1994 to obtain more accurate volumes for their discoveries, they had already compiled an impressive list of the largest and tallest coast redwoods. On that first trip Michael showed me about 20 of what he thought were the largest, which I then measured. Of the 20 largest known coast redwoods (by volume), 15 are located along Prairie Creek in Prairie Creek Redwoods State Park; the Arco Giant is along Prairie Creek, but just over the boundary in Redwood National Park.

Then came the late 1990s, and a young canopy researcher named Steve Sillett. Steve was smitten hard by the big-tree bug and has discovered or co-discovered several new tall trees, as well as the Grove of Titans. Steve's rope-based tree research has documented the astonishing ecologic complexity of giant redwood crowns. Many of the more complex trees listed here were directly measured by Steve and some of his students. These include the three trees in the Grove of Titans, Iluvatar, and Adventure. Another recent discovery is the world's tallest known living thing, the Stratosphere Giant, which stands 368.6 feet tall. ▲

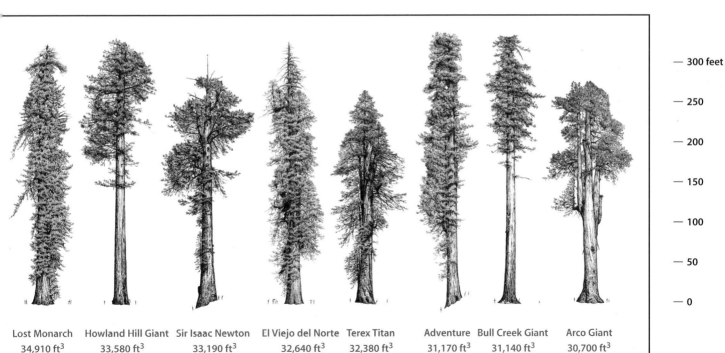

Lost Monarch	Howland Hill Giant	Sir Isaac Newton	El Viejo del Norte	Terex Titan	Adventure	Bull Creek Giant	Arco Giant
34,910 ft³	33,580 ft³	33,190 ft³	32,640 ft³	32,380 ft³	31,170 ft³	31,140 ft³	30,700 ft³

— 300 feet
— 250
— 200
— 150
— 100
— 50
— 0

Del Norte Titan

Volume	36,890 ft^3	1,045 m^3
DBH	23.7 ft	723 cm
Height	307 ft	93.6 m
AF Points	1,222	

The largest known coast redwood remained unknown until May 1998, when Michael Taylor and Steve Sillett stumbled across it after a long day of exploration in Jedediah Smith Redwoods State Park. The date was May 11, truly a historic day in big-tree history, commemorated as the Day of Discovery. After an all-day bushwhack through the heart of Jedediah Smith, and after finding the largest known Douglas fir in California, the exhausted pair entered what is now known as the Grove of Titans. Their first encounter was with the Screaming Titan, a double tree with a fused base. Michael first saw only the massive fused trunk of the tree, and, weary after a long day, named it after his reaction. Later, on descending into the main part of the grove, the pair created some history. The first-, third-, and sixth-largest known coast redwoods are in the Grove of Titans, in a park that before the Day of Discovery was thought to have only one of the really large known trees.

The Del Norte Titan sits on the floodplain of Mill Creek as it travels through Jed Smith Park, the alluvial soils apparently providing the tree with everything it could possibly want. My first view of the grove was the same that Michael and Steve had had on the Day of Discovery, and the Del Norte Titan is easily the most impressive coast redwood I have seen. Two large reiterations peel off at 106 feet up, causing the trunk to swell in the east–west direction, although from the north this gives the first 100 feet of the tree a very columnar appearance. One of these reiterations is over 5 feet thick and 155 feet tall in its own right. Seven other major reiterations and dozens of lesser ones decorate this tree which, at nearly 37,000 cubic feet, is the fifteenth largest known tree in the world (after 14 giant sequoias)!

The Del Norte Titan has been the subject of an ongoing study of redwood crown architecture and epiphyte distribution, as have several other redwoods listed here. Detailed, direct crown and trunk measurements have been collected by Steve Sillett and his students from Humboldt State University, and their data were used to aid my estimates of wood volume for these trees. Redwood crowns are often quite complex, and the view from the ground is often at least partly obscured by foliage and/or trunks. This is very much the case with the Del Norte Titan. The lower third and the upper third are visible from var-

At 100 feet off the ground, above the dominating main trunk, the first and largest of the Del Norte Titan's 43 reiterations emerge. Even though they encompass an astounding volume of 3,500 cubic feet, at least three other redwoods have still more.

ious vantage points, but the middle third is very well hidden by its own dense crown and several nearby trees. Fortunately, more detailed data of this kind were available for several of the most complex crowns, such as the Del Norte Titan carries. ▲

The massive, slow-tapering first 100 feet of the Del Norte Titan, the largest known redwood, do not hint at the extremely complex architecture of the next 200 feet.

Iluvatar

Volume	36,470 ft³	1,033 m³
DBH	20.1 ft	614 cm
Height	300 ft	91.4 m
AF Points	1,084	

This tree, the largest in California's Prairie Creek Redwoods State Park, is named for the Creator of the Universe in Tolkien mythology—an appropriate name for what several of us feel, looking at the supporting data, is the most architecturally complex tree on earth. This unusual tree has a most impressive, very full crown that occupies over 50,000 cubic yards of space. Volume of this kind is hard to conceptualize, but the crowns of some of these redwoods are among the world's largest—and that includes the crowns of the giant Montezuma cypress in Oaxaca and the giant banyans of India. This tree also has an irregularly shaped base. Almost triangular in cross-section, the base is buttressed to support the large, reiterated trunks that emerge fairly low on the main trunk.

Iluvatar was one of the more difficult trees to calculate volume for, as the circular and even the elliptical formulas proved insufficient for the task. A footprint, or map of the tree base, was used to calculate the cross-sectional area of the stem. Also, the massive size and number of reiterations (134) made it very difficult to measure from the ground. Reiteration volumes were obtained directly by Steve Sillett and some of his students who are studying the crown structure, epiphytes, microclimate, and arboreal salamanders of several trees in the grove.

The tree's breast height diameter is slightly over 20 feet, tapering to 12.5 feet at 115 feet up, where the first of many reiterations begins. The lowest of these is over 8 feet in diameter itself, and gives rise to a series of trunks, each in turn having trunks of its own. This sympodial growth form carries the crown of this trunk system nearly 80 feet out from the main trunk. Three other major trunk systems are found in the tree, along with dozens of smaller ones, and nearly all of them are healthy and covered with foliage. What is most mind-boggling to me is how these huge trunks, supported so far from the main trunk, are able to exist—after all, this is just wood. My theory has to do with the branch and trunk fusions. Many of the larger trunks have branches fusing them to other trunks. That is, a branch from one trunk, after rubbing against another trunk for a few centuries, has fused with the other trunk. All of the wood

A closer view of the complex architecture of this amazing tree. The abundant branch–branch and branch–trunk fusions of Iluvatar weld this impressive assemblage together, making it difficult to imagine the giant structure ever failing.

produced by these trunks and branches in the years that follow only serves to make these bonds stronger. These fusions then act, like the triangular beams on the Eiffel Tower, to create a gridlike frame that becomes stronger than the original architecture of the tree. Many of these trunks with fusions actually increase in diameter above the fusion, indicating a "short-circuit" of the normal flow of water and nutrients within these stems. Iluvatar tops out at 300 feet, having accumulated well over 36,000 cubic feet of wood in its trunks, making it the second-largest known coast redwood. This measure means the Del Norte Titan and Iluvatar are the only known living coast redwoods having over 1,000 cubic meters of wood. ▲

Even four of my colleagues do not block much of the huge base of Iluvatar, a tree with the larges known redwood crown. The single trunk first ramifies at 120 feet, where a huge arm that is nearly 9 feet thick emerges. In all, 134 separate trunks are encountered, with a volume that totals over 4,400 cubic feet.

Lost Monarch

The Lost Monarch, in the Grove of Titans, has the largest basal diameter known for a living coast redwood. Discovered only a few minutes before the Del Norte Titan, it was initially thought to be the largest. Indeed, it does have the largest single redwood trunk known. Some very large basal sprouts on the back side of the tree prevented a tape from being stretched around the tree, so the final measurements had to wait for the lasers to indirectly measure the size of the lower trunk. While directly measuring other trunk diameters on the Lost Monarch, Steve Sillett observed that nearly all of the branches above 200 feet had been killed in a crown fire in the distant past. The living branches in its upper crown have all sprouted from the scorched trunk since the fire. While the tree has a slightly larger trunk than either the Del Norte Titan or the Howland Hill Giant, it has only a few quite small reiterated trunks.

The base is my favorite portion of this tree. The tree sits on the floodplain of Mill Creek in Jedediah Smith Redwoods State Park, situated between the creek and a marsh and up against the toe of a slope. The enormous base, nearly 30 feet thick, vaults out of the marsh like a volcano. The massive roots of the tree also snake out into the marsh, and are still visible nearly 100 feet beyond the tree.

The opposite side of the marsh provides a marvelous viewpoint of the tree, which is the one I chose for the drawing. Visible here are two huge, down-sloping branches that extend from the left side of the tree, each over 70 feet long.

The Lost Monarch illustrates one of the many problems tree measurers face—trees with several basal trunks. While reiterated trunks are obviously part of the same tree (because there is only one stem as the tree leaves the ground), with basal sprouts the relationship is not so clear. In this case, two large "trees" sprout at the base of the Lost Monarch and are fused with it for the first 20 feet or so, before becoming individual stems. I consider these to be clearly part of the same root system, yet I do not include

Volume	34,910 ft³	989 m³
DBH	25.2 ft	768 cm
Height	321 ft	97.8 m
AF Points	1,290	

them in my measurements because they are separate trees. In the case of some trees, the fusion is so complete and occurred so long ago that it is very difficult to tell if the tree was originally single-trunked or not. DNA sampling will not help, especially with redwoods, for they are such prolific sprouters that we may find entire groves that constitute only a single genetic individual. ▲

Although the Lost Monarch was discovered in early 1998—comparatively recently—its lower trunk is the largest known for a redwood.

Howland Hill Giant

Volume	33,580 ft³	951 m³
DBH	19.8 ft	602 cm
Height	329 ft	100.3 m
AF Points	1,092	

The rain forest of the western part of Jedediah Smith Redwoods State Park is home to this tree, the Howland Hill Giant. While its diameter is a modest 19.8 feet at breast height, this tree has a slow taper, and is still over 14 feet thick at the height corresponding to the top of the photo.

The Howland Hill Giant tree is a great example of a really large coast redwood that was scarcely noticed and that went unnamed until 1990, when Michael Taylor first spied it growing right along a popular road in California's Jedediah Smith Redwoods State Park. Other nearby trees had even been named and much publicized as giants although lacking any supporting data. The Stout Tree, for example, has been touted as the "most massive" redwood. It is a nice tree, but my measurements indicate that dozens of more massive redwoods exist. Perhaps a giant tree is good enough for most people. Yet with the Howland Hill Giant we have a situation where one of the greatest giants was seen by thousands, yet ignored.

On the other hand, perhaps this situation reflects the fact that the Howland Hill Giant has a relatively small breast height diameter for one of the really big redwoods. Nevertheless, it has a very slow taper, and keeps a huge trunk to over 300 feet—to become the only tree on earth over 6 feet thick at a point 300 feet up. This is another good example of how the point system, which is biased toward a tree's diameter at 4.5 feet, is a poor predictor of volume. A statistical regression study of the diameters of the 33 largest coast redwoods indicated that the diameter measured at 50 feet above the ground is the best indicator of tree size—understandably a measurement few people take. Michael Taylor's ability to see past DBH has enabled him to find most of the world's largest known redwoods. ▲

Sir Isaac Newton

Volume	33,190 ft³	940 m³
DBH	23.0 ft	701 cm
Height	311 ft	94.8 m
AF Points	1,203	

This fifth-largest coast redwood was briefly the national champion during the mid-1990s, and combines a gigantic base (23.0 feet DBH) with good height (311 feet) and a massive trunk (33,190 cubic feet). Although my measurements indicate that the Newton is one of the largest, there is another far taller tree with a larger DBH diameter that I do not even include in this book. That tree is the Godwood Creek Giant, and it racks up a whopping 1,309 AF points. At 361 feet it is one of the tallest, and it has the second largest known DBH for a living redwood—24.4 feet. However, the trunk of the Godwood Creek Giant has a rapid taper that reduces its volume to the point where it is not even in the top 20 trees.

The Sir Isaac Newton Tree is one of several champion trees located along Prairie Creek in the California state park of the same name, which contains true rain-forest environments, unlike many surviving old-growth redwood areas. Rainfall within the park ranges from 80 to 110 inches per year, as opposed to the 50 to 60 inches received by the more famous groves of Humboldt Redwoods State Park and the Avenue of the Giants. Because of this moisture, the forests have a healthy mix of tree species—including western hemlock, Sitka spruce, Douglas fir, Port Orford cedar, Pacific yew, bigleaf maple, and red alder—along with the coast redwood.

While the Newton was for a while the largest known redwood, I have yet to meet someone who is a big fan of this tree, and I've seen people frown or grimace when I mention it; others dismiss it as "ugly." The tree is heavily decadent—reiterated trunks hide much of the main stem, and the top is dead. Despite all this, or perhaps because of it, I am drawn to this tree. Perhaps the giant burl near the base, weighing several tons, combined with the tree's overall gnarl,

The huge burl above the onlooker in this view of the Sir Isaac Newton weighs over 20 tons, yet it is a relatively minor blemish on the base of this enormous tree.

gives it its charm. After all, a little decadence can be a good thing. ▲

El Viejo del Norte

Volume	32,640 ft^3	924 m^3
DBH	22.1 ft	674 cm
Height	324 ft	98.8 m
AF Points	1,177	

Another monumental tree in the Grove of Titans, El Viejo is the character of the grove. Certainly a contender for the gnarliest tree alive, El Viejo is without question the gnarliest coast redwood I have seen. The tree has every necessary element of character—huge fern mats, massive reiterations, massive fused branch networks, great size, asymmetry, and a dead top. The Lost Monarch and El Viejo Trees stand side by side, directly across the creek from the Del Norte Titan. On the Day of Discovery, this was the second giant coast redwood spotted in the Grove of Titans. As Michael Taylor and Steve Sillett entered the grove at the end of a long day's bushwhack-ing, the first tree they encountered was the Screaming Titan. After the letdown of that double tree, they found El Viejo only a short distance beyond, and the rest is history.

The main trunks of El Viejo del Norte and the Lost Monarch are nearly identical in form, although the Lost Monarch's is pro-portionally larger. Both trees have huge bases that quickly taper to fairly modest upper trunks that reach nearly the same height. The main features that set El Viejo apart are the two sets of massive fusions that occur on the lower trunk. Initially it was difficult to ascertain how these might have developed, but through detailed measurements, sketches, and analysis the mystery has been uncov-ered. Branch fusions are fairly common in giant coast redwoods, yet these enormous masses of live wood remain a source of con-fusion as well as amazement. Here, the swamp that these masses of wood now jut out into was formerly the stream bed, and the tree developed a large number of long, downward-sloping branches. Many of these fused, broke off and then fused, or broke off, generated reiterations, and then fused. The result is a complex, fused network of wood that gives this gravity-defying structure the strength to persist.

Above all of this, at about 260 feet, is one of the largest fern mats known. A large horizontal branch that gives rise to sever-al small reiterations is completely covered with a thick growth of the leatherleaf fern (*Polypodium scouleri*) and huckleberry bush-es. The mat measures 25 feet long by 6 feet wide and is about 3 feet thick—making up a veritable skybound forest floor. This sur-prising element provides the perfect finish for a most interesting tree. ▲

This view of El Viejo del Norte gives an idea of the tangle in this gnarliest of redwoods. The huge growth on the side of this tree is the outcome of centuries of branches growing, breaking, resprouting, and fusing. The result is a complex mass of wood that initially had us baffled, and still has us astounded.

Terex Titan

Volume	32,380 ft³	917 m³
DBH	21.3 ft	649 cm
Height	262 ft	79.9 m
AF Points	1,087	

The Terex Titan is one of the gnarliest redwoods. It has such a grotesque, prehistoric look to it, and is so heavily guarded by overgrown brambles, that visitors approaching its great hulking mass may feel transported back to the Mesozoic era—one would hardly be surprised to see Brachiosaurs tromping past. While the upper crown of this tree was sheared off centuries ago, the reiterated trunks have restored much of the tree's original foliage volume. Based on the huge branch scars and the look of the sheared-off top, the original tree must have had a crown structure similar to the Iluvatar. The Terex Titan acquired its name from the world's largest truck, a 604-ton, 3,500 horsepower General Motors vehicle used in the giant open-pit mines of Utah and Nevada. Ron and Michael had fun when naming their trees, and this one seems awkwardly appropriate.

The Titan is another of the many giants located along Prairie Creek in California's Prairie Creek Redwoods State Park, truly one of the forest jewels of the world. Preserved in the early 1920s by generous donations from the Save-the-Redwoods League, this park contains what may be the finest redwood forest remaining. Currently designated as a World Heritage Site and Man in the Biosphere Preserve, the small, 14,000-acre park contains some of the world's largest trees. Because the park sits right alongside the ocean, the wind-blasted forest does not contain the tall trees abundant at interior locations like Humboldt Redwoods State Park. It does, however, contain 15 of the 20 largest known redwoods. Nearly all of these giants show the ravages of past storms, but their seemingly eternal life allows

While one might suppose that a tree as immense as the Terex Titan might be visible from a long way off, the dense rain forest hides this tree until one is very close.

them to resprout new foliage and persevere, as the Terex Titan is in the process of doing today. ▲

Adventure

Volume	31,170 ft³	883 m³
DBH	16.2 ft *	495 cm *
Height	334 ft	101.8 m
AF Points	967	* Measured at 6'2

The Adventure, like the Howland Hill Giant, achieves its great size by having a very large upper trunk. The lower trunk is smaller than the other coast redwoods listed here, but by 100 feet it has caught up to the giants. When Michael Taylor first pointed out the tree to me, I thought it smaller than several others I had seen; however, I did take one set of preliminary measurements, and when I worked up the data it was clear that this indeed might be one of the really large ones. From 150 to 200 feet, the Adventure has the largest trunk of any known coast redwood, and by 300 feet it is one of only three trees—of any species—to still be over 4 feet thick.

The Adventure gets its name from its precarious position as well as the adventure several of us had when trying to measure the tree. The tree is easily visible from the trail along Prairie Creek, but that is where the simplicity stops. The tree is across the creek from the trail, and even though it is near the creek, there is an abrupt, 10-foot cliff where the creek has undercut the bank. All around are very steep slopes, and even wrapping a tape around the tree turned out to be an adventure. With its base right on the creek on a very steep slope, the tree is fully exposed on the creek side and fully obscured on the uphill side, while almost the entire length of the visible side of the tree is clothed in foliage. Several very healthy reiterated trunks aid in this covering. Altogether, these circumstances meant the laser station had to be moved to seven different locations in order to get an accurate volume estimate. ▲

Michael Taylor poses with the Adventure, one of his early discoveries. Located on a natural edge, with one side fully exposed along Prairie Creek, it is still one of the tallest known trees within California's Prairie Creek Redwoods State Park.

Bull Creek Giant

The largest known tree growing in the famous Rockefeller Forest within California's Humboldt Redwoods State Park is the Bull Creek Giant. The lower Bull Creek flats are well known for containing the world record stand for biomass—this is the place that has more wood per unit of area than anywhere else on the planet. The Bull Creek Giant, less dramatic than most of the largest redwoods, does not have the big branches or unusual form of many of the great ancients of Prairie Creek. I attribute the lack of these characteristics to the tree's being much younger than the giants at Prairie Creek, although others think it may be very old. The tree has a large basal buttress that rapidly tapers to 16 feet thick at 11 feet off the ground, and that is where the taper slows—dramatically. The huge shaft rises to over 160 feet before the first branches are reached, at a point where the trunk is still over 10 feet thick. The trunk diameter does not drop below five feet until the 310-foot mark is reached, making it the second-largest known tree on earth at that height.

The differences between the coast redwood forests of Prairie Creek and those of Bull Creek are great. Prairie Creek is a rain forest, and the forests there are more open, allowing for abundant western hemlock and Sitka spruce associates and a very dense shrub layer. The alluvial Bull Creek forests are dense, nearly pure redwood forests, much drier, and largely free of understory shrubs. The forest floor is often carpeted by wood sorrel (*Oxalis oregana*) and sword ferns (*Polystichum munitum*). The hike along the south side of Bull Creek from Rockefeller Forest eastward to lower Bull Creek Flats passes through one of the finest forest formations on earth. Mile after mile of amazing redwood forests are encountered. This is also the tallest forest canopy on the planet, encompassing the highest density of trees 330 feet or taller in the world, including 86 trees over 350 feet, and 18 of the 26 trees known to be taller than 360 feet. ▲

Volume	31,140 ft³	882 m³
DBH	22.3 ft	679 cm
Height	332 ft	101.2 m
AF Points	1,190	

The trees sharing the alluvial flats along Bull Creek, home of the Bull Creek Giant, often consist of a single tree species, very different from the diversity of species found in rain forests. Growing above a carpet of wood sorrel and ferns, these alluvial forests more than compensate by being the tallest and densest on the planet.

Arco Giant

Volume	30,700 ft³	869 m³
DBH	24.4 ft	745 cm
Height	265 ft	80.8 m
AF Points	1,211	

The Arco Giant defines the word "character," with its multiple reiterated trunks, burls, snapped-off tops, great vigor, spiral bark patterns, and abundant sites for epiphyte accumulation. Standing under this monarch and gazing at its massive crown, one will certainly be in awe, as I always am when visiting this favorite coast redwood. The combination of the tree's enormous footprint with its very intense level of gnarl makes this a tree for the ages.

The Arco Giant is the largest known tree in Redwood National Park. The tree is just south of the prairie for which the creek was named and adjacent to the boundary of Prairie Creek Redwoods State Park. The property was purchased from the Arcata Redwood Company when the national park was created in 1966. Of the ten Coast Redwoods listed here, this is the only one that was not discovered or co-discovered by Michael Taylor. An earlier picture of the tree appeared in a July 1964 *National Geographic* article that discussed the newly found "tall tree" along Redwood Creek, but January of 1998 was hard on this tree, as the right top (as seen in the drawing) sheared off during a winter gale. The view shown indicates the extra width of the trunk, which is very irregular in cross-section and flares out to support the multiple reiterations. A view from 90 degrees to the left or right side of the tree shows a more normal taper to the trunk. ▲

The massive base of the Arco Giant dominates as my son gives an idea of the scale in this view of a spectacular conifer—the largest known tree in Redwood National Park.

WESTERN RED CEDAR *Thuja plicata*

Canoe cedar is a tree of the utmost grandeur, its boughs sweeping from the narrowly conical crown downward and outward with majestic benevolence.
—*Donald Culross Peattie, 1950*

Western red cedar is a tree that typifies the Pacific Northwest coastal forest environment. The tree occurs from sea level near the ocean to 6,000 feet in the Cascades, and while it is often associated with swamps or other poorly drained soils, it can also occur in well-drained or even dry environments. The ecology of western red cedar is less predictable than for other tree species in Pacific Northwest forests. It has a long life-span, in part due to its highly decay-resistant wood. Many of its associates will quickly rot and decay once a major part of the crown has died, but western red cedar does not. Its wood will resist decay and will support the remaining living crown. Red cedar crowns are, however, very sensitive to drought—the tops will often die back in a hot, dry year. A new leader will then develop from a live twig lower in the crown. This process, repeated over time, creates dozens of tops, most of which are dead.

Western red cedar was the tree most important to the Northwest Coast Indians, who used the wood as a raw material to make canoes, houses, boxes, and a host of other useful objects. The bark and roots were woven into clothing, bowls, baskets, and many household items. Totem poles, characteristic monuments of the Northwest Coast Indians, were also made from the durable wood. After Western Europeans invaded the Pacific Northwest, they found the old-growth wood of western red cedar highly valuable as well. Shingles and shakes were easily split from red cedar wood, and this was a thriving industry for most of the past century. The rapid depletion of old-growth red cedar has left this

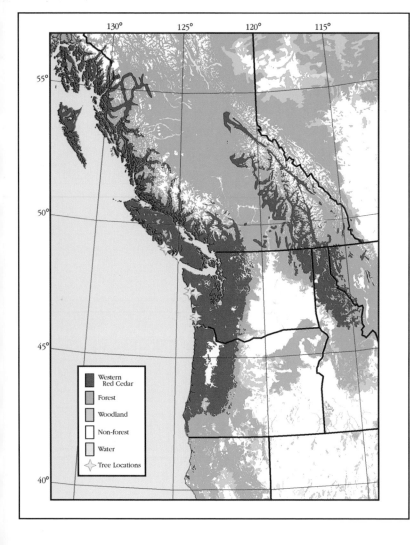

Western
Red Cedar
Forest
Woodland
Non-forest
Water
Tree Locations

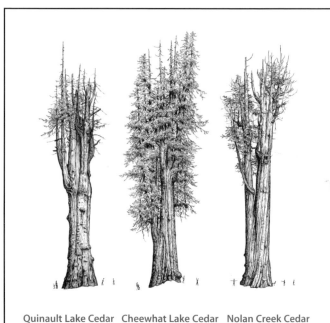

Quinault Lake Cedar
17,650 ft³

Cheewhat Lake Cedar
15,870 ft³

Nolan Creek Cedar
15,330 ft³

industry high and dry. The second-growth cedar that has followed in the aftermath of logging does not have the desirable qualities of the old-growth wood, so we will have to wait another century or so to have this great wood resource again.

Even though this species is a common component of many Pacific Northwest forest types, the truly giant western red cedars grow only in the coastal rain forests. Cascadian foresters often brag about their huge red cedars, but I have yet to see one that even approaches the size of those seen in this book. At present, over a dozen trees known to be larger than 16 feet in diameter have been recognized, and probably many are yet to be discovered. The largest red cedars are found on the western Olympic Peninsula and on the west coast of Vancouver Island. While the Olympics still have a few unexplored areas, the chances of finding new records there are diminishing. Vancouver Island and the upper British Columbia mainland, however, have vast (albeit dwindling) unexplored areas of cedar forest, such as those in the Clayoquot Sound and neighboring areas. ▲

Left: Giant western red cedars are well known to visitors in the lowland river valleys of the Olympics or the North Cascades. As huge as these trees are, much larger individuals may be found in the dense forest jungles along the coastal plain of Washington and Vancouver Island.

Right: In this turn-of-the-century Darius Kinsey photo, we see the largest known recorded western red cedar. The trunk measured over 70 feet in circumference, and from the appearance of the single stem no doubt had the wood volume to back the claim for this tree as the largest red cedar ever known. (D. Kinsey Collection, Whatcom Museum of History and Art)

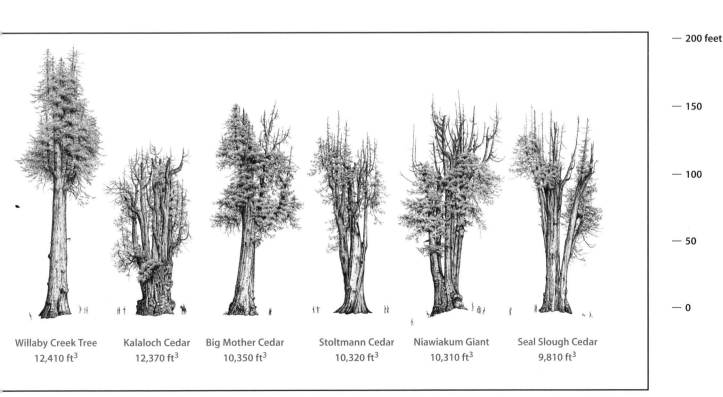

Willaby Creek Tree	Kalaloch Cedar	Big Mother Cedar	Stoltmann Cedar	Niawiakum Giant	Seal Slough Cedar
12,410 ft³	12,370 ft³	10,350 ft³	10,320 ft³	10,310 ft³	9,810 ft³

— 200 feet

— 150

— 100

— 50

— 0

Quinault Lake Cedar

Volume	17,650 ft³	500 m³
DBH	19.5 ft	594 cm
Height	174 ft	53.0 m
AF Points	920	

Growing on the north shore of Quinault Lake, this tree was first recognized as a giant among cedars during the early 1900s. When the first national Big Tree List was published in April 1941, this tree was on it, nominated by F. W. Mathias of Hoquiam, Washington. At that time it was recorded as being 62'8" in circumference (close to what I measured in 1993) but only 100 feet tall (a poor estimate). Owing to this short height estimate, the Kalaloch Cedar replaced it as national champion in the 1950s, and the Nolan Creek Cedar replaced both in the 1970s. It wasn't until I remeasured the Quinault Lake Cedar in 1993 that a more accurate height was obtained, giving it enough points to reclaim the title. As it turned out, even this was an underestimate, since the tallest trunk was obscured from my vantage point at the time. In my 1996 book, *Champion Trees of Washington State,* this tree is listed as out-pointing every other tree in Washington (931 points), and second in diameter to the Kalaloch Tree. Based on wood volume, it is the largest tree in the state.

The Quinault Lake Cedar is hollow at the base, with several room-like chambers. The nickname "house-tree" was thus applied to it, as it has not only a living room, but a kitchen and master bedroom as well (although, to be quite honest, the accommodations are too rustic for my taste). Its single trunk, which extends to over 70 feet as a 15- to 12-foot-thick column before breaking up into several massive reiterations, gives it the volume needed to be Washington's largest tree and the world's largest known western red cedar. In fact, this tree may be the largest tree in the world outside of California. That is, at least until New Zealand's Tane Mahuta (a large kauri, *Agathis australis)* or some as yet undiscovered red cedar along coastal British Columbia takes this title away.

The tree is, however, barely alive. The only part of this tree still living is a 2-foot-wide strip of bark that goes up the main trunk and spirals its way up one of the smaller reiterations. The recent addition of a rather wide

A view of the bizarre crown of the Quinault Lake Cedar illustrates some of the reasons why quantifying the huge amount of wood in these eccentric trees can be a difficult job.

trail around the base of the tree will do nothing to help with the health of this last, small living root system. Cedars, however, are very resistant to decay. That little fragment of life on this once-great giant could easily survive several more centuries and grow to be much larger than it is today. Conversely, this small piece could easily break off in a storm or have its roots killed by excessive trampling, ending the life of this giant among giants. ▲

The great bulk of the Quinault Lake Cedar, the world's largest known western red cedar, dwarfs the visiting couple here. This tree is one of a number of arboreal attractions in the Quinault Lake area of the Olympic Peninsula.

Cheewhat Lake Cedar

Volume	15,870 ft³	449 m³
DBH	19.2 ft	584 cm
Height	182 ft	55.5 m
AF Points	917	

The largest known western red cedars have not yet been discovered. Why? After visiting the forests on the west coast of Vancouver Island you will understand. Drenched by 10 to 20 feet of rain per year, laced by raging torrents, broken up by fragmented swamps filled with icy muck, filled with downed wood, and lodged in a dense understory of tough, thick, and often thorny shrubs, these forests are no friend to the casual hiker or recreationalist, and have generally been explored only immediately before being logged. This is the home of Bigfoot and ghost bears and other creatures that might find their homes only in a forest ten thousand years old. Fire is a stranger, and through thousands of years without it the cedars have grown older and more numerous, until they have come to dominate whole blocks of wet, swampy lowlands and valley bottoms. Pacific Rim National Park, Carmanah and Walbran Valley Provincial Parks, and plenty of as-yet-unprotected areas are packed with huge cedars.

The Cheewhat Lake Cedar, the largest known tree in Canada, was not discovered until 1988. It is only about 1 kilometer from a mainline road, but the brush in these forests is not to be believed. Bushwhacking takes on a new dimension on the west coast of Vancouver Island. Dense salal and huckleberry bushes up to 30 feet tall block your way. Every surface is covered with moss. Giant logs are strewn about with abandon like some nightmarish game of Tinker Toys. Caulks (pronounced "corks") on your boots are a must, as one slip could mean disaster.

At the 1996 summer solstice, Erik Piikilla and I descended through a clearcut before entering Pacific Rim National Park to see the tree. We passed many other large cedars on the way. The Cheewhat Lake Cedar presents itself as a wall, as is obvious from the photo. Unlike many of the other giant cedars described in this book, this one is still very healthy; the cambium is intact for about 90 percent of the circumference, and even the small scar where cambium is absent does not extend very far up the tree. Although the tree's lower 40 feet appear almost identical to the Quinault Lake Cedar in size, above that point the trunk breaks up into multiple stems. The volume of the multitude of reiterations is enough to make the Cheewhat Lake Cedar the second largest known western red cedar, but I think even larger trees may be lurking in the rain forests of Vancouver Island. ▲

Canada's largest tree, the Cheewhat Lake Cedar, lies hidden among a dense rain-forest tangle on Vancouver Island's west coast. Other giants await discovery in British Columbia's vast coastal rain forests.

Nolan Creek Cedar

Volume	15,330 ft³	434 m³
DBH	18.5 ft	565 cm
Height	171 ft	52.1 m
AF Points	884	

The bleached wood of the nearly dead Nolan Creek Cedar gleams in the afternoon sun on a rare sunny day in the Olympic rain forest.

A visit to the Nolan Creek Cedar is a surreal experience. The tree stands in an area of rolling hills that were logged in the late 1970s. The young forest of trees growing up now are 10 to 15 feet tall, green and thriving. In stark contrast is this enormous tree, probably 2,000 years old, nearly dead, with its wood bleached silvery-white by sun and the elements. The tree was discovered in 1977 when the Washington State Department of Natural Resources was planning a timber sale on one of its coastal rain-forest properties. The tree was spared because it was discovered to be a national champion, but was forced to exist in a denuded landscape. As the tree's fluted trunk was originally measured, the tree was 61 feet in circumference (19.4 feet in diameter) and stood 178 feet tall to its dead, multiple tops. Only a small portion of living bark now spirals its way up the tree, keeping a few small tufts of foliage alive. Ironically (and we assume accidentally), this small part of living bark was sawed into when a wooden walkway designed to protect its roots was built around the tree.

From certain angles, the Nolan Creek Cedar looks larger than it is. The trunk splits in two partway up, and so gives the impression of one massive trunk from several viewpoints. Above the 20-foot diameter base, the tree tapers to a diameter of 16 feet before splitting into 13- and 7-foot trunks. These then split and resplit into a candelabra with dozens of tops. Although mostly dead, the behemoth is still sound and easily capable of living for several more centuries before the elements finally shut down the metabolic activity in this, the third-largest known western red cedar. ▲

Willaby Creek Tree

Volume	12,410 ft³	351 m³
DBH	18.0 ft	550 cm
Height	195 ft	59.4 m
AF Points	888	

The Willaby Creek Tree changed my way of thinking about the giant trees of the Olympics. I had assumed that since most of the alluvial areas had been explored, the potential to find new champions was dwindling. This tree shows that fairly steep hillsides can harbor giant trees within the rain-forest environment, opening up vast new areas as potential sites in which to hunt for big trees. For example, this tree and several very large Douglas firs were found well above the flats surrounding the south shore of Quinault Lake in the Olympics. I have known about this tree for at least ten years, but I don't know who first discovered it. I have often taken people to see what I call the Miracle Acre—a stand of 350-year-old Douglas fir that has held our Northwest biomass record since the 1950s. The Willaby Creek Nature Trail passes through this grove of towering 270- to 300-foot trees, packed in at up to 30 per acre. The trail map shows some other trails, including a spur trail that travels along a bench above the lake, crosses Willaby Creek, then climbs steeply up the slope to the big cedar.

Unlike most of the other cedars listed here, the Willaby Creek Tree is quite healthy. The full crown is supported by a fully living stem, with live cambium all the way around. It is also the tallest cedar listed here, and probably also the youngest. This tree shows that what may be no more than a 600-year-old "youngster" can get huge. While the 18-foot DBH is respectable, the trunk tapers rapidly, so that by 30 feet up is it already down to 12 feet thick. However, the main trunk does not split until 77 feet up, where the stem is still 9.7 feet in diameter. Thanks to this long, single stem, the Willaby Creek Tree accumulates enough volume to compete with its much older relatives listed on these pages. ▲

Yet another Quinault giant, the Willaby Creek Tree was the first of the giant cedars found growing on a fairly steep slope—opening up tremendous potential for finding new champions in this area.

Kalaloch Cedar

Volume	12,370 ft³	350 m³
DBH	19.6 ft	599 cm
Height	123 ft	37.5 m
AF Points	877	

Near Kalaloch Lodge, in the strip of Olympic National Park along the Pacific Coast, you can easily find this old, weather-beaten veteran. First noted in the 1950s, the Kalaloch Cedar was the national champion from 1955 to 1977, when the Nolan Creek Cedar was discovered. Signs and a nearby parking lot give thousands of park visitors easy access to this rain-forest giant, now a "sacrificial tree" sadly showing signs of wear. The short trail to and around the tree has become a pedestrian highway, where the soil is densely compacted in a band wide enough to drive a vehicle on. This is a recipe for infection and death for the tree's root system.

Many have scoffed at this tree, exclaiming that it is not one tree, or that they have seen much larger trees elsewhere. Indeed, although the very gnarly base, covered with large burls, ferns, shrubs, and some rather large hemlock trees makes it difficult to tell, I believe it is a single tree. The short but thick trunk gives rise to no less than 12 major reiterations and countless lesser trunks. The Kalaloch Cedar is easily one of the gnarliest trees in this book, and a particular favorite of my wife, Kathy, who enjoys seeing this tree when we are in the area. This cedar was difficult to measure because of its extremely asymmetrical trunk and the numerous reiterations. ▲

The heavily visited Kalaloch Cedar is located along Highway 101 in the coastal strip of Olympic National Park. Even though this gnarliest of cedars is only partly alive, it provides support for a whole aerial garden—including two full-size hemlock trees.

Big Mother Cedar

Volume	10,350 ft³	293 m³
DBH	18.5 ft	564 cm
Height	154 ft	46.9 m
AF Points	865	

As Adrian Dorst piloted the skiff across the calm waters of Clayoquot Sound, the cool, moist air of the December day began to settle in around us. Our destination was Meares Island, one of the more prominent features of the sound, and one steeped in controversy—loved by some people for its aesthetic rewards and by others for its merchantable timber. As we approached, the mist covering the island occasionally parted to give us glimpses of the red cedar forests that blanket its lower slopes.

With me on that day were Adrian, a local photographer; Chris Earle, a friend and fellow conifer enthusiast; and Doug Chadwick, writer for *National Geographic*. Adrian had been living in Tofino, in the heart of Clayoquot Sound, for the past 28 years, and had discovered many of British Columbia's record trees over the years. Like me, he was keenly aware of the weak relationship between DBH and tree size, and we were checking several of his contenders to see if they were champions.

When Adrian first saw the Big Mother over 10 years ago, there was no trail, but the tree grows only a few hundred yards from the island's rocky shore. The name comes from the repeatable part of the exclamation he uttered upon first seeing the tree. Like many of the large red cedars, the tree's lower trunk is festooned with burls and hemlock seedlings. Above rises a massive, fluted trunk that supports a large head of reiterated trunks. While many of the reiterations are dead, the tree is quite healthy and

Big Mother Cedar is the largest known tree in Clayoquot Sound, a controversial area renowned for breathtaking scenery and notorious for denuded hillsides. This area is vast, however, and trails are scarce. Bigger trees are most certainly waiting to be discovered in the glorious rain forests around Tofino.

carries a large crown. These dead trunks are a characteristic of large old red cedars—a trunk will die back during some stressful event but the tree will send up a new leader upon recovering. The dead trunk then remains intact for centuries, leaving a legacy of gnarl for us to enjoy. While the Big Mother Cedar is not as large as some of the red cedars elsewhere, it is large enough to join the exclusive 10K club of trees over 10,000 cubic feet in volume, a truly elite class! ▲

Stoltmann Cedar

Volume	10,320 ft³	292 m³
DBH	19.4 ft	591 cm
Height	146 ft	44.5 m
AF Points	890	

Randy Stoltmann, who began British Columbia's version of the Big Tree Program and is credited with numerous tree discoveries, died in 1994, just as we were beginning to realize that wood volume is perhaps a better method of comparing trees than are points. Western red cedars were always his favorite, and when he first visited the Clayoquot Arm Recreation Site on Kennedy Lake, I'm sure he wrapped his tape around many trees before concluding that the Clayoquot Arm Cedar was the largest. As you may imagine when you look at my drawings of this gnarliest of species, red cedars are incredibly difficult to measure accurately.

The Stoltmann Cedar is the largest of many giant cedars around Kennedy Lake in Clayoquot Sound. The tree is named for British Columbia big-tree pioneer Randy Stoltmann, who considered western red cedars his favorite trees.

True, at 21 feet the Clayoquot Arm Cedar has one of the largest diameters on record, but the base consists of a huge, burly pedestal atop which a moderately large tree sits. Because this is quite evident from the pictures I had seen of the tree, I almost decided not to visit the site.

One evening in Tofino when a few of us had some time to kill, we took the half-hour drive out to the recreation site to check out the cedars. Randy's hiking guide provided a nice trail description. The trail has many fine cedars, but once the massive wall of the Stoltmann Cedar came looming into view, we knew we were gazing at the largest tree in the stand. I felt privileged to name the tree—his favorite species, and a tree he was familiar with, in the center of the world's finest cedar forest—after Randy. The enormous, fluted trunk spirals its way up, splitting off once, twice, and ultimately into nine main trunks before reaching its 146-foot dead top. I took a few measurements in the waning light, but had to return to the tree later to finish gathering the very complex data set this tree provided. ▲

Niawiakum Giant

Volume	10,310 ft³	292 m³
DBH	17.3 ft	527 cm
Height	154 ft	46.9 m
AF Points	820	

Bart Kenworthy, who rediscovered the Niawiakum Giant in the second-growth forests of the Willapa Bay region, stands on top of the tree's burly base, as Kathy and I look on.

Bart Kenworthy is a gifted wood sculptor from the Willapa Bay area who has explored much of that part of southwestern Washington for sculpting material. He found the Niawiakum Giant near the headwaters of the Niawiakum River and immediately recognized it as exceptionally big. The area was logged years ago except for this tree, so it now grows in a dense stand of second-growth cedar owned by Weyerhaeuser. The unusual shape of the tree's base may have saved it: low-forking trees are very dangerous to cut. Bart first showed me the tree in 1992, in time for the third edition of the Washington Big Tree Program listing but before I had laser equipment. Once the laser allowed me to measure tree volumes, I knew I had to return to this giant to see how its hugeness compared with others.

I returned in 1998, and Bart took me up there. As seen from a distant road, the top of the tree—that is, all its many tops—is easily visible as it towers above the surrounding second-growth forest. Although the highest tops are dead, the Niawiakum Giant has intact cambium, is quite healthy, and supports a hefty crown. The huge and highly irregular base quickly divides into five main reiterations and then into dozens of smaller ones. Each one of the main trunks has a volume measuring between 880 and 1,600 cubic feet. These, together with the short trunk, add up to one of the largest cedars known today. ▲

Seal Slough Cedar

Volume	9,810 ft³	278 m³
DBH	18.5 ft	564 cm
Height	150 ft	45.7 m
AF Points	861	

Just a few air-miles from the Niawiakum Giant is another Weyerhaeuser property, this one clearcut save for one lonely tree—the Seal Slough Cedar. At the site, gazing out across the clearcut landscape, one can see dozens of huge cedar stumps from trees cut during the original railroad logging that occurred back in the twenties or thirties. Interestingly, after the more recent clearcutting, those old-growth stumps were the source of an additional harvest equal to or exceeding that of the second-growth trees. The stumps themselves are harvested by "cedar rats," folks who cut up these huge structures into bolts, the short blocks of wood used in making cedar shakes. Each stump can be converted into several pallets' worth of bolts, and that can turn a tidy profit.

A group of visitors cluster at the base of the Seal Slough Cedar, a huge, solitary tree left after logging near Willapa Bay in southwestern Washington.

The Seal Slough Cedar, like the Niawiakum Giant, was probably never cut because of its unusual base. Easily visible among the cracks in the trunk of this tree are cedar roots growing in the tree's own rot. The center of the tree is partially decayed and the roots find this moist location ideal. It's ironic that wood the tree laid down centuries earlier is now fueling the production of new wood on the outer skin of the same tree. A half a dozen hemlocks were also sharing this fertile pocket, but most were removed during the logging. The greater than 18-foot-thick trunk tapers to a little under 15 feet at 20 feet above the ground before splitting off into two massive trunks. The largest of these is a 10-foot-thick column that continues for another 30 feet before splitting and resplitting itself. The top consists of dozens of tops, most of which are dead. Enough foliage remains, however, to keep this tree alive for centuries to come, assuming of course that it escapes any catastrophe brought on by its newly exposed condition. ▲

DOUGLAS FIR *Pseudotsuga menziesii*

Douglas spruce possesses a constitution which enables it to flourish through thirty-two degrees of latitude, and the rapidity of its growth and its power of reproduction make it the most valuable inhabitant of the great coniferous forest of the northwest, which it ennobles with its majestic port and splendid vigor.
—Charles Sprague Sargent, 1901

Douglas fir is the most important timber tree in the world, and is perhaps the most recognized tree in the Pacific Northwest, for good reason: this one species of tree has fueled the economies of Oregon, Washington, and British Columbia for the last 150 years. This is the tree that supported the great boom of lumbering in the Pacific Northwest during the late nineteenth and early twentieth centuries. Even though the old-growth logging era is almost over, the second-growth Douglas fir

timber also has many desirable properties. Good-quality dimension lumber and plywood is readily obtained from trees as young as 40 years.

The largest Douglas firs are now gone. This statement is probably more accurate for this species than for any other western tree. For most of our western giants, such as giant sequoia, Sitka spruce, and western red cedar, the largest dimensions ever recorded are represented by existing trees, or trees only slightly larger. But with Douglas fir, our current giants are the leftovers from logging or isolated individuals in more remote parts of the tree's range. The haunting grounds of giant Douglas firs were the Coast Ranges and the lower slopes of the western Cascades in Oregon and Washington. The productive, low-elevation areas are almost exclusively in private hands and were the first to be logged. The groves at Quinault Lake in the Olympics are about the only old-growth forests remaining that have these perfect conditions. It is no

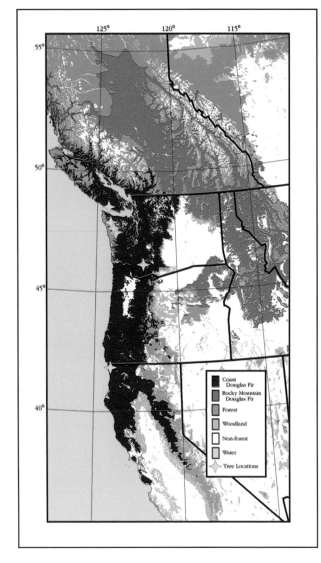

Coast Douglas Fir
Rocky Mountain Douglas Fir
Forest
Woodland
Non-forest
Water
Tree Locations

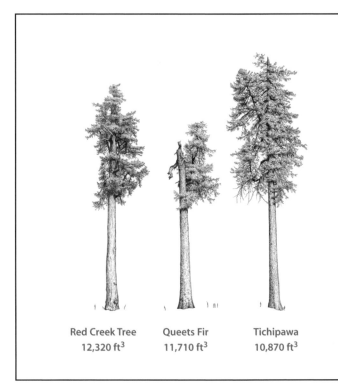

Red Creek Tree	Queets Fir	Tichipawa
12,320 ft^3	11,710 ft^3	10,870 ft^3

Top: Windswept Douglas firs along the Washington coast give little hint of the grandeur they achieve when protected by forest and allowed to reach their potential.

Left: The most structurally complex forests in the Pacific Northwest are old forests that contain a high proportion of Douglas fir. Excepting the ancient redwood forests, these forests contain the highest biomass of any forest type on earth.

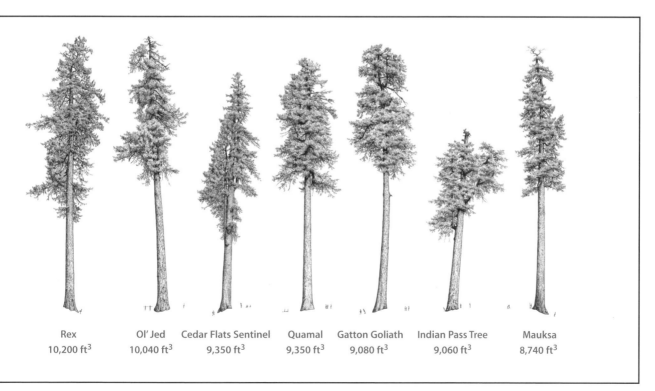

Rex	Ol' Jed	Cedar Flats Sentinel	Quamal	Gatton Goliath	Indian Pass Tree	Mauksa
10,200 ft³	10,040 ft³	9,350 ft³	9,350 ft³	9,080 ft³	9,060 ft³	8,740 ft³

— 300 feet
— 250
— 200
— 150
— 100
— 50
— 0

The impressive base of the Mineral Tree is only slightly bigger than the largest trees we have today. The upper trunk, however, was much larger, maintaining a thickness of 6 feet at 230 feet off the ground—making this tree the largest Douglas fir ever recorded. (Photo courtesy U.S. National Archives)

surprise, then, that five of the ten largest known trees of this species are found there.

Dozens of old photographs show lumberjacks in the process of felling a giant tree somewhere. The Mineral Tree was the largest Douglas fir ever recorded. It stood near the small logging town of Mineral, southwest of Mount Rainier, and was well known by locals. Richard McCardle, an early forester at the University of Washington, used to take students to see and measure this tree. Although the top was broken, the piece of it lying on the ground was measured at 168 feet in 1911, and again measured at 160 feet in 1925; the difference was probably owing to the smaller top section having decayed. The standing bole was measured several times, most recently in 1925. This lower section was 225 feet, making the original total height of the tree 393 feet, far taller than any tree living today. Picnickers had the nasty habit of building fires against the tree, which eventually hollowed it out enough for McCardle and a friend to count 1,020 rings before the tree toppled in 1930.

Douglas Fir Wars

The story of the Douglas fir in the National Big Tree Register is basically the story of the Queets Fir. The Queets Fir first came to notice in December 1940 when a letter reached the American Forestry Association soon after its request for people to submit nominations of the largest trees in the country. The letter had been sent by Preston Macy, the first superintendent for Olympic National Park. His measurements included a height estimate of 170 feet. During the summer of 1941 a giant tree near Seaside, Oregon, was discovered on Crown Zellerbach land by forester Les Lloyd, and another nomination was submitted to the AFA. By July of 1941,

Preston Macy had returned to the Queets Tree to get updated measurements and found the tree to be 17'1" in diameter and 221 feet tall. The Queets Fir thus took the title away from the Oregon tree by virtue of its 17'1" diameter, a number Oregonians were uneasy about. It held this title until September 1962, when the tensions built up enough to get the governors of the two states involved. A group of judges was assembled to measure the mighty Queets Fir and Oregon's largest, now called the Clatsop Fir, located near Seaside, along Klootchy Creek. The judges included the famous early foresters Leo Isaac and Thornton T. Munger. Here are the numbers they obtained:

Results of 1962 survey	Clatsop Fir Oregon	Queets Fir Washington
Diameter at breast height, feet	15.48	14.46
Height to broken top, feet	200.5	202
Total tree height	202	221
Diameter at broken top, feet	4.5	6.7
Gross volume outside bark, cubic feet	10,095	14,063
Average crown spread	65	61
Total AFA points	819	781

The Oregon tree was crowned champion based on points; it came out 38 points higher than the Queets Fir, largely due to a larger basal diameter, although the Queets Fir was much larger in terms of volume. One problem in obtaining measurements lay in the fact that the Clatsop Fir stood on a slope, and a tape placed 4.5 feet above the average ground level ended up at ground level on the high side of the tree. The point was moot, however, because two months later the famous Columbus Day storm blew through the Pacific Northwest, and a month after that the Oregon tree went down.

And so the Queets Fir was champ for one more decade, when Lance Finnegan found another giant growing in Oregon in 1971. This tree, called the Finnegan Fir, had a breast height diameter of 13 feet, much thinner than either the Clatsop or Queets Firs. With 810 points, it was easily able to hold the new record, thanks to its intact top that was 302 feet high. Located in the Coos Bay area, an area famous for large and tall Douglas firs, it regained the title for Oregon. The official pronouncement of the new champion did not come until 1975, which turned out to be unfortunate because this record, too, was short-lived. Slightly more than five months after it had been crowned champion, it fell in a violent storm. Again the Queets tree

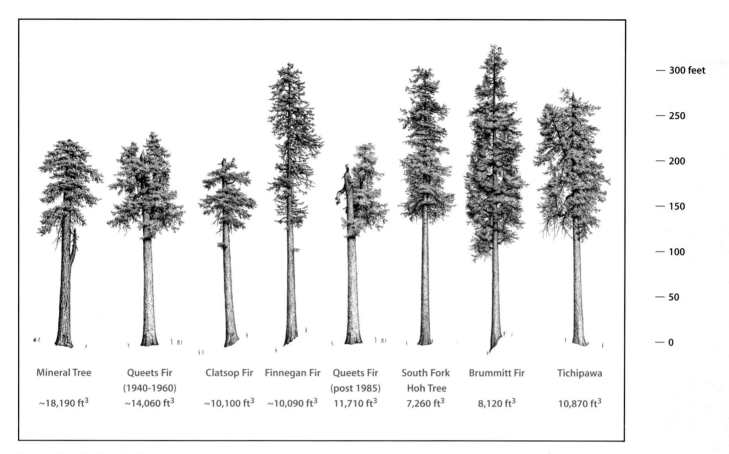

Mineral Tree	Queets Fir (1940-1960)	Clatsop Fir	Finnegan Fir	Queets Fir (post 1985)	South Fork Hoh Tree	Brummitt Fir	Tichipawa
~18,190 ft³	~14,060 ft³	~10,100 ft³	~10,090 ft³	11,710 ft³	7,260 ft³	8,120 ft³	10,870 ft³

— 300 feet

— 250

— 200

— 150

— 100

— 50

— 0

Former champion Douglas firs

regained the title. It seemed as if the gods on Mount Olympus were looking after their own.

In 1988, I nominated a tree in the Olympics, a tall and youthful one with an 11.9-foot diameter and a beautiful crown that reaches 298 feet into the sky. I was told of this tree by Bob Wood, author of several books on the Olympics, including *Olympic Mountains Trail Guide*. Jerry Franklin, forestry professor at the University of Washington, had also seen the tree and considered it the most perfect specimen he had ever seen. While this tree has enough points to share the title with the Queets Fir, it is very slender, and today I know of nearly two dozen trees that are larger.

One very tall tree took the record back to Oregon in 1989, when another Coos Bay area tree, the Brummitt Fir, was measured and nominated. At 329 feet tall, the Brummitt Fir is the tallest known Douglas fir, and one of the most perfect specimens in existence. This is another case, however, where a tall, youthful tree claimed the record due to its point total. This tree held the record for nine years, and that became the first time Oregon had held the record for more than a few months.

Washington reclaimed the title in 1998, a year when a number of giant Douglas firs were discovered, including six of the ten largest known specimens. We now know of four trees that outpoint the Brummitt Fir, all of which have higher volumes. The largest Douglas fir of all, however, is a tree that is in neither Oregon nor Washington. Called the Red Creek Tree, it is in British Columbia, and is not only the largest Douglas fir, but the largest member of the pine family. ▲

Red Creek Tree

Volume	12,320 ft³	349 m³
DBH	13.9 ft	423 cm
Height	242 ft	73.8 m
AF Points	784	

The Red Creek Tree is the largest known Douglas fir and the largest known member of the pine family. Whether the Queets Spruce, the Queets Fir, or the Red Creek Tree was the largest known individual in this family had been debated for some time. The Red Creek Tree is the last of an elite class of giants that once covered much of southwestern British Columbia. The area was heavily logged for over a hundred years, and very few old giants like this remain.

Although the tree has been wracked by time and the elements, it still maintains a large and healthy crown. The huge branches and snapped top attest to the tree's great age and once greater height.

The Red Creek Tree was discovered in 1976 by a logging-road survey crew. As the story goes, one crew returned to camp that evening with stories of the giant tree they discovered, but the other crew looked puzzled. They could not understand how they missed it because they found the remnants of the second group's lunch at the base of the tree.

I first visited the tree in 1988, when Al and Mary Carder drove me out to Port Renfrew to see it. Al Carder is the author of *Forest Giants of the World, Past and Present,* an authoritative and engaging account of historical and living giant trees from all over the world. Al notified the world of his new discovery, and the tree has now been preserved and has been the subject of several newspaper articles, posters, and postcards. However, it was not until 1998 when I revisited the tree to collect volume measurements that I uncovered the fact that it was indeed the largest known.

Even though it grows just a few miles from the ocean and several large neighboring trees have been logged, an intervening ridge shelters the Red Creek Tree from storm winds. The Queets Fir has a larger basal diameter, and there are hundreds of Douglas firs that are taller, but the massive trunk of the Red Creek Tree has no peer. The Queets Fir is the largest Douglas fir for the first 13 feet, but the Red Creek Tree is larger above that point, and is the only known tree on earth (excepting coast redwoods and giant sequoias) to be 7 feet thick 144 feet off the

This view of the Red Creek Tree only hints at some of its gnarl and complexity, the mark of centuries of storm damage and regrowth.

ground. There are plenty of western red cedars, Sitka spruces, and other trees elsewhere in the world with larger basal diameters, but I know of none that sustain such a massive pillar of wood to such a great height. I'm sure that many proud Americans will be miffed to hear that the largest Douglas fir tree is a Canadian, but all I can say to them is "I've looked—show me a bigger one!" ▲

The columnar lower trunk is unmistakable in this misty view of the Red Creek Tree, the largest known Douglas fir. While its base is smaller than that of the Queets Fir for the first 13 feet, the Red Creek Tree is larger from there on up.

Queets Fir

Volume	11,710 ft³	332 m³
DBH	15.9 ft	485 cm
Height	200 ft	61.0 m
AF Points	809	

The Queets Fir is the largest known Douglas fir still standing in the United States, although most of the original top is gone. This mighty tree, which once easily approached 300 feet tall, has been ravaged by centuries of coastal winds until only a giant 175-foot trunk with two large branches remains. These branches, once at the base of the original crown, are the only living branches left on this behemoth. When standing next to the tree, one can get a sense of how massive some of the historic trees were. Now just a shell of its former glory, this tree and the Red Creek Tree are the only Douglas firs left that really rival the size of the largest trees taken by the loggers. One of the surviving major branches on the Queets Fir has now turned upright and is regenerating a new crown.

The Queets Fir, located on the Queets River Trail in Olympic National Park, has long been recognized as an extraordinarily large tree. When it was first discovered, the top had been snapped off at a height of 202 feet, and the remaining crown topped off at 221 feet. It kept this appearance from about 1940 until the winter of 1985–86, when a winter storm sheared off another 25 feet of trunk, taking most of the live crown with it. All that remained of its crown were the lower branches that persist today. The *early* measurement of 17'1" was hard to swallow for many people. The official measurement from 1962 was 14'5". Why such a big discrepancy? The judges from 1962 admitted that they had trouble assessing where true ground level was. What happens with big Douglas firs is that a "skirt" made up of bark sloughing off over the centuries develops at the base of the tree. This cone of bark is good rooting material and is the reason for the hemlock minions that usually accompany big Douglas firs. But when people visit one of these trees, they naturally want to touch the tree, which means walking on and compacting this skirt. The Queets Fir has been visited so often for so long that this skirt is now a trail around the tree about 3 feet above ground level. This may explain the differences in measurement, as the

original measurement was made when the tree had an untrammeled base that allowed them to see the real ground level. The 1962 measurement was made from the top of the skirt, which is why it is smaller than my measurement, taken from the true ground level.

I first visited the tree in 1987, too late to have seen it in its former glory. I returned to the tree twice in 1998, and my photos indicate that the crown had grown. But ultimately the tree is doomed: once the rot at the top of the tree penetrates farther and the last two branches break off, the Queets Fir will be a giant snag. And even though we now know that the Red Creek Tree is larger, the Queets Fir has played a big part in the history of Douglas fir records. ▲

A close-up of the weather-beaten remnant of the crown of the Queets Fir gives a good idea of the tree's complexity. It is one of the last of an elite class of trees that we can now only read about.

The mighty Queets Fir has been through a millennium of rain, storms, and occasional sunshine in the remote Olympic rain forest, and has a nearly 16-foot-thick trunk to show for it.

Tichipawa

Volume	10,870 ft^3	308 m^3
DBH	13.4 ft	408 cm
Height	281 ft	85.6 m
AF Points	804	

It was March of 1998 and we had gathered to chat after a local scientific meeting. Steve Sillett, my coast redwood–loving buddy, was in town and we were going to the Quinault Lake area on the Olympic Peninsula the next day to check out some trees. Dave Shaw, another tree friend, was also there and just happened to mention that about five years ago he'd measured a 13-footer in that vicinity. I was stunned. "What! And you never told me?" Yes, he had known about it, but figured I had already found all of the giants. It was a nice compliment, but in a park of one million acres that's a difficult task.

The next day we headed for Quinault Lake and the tree. After a couple hours of bushwhacking (we first circled the target area to make sure we didn't miss anything), we saw the top of a tree that had a huge trunk and some impressive, reiterated trunks. We immediately knew we had found it and what a wall of wood it was. Even though the tree was in an area with many other large Douglas firs, it stood out as being in a different league.

At 13.41 feet in diameter, it has the fourth-largest known DBH of any Douglas fir, and with a volume of 10,870 cubic feet, it ranks third. As the drawing shows, the main trunk is broken off at a height of over 275 feet, where it is still two feet in diameter. This suggests that the tree was once at least 300 feet tall. It is over 7 feet in diameter at 110 feet off the ground, and this accounts for its impressive volume. The upper crown is dominated by three massive reiterations, which not only support much of the tree's foliage, but also add to the astounding character of the tree. The mighty tree reminded my wife, Kathy, of a thunderbolt, so that was the name we gave it, using the native Quinault word. ▲

Tichipawa is the "Thunderbolt" of the Quinault rain forest. The tree, first measured in 1998, convinced me that new champions are sometimes right around the corner.

Rex

Volume	10,200 ft³	289 m³
DBH	13.0 ft	396 cm
Height	302 ft	92.1 m
AF Points	807	

Rex Nemorensis, the self-proclaimed King of the Forest in ancient Celtic lore, is yet another big Douglas fir from Quinault. As Steve Sillett so aptly put it in an e-mail I received after calculating this tree's volume, "Quinault now has five of the top ten Douglas firs. . . . It's not fair." Fair or not, the Quinault area, in my mind, is typical of what many areas in the Coast Ranges of Oregon and Washington must have been like before logging. Quinault just happens to be the only

one left, thanks to the fact that it occurs near the only national park in the huge California-to-Alaska coast forest ecosystem to be established before the 1960s, by which time the loggers had pretty well taken their pick of the biggest big trees. The Quinault forest was preserved, along with the rest of Olympic National Park, back in 1938, when loggers were still chipping away at the edges of this forest. We found Rex a year after Tichipawa, again on the day after the conclusion of the Northwest Scientific Association Meeting, which was held in Tacoma in 1999, when we went out to finish exploring the grove of giants reported by Peter Erben two years earlier. We spent most of the day off trail, thrashing a sinuous course between the trail and the steep slopes that bound the Quinault Valley. The grove contains at least three 12-footers (the three listed here), and over a dozen that are 10 feet or greater in diameter. Rex was the last tree visited on this long and soggy day of bushwhacking.

Rex stands astride a moist seep on a high bench in the Quinault Valley. It was getting late, and we were all tired and ready to leave when Chris Earle spied this tree upslope as we were heading down. Of the six of us out on this day of exploration, not one had any doubt that this was the largest tree we had seen all day. Consequently, we had to thrash our way back in a few weeks later to make measurements. While its 13-foot diameter is exceeded by a few other Douglas firs, the columnar trunk holds its diameter to a great height. At 120 feet the trunk is still nearly 7 feet thick, at 220 feet the trunk is 4.5 feet thick, and the live top towers 302 feet above the earth. ▲

The Rex was a 1999 addition to the growing number of giant firs found and measured on the south shore of Quinault Lake, giving that area five of the ten largest known Douglas firs.

Ol' Jed

Volume	10,040 ft³	284 m³
DBH	13.6 ft	414 cm
Height	301 ft	91.7 m
AF Points	829	

California used to be considered well south of the range of giant Douglas firs. Even though there are large areas of Douglas fir forests in northern California, and these trees are often the largest species of trees in the stand, their size can't compare with the giants in the Olympics. Or so I thought before I saw Ol' Jed. This tree is in a remote location within the heart of Jedediah Smith Redwoods State Park. It was first identified on the Day of Discovery, a day when several of the largest known coast redwoods were also found. The day started when Michael Taylor and Steve Sillett, after looking at maps and air photos, figured that the West Fork of Clark's Creek was one of the last remaining areas to explore for big coast redwoods (Michael and I had already explored the lower reaches of both the East and West Forks). The basin did indeed have some large trees, including a coast redwood 357 feet tall, the tallest tree known in the park. While trying to skirt a ridge and come back through East Fork, Michael and Steve got disoriented and stumbled into another basin—the topographic maps of the area are crude and several features do not show up on them. While descending to the creek, they came upon Ol' Jed. It had been only two months since Steve had accompanied me as we found Tichipawa, which became the national champ, and his initial impression was that Ol' Jed was larger.

Two months later I made the daylong trip out to see their discoveries. Although we tried a different route, we had the additional burden of lugging the laser equipment around with us. The tree measured out as being much taller than the other large Douglas firs I had seen up to that time. In fact, it was growing in a coast redwood forest and was taller than all of the surrounding redwoods! Normally, Douglas firs are embarrassed by the giant coast redwoods in these forests, which grow taller and larger, and live much longer. Ol' Jed, however, sits at the confluence of two small creeks, in a site that brings it plenty of light and moisture to support the competition with its redwood cousins. Ol' Jed easily has more points than any other Douglas fir thanks to its

Ol' Jed is the first truly giant Douglas fir from California, and is pictured here with Steve Sillett, who discovered the tree, and who has made the arduous all-day bushwhack out to visit it three times.

huge base and lofty height, even though the rapid taper of its lower stem gives it a wood volume smaller than four other Douglas firs. Nonetheless, this tree still makes the elite 10K club (10,000 cubic feet wood volume). California finally showed us a respectable Douglas fir. ▲

Cedar Flats Sentinel

Volume	9,350 ft³	265 m³
DBH	11.8 ft	361 cm
Height	264 ft	80.5 m
AF Points	726	

On the southeast slope of Mount St. Helens sits a tiny piece of forest called Cedar Flats that has long been one of my favorite places to go to see classic, old-growth Douglas fir forest. The place was set aside as a Research Natural Area to preserve some outstanding cedar swamps, but for me the real attraction has always been the several acres of massive, tall Douglas firs, growing here among their ever-present minions, hemlocks and cedars, amid a beautiful setting. Forests such as this were once commonplace in this part of the Cascades, but were logged long ago. This stand would also be gone were it not for the Research Natural Area, set aside in 1946.

Years ago, Steve Sillett mentioned to me

It wasn't until 1999 that a Douglas fir from the Cascades was found that could compete with the coastal giants, and the Cedar Flats Sentinel was it. Poised on a bluff, the Sentinel is surrounded by one of the finest Douglas fir forests remaining.

that he had once seen a big tree in the Cedar Flats grove, off the trail and near the bluff. One morning in August 1999 as I was helping teach a field class on ecological recovery at Mount St. Helens, I found a couple of early morning hours to get out alone in the stand for photography. The early morning fog provided some excellent lighting conditions in the forest, and as the stand is not very large I soon stumbled upon the tree Steve had seen years earlier. My first impression was that it was much larger than any other tree in the grove, and upon reaching the tree I thought it could even be the largest tree in the Cascades. It grows like a sentinel on the edge of the bluff, overlooking the vast floodplain of the Muddy River. As I had only my camera with me at the time, I forded the icy river to get a rough estimate of the size and then returned a few weeks later with the lasers to get detailed measurements. My estimates turned out to be fairly close, but I had erred on the small side. The tree was larger than I had guessed. Once I had returned home and calculated the numbers, it was a pleasant surprise to find how big it really was. Not only was it the largest tree in the Cascades by a fair margin, but it had surpassed even some of the Quinault Douglas firs to rank sixth overall. ▲

Quamal

Volume	9,350 ft³	265 m³
DBH	12.6 ft	384 cm
Height	276 ft	84.1 m
AF Points	766	

The Quinault region is home to many of our largest Douglas firs, due partly to the fantastic growing conditions found there, partly to the fortuitous fire history, and partly to the logging of many other prime tree-growing areas in the Pacific Northwest. Peter Erben, recreation planner for the Quinault District of the Olympic National Forest, was bushwhacking in the area east of the main established trails when he stumbled upon a magnificent grove of giant Douglas fir. One of the established trails in the Quinault area passes through what big-tree fans and foresters call the Miracle Acre, a grove of large Douglas fir that currently holds the record for biomass (weight of wood per acre) in the Pacific Northwest. The Miracle Acre is a stand of 350-year-old trees that are 4 to 8 feet in diameter, packed in at up to 30 trees to the acre, and averaging 285 feet tall. While the individual trees in the stand are large and impressively tall, none of these youngsters are giants when compared with the trees in this book. The grove that Peter found has far fewer big trees per acre but makes up for this fact by having much larger trees. Probably in the 500- to 600-year-old age range, the trees in this grove range from 7 to 13 feet in diameter.

Quamal is perhaps the second-largest tree in the grove, has a magnificent symmetrical form, and is also quite photogenic. Peter considers this tree the finest in the grove, a statement for which he will receive little argument from me. Visitors are enveloped by a sense of beauty and perfection in the presence of this tree, so we named the tree for the Quinault word for "beautiful." Although the top was once broken out, this feature is well hidden by foliage. The lower trunk is truly massive and rises arrow-straight through a lower canopy of lesser trees to support the massive crown. The 12.6-foot DBH tapers to 10 feet at a height of 25 feet, and above that tapers more slowly; it is still 8 feet in diameter 80 feet off the ground. The trunk volume, 9,350 cubic feet, ranks it as the seventh-largest Douglas fir known. ▲

Quamal, one of the most photogenic of its species, grows in what I consider the Northwest's finest forest and stands on a lovely terrace high above Quinault Lake.

Gatton Goliath

Volume	9,080 ft³	257 m³
DBH	13.0 ft	397 cm
Height	295 ft	89.9 m
AF Points	798	

Gatton Creek tumbles out of the well-watered mountains above Quinault Lake as it passes through some of the finest Douglas fir forest remaining. At one time I had three favorite stands that I considered to be the best examples of old-growth Douglas fir, but when I saw this stand during the summer of 1998, I knew that I had probably found the finest surviving stand of Douglas fir. When Peter Erben punched a trail through this stand in 1997, he little realized the signifi-

cance of his find. He used part of an old, abandoned trail to the Colonel Bob Wilderness Area and then connected with existing loop trails in the south shore area. Along with this tree, the grove contains the Rex and Quamal trees, listed above, as well as a dozen or so other trees greater than 10 feet DBH.

A full 13 feet thick at breast height and 295 feet tall, the Goliath dwarfs neighboring Douglas fir and western hemlock trees. The tall, sweeping bole zooms upward to over 150 feet before the first branches are encountered, and then an equally impressive, huge crown sits at the top, well above the surrounding forest. At over 250 feet, where there is a massive break, the stem is still 3 feet thick, at which point three reiterations take over and carry the crown to its present 295-foot top. Before this break, which must have occurred more than a century ago, the tree was likely over 300 feet tall. While this tree has a wood volume of over 9,000 cubic feet, there may well be larger trees yet undiscovered in this large and only partly explored area of Olympic National Forest. ▲

The Gatton Goliath, located just a stone's throw from Quamal, has a sweeping bole that is both taller and with a larger base, yet slightly smaller, than its beautiful neighbor.

Indian Pass Tree

Volume	9,060 ft³	257 m³
DBH	11.6 ft	353 cm
Height	198 ft	60.4 m
AF Points	650	

The Bogachiel Valley in Olympic National Park has very old forests on the slopes rising above the spruce–hemlock forests of the valley floor. The forest on the upper glacial terraces have been undisturbed for millennia, their pioneer Douglas fir long dead in most areas, replaced by late-successional species such as hemlock and cedar. In 1992 Randy Stoltmann, on advice obtained from Bob Wood, began to explore the Indian Pass area. A section of the Bogachiel–Calawah Trail passes through an area with scattered surviving Douglas fir. A vast flat 400 feet above the river stretches across the pass and is dominated by climax Pacific silver fir and western hemlock forests. Where the flat runs into Rugged Ridge, a steep, south-facing slope, the forest changes to a mix of young and mature Douglas fir, the result of recent fires. At its west end, however, where the ridge disappears into the flat, there is a small knoll that is separated from the main ridge by a wetland. This wetland must have protected the knoll from one or more fire episodes, for the knoll is covered with extremely old Douglas firs. Most of these trees are now dead, but the largest still survives.

This is the Indian Pass Tree, a tree first noticed and measured by Randy Stoltmann in August of 1992. Six years later to the day, Steve Sillett and I revisited the tree and found it to be still alive and dominating its small knoll. Several giants in the vicinity appeared to have died within the last couple of years, including one with probably the largest branches either of us had ever seen on a Douglas fir. We confirmed Randy's origi-

The Indian Pass Tree is a surviving remnant of an ancient fir grove deep within the rain forests of the Bogachiel Valley. It and a few other surviving Douglas firs are all that remain in this thousand-year-old forest.

nal measurements: the tree was nearly 12 feet in diameter and rose 198 feet to a broken top. The lower 60 feet of trunk is very columnar and extremely large, as it is still 9 feet in diameter at that point. The next 100-foot segment is much smaller, with the trunk losing considerable size after the first reiteration is reached at 80 feet. However, the bulk of the lower section allows the tree to amass over 9,000 cubic feet of wood, making it the ninth-largest known Douglas fir as of this writing. ▲

Mauksa

Volume	8,740 ft³	247 m³
DBH	11.9 ft	363 cm
Height	290 ft	88.4 m
AF Points	754	

Only three of the ten largest Douglas fir trees listed here had been discovered by early March of 1998—the Red Creek Tree, the Queets Fir, and the Indian Pass Tree. But the next six months saw more giant Douglas firs discovered than in the entire history of the Big Tree Program. The first of these spotted was Mauksa, which is easily visible from a major road. The Quinault area has so many giant Douglas firs that another 10-footer,

about 250 feet tall, was no big deal. What looked to be a 10-foot-diameter tree, however, turned out to be nearly 12 feet, and the 250 feet was actually 290 feet. We stumbled upon Mauksa while searching for the still larger Tichipawa, described above. This tree is so close to the road that it still amazes me that no one had noticed it before—and so much so that it seems to laugh at me whenever I drive by. We named it Mauksa, which is Quinault for "one who laughs all the time."

Mauksa is situated above a small, unnamed creek that drains part of the glacial terraces above Quinault Lake in Olympic National Forest. The skirt or "cone" of old bark that accumulates at the base of ancient Douglas firs is particularly well developed in this tree. This tree's ability to deceive the senses (at least mine) seems to be related to its extremely heavy trunk—the section from 50 to 150 feet is comparable to many of the larger trees listed above. Above that, the top 100 feet of this tree are very slender, the stem snaking its way high into the sky. ▲

In the rainforests of Quinault, any exposed surface is a potential growing site. As such, most of the big trees have accumulated minions of hemlocks around their bases. In time these, too, can become giants. Kathy is seen here partway up the slope of the Mauksa.

SITKA SPRUCE *Picea sitchensis*

No tree in the American forest grows with greater vigor or shows stronger evidences of vitality, and there are few more beautiful and impressive objects in the forests of temperate North America than one of these mighty spruce trees with its spire-like head raised high above its broad base of widely sweeping and gracefully upturned branches.
— *Charles Sprague Sargent, 1901*

Sitka spruce is the world's largest species of spruce. While most of the world's spruces are found in montane, boreal, or, in many cases, timberline surroundings, Sitka spruce is a coastal species. The rain-forest environments along the coast of the Pacific Northwest are where it makes its home, and throughout most of its range it is restricted to within a few miles of the coast. It can be seen at its best, however, in the Oregon Coast range, the Olympic Peninsula, and Vancouver Island, where it will stray up to 20 miles from salt water along the floodplains of large rivers. At their northern extent, Sitkas grow as a stunted shrub-form on the eastern end of the Alaska Peninsula and Kodiak Island. Near the southern end of their range, Sitka spruce are abundant as riparian trees towering 300 feet high in California's Prairie Creek Redwoods State Park, yet only 60 miles further south, at Cape Mendocino, the trees abruptly reach their southern limit.

As is true for many important timber species, the largest specimens of Sitka spruce fell to the saw and ax long before any detailed measurements were made. The wood of Sitka spruce is highly valued, often being touted as having the highest strength-to-weight ratio of any wood. This combination made it ideal for early aircraft, propellers, boat components such as masts, and ladders. The resonant quality of its clear wood has also made it the best for forming soundboards in pianos and guitars.

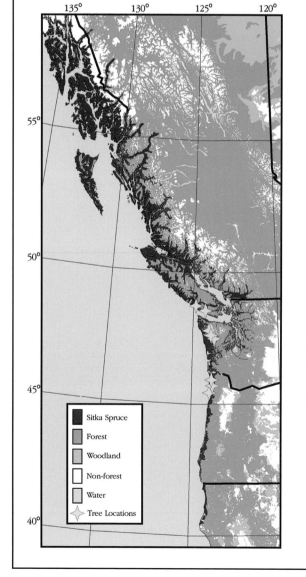

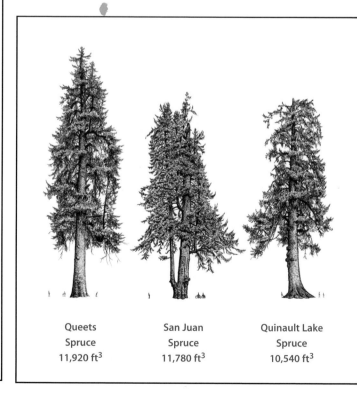

Queets Spruce 11,920 ft³

San Juan Spruce 11,780 ft³

Quinault Lake Spruce 10,540 ft³

The rain forests of the Pacific Northwest are the ultimate place to study the nurse log phenomenon, and no species displays this characteristic better than Sitka spruce. Here is one of the giant nurslings that survived (most nurse log seedlings don't), its roots now forming an archway big enough to walk through.

Sitkas were heavily exploited during the early part of the twentieth century when many of the aircraft used during two world wars were constructed of spruce cut from the coasts of Oregon and Washington. An entire division of the Army (the Spruce Railroad Division) was devoted to quickly getting large quantities of spruce to the mill for wartime use.

Sitka spruce generally propagates on nurse logs. As a result, ancient specimens often have inflated buttresses where the roots have swallowed the log they grew on. If the log was large (such as another spruce), such buttressing may still be apparent several centuries later. Fantastic basal diameters have been attributed to this species, but these giant bases may or may not be supporting a giant tree. Because of this, there is a poor cor-

relation between the basal size of Sitka spruce trees (their DBH) and their total volume. This species is largely responsible for my own reluctance in using DBH to judge size. One of the first national champion trees that I nominated was the giant spruce at Quinault Lake. This tree has the largest known basal diameter for a spruce—most likely the result of having started life on a nurse log. The buttresses are huge, resulting in strong disagreement as to where to measure the circumference. When you are measuring at breast height on this tree, moving the tape a few inches up or down could change the circumference by several feet. The Klootchy Creek Giant has a similar configuration, with the result that both trees have huge point totals (both over 800 AF points), even though at least two other trees are larger than these two.

Another giant spruce is located in the Queen Charlotte Islands off the coast of British Columbia, but I was not able to get up there in time for this book. The tree is located on Windy Bay on Lyell Island and is locally famous. I have seen a photo of the tree, and according to the BC big-tree web page (*Big Trees of British Columbia*), the tree is 174 feet tall and 14.2 feet in diameter. While the height is not impressive, the trunk diameter is. From the photo, it appears that this tree also has a slow taper. Once measured, this tree could easily make the Top Five—it could even be the largest spruce in Canada. ▲

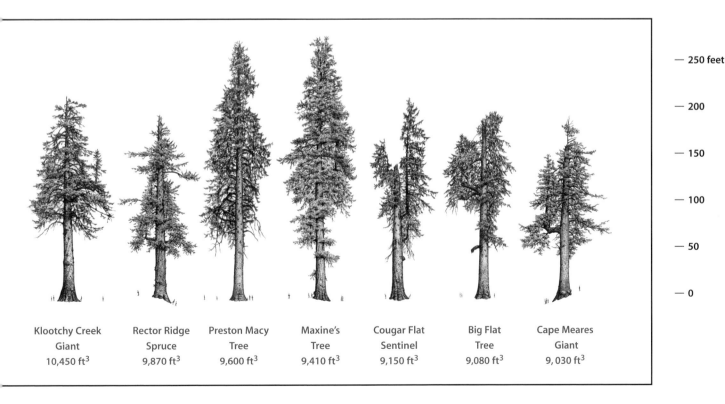

Klootchy Creek Giant	Rector Ridge Spruce	Preston Macy Tree	Maxine's Tree	Cougar Flat Sentinel	Big Flat Tree	Cape Meares Giant
10,450 ft³	9,870 ft³	9,600 ft³	9,410 ft³	9,150 ft³	9,080 ft³	9,030 ft³

— 250 feet

— 200

— 150

— 100

— 50

— 0

Queets Spruce

Volume	11,920 ft³	337 m³
DBH	14.9 ft	455 cm
Height	248 ft	75.6 m
AF Points	832	

The Queets Spruce has been recognized for decades. Unlike many other rain-forest spruces, this tree does not have the big buttresses or flaring root systems common in this species. For this reason other big Sitka spruces have occupied the pages of *American Forests* over the years, but this tree was never one of them. This is another example of the way DBH can lead us to choose smaller, bell-bottomed trees over the true champions. Because spruces nearly always start life on nurse logs, their buttressing can be quite large. For example, the current point champion, the Quinault Lake Spruce, has 882 points compared with the Queets Spruce's 832, even though the Queets Spruce is more than 50 feet taller.

The Queets Spruce is the world's largest spruce and is just shy of beating out Douglas fir for the title of the largest member of the pine family. Bob Wood first told me about this tree during the late 1980s when I began measuring western trees. He indicated that it had a huge, 15-foot-thick trunk, and that it was taller than the tree at Quinault Lake. He also mentioned that a recent study on the growth of this tree indicated that the growth rings are still relatively large, so that the tree adds a foot to its circumference every 35 years or so. Because the tree has over 6,000 square feet of living cambium, the tree produces about 40 to 50 cubic feet of wood per year, making it one of the fastest growing trees on the planet. This is a productivity rate equivalent to a quarter acre of healthy forest in the same stand. Even though the Queets Spruce does not have the largest diameter for a spruce until 112 feet from the ground, the heavy upper trunk more than makes up the differ-ence. The tree is situated near the Queets Campground in Olympic National Park, but it is off the road and behind a screen of vine maples, so its massiveness is missed by many.

I estimate the age of the Queets Spruce at 350 to 450 years, which may seem conservative to some. The fast growth rates and the wonderful growing conditions, along with the shape and condition of the tree, led me to this conclusion. For the same reasons, however, I put the Queets Fir in the 1,000-year

The gnarly lower crown of the Queets Spruce has several huge, epiphyte-laden branches that have decided to become trees themselves.

range. In any case, the two trees are near twins in trunk dimensions, at least up to the point where the Queets Fir is broken. For this reason only the Red Creek Tree is a larger member of the pine family. Historically, there is strong evidence that many trees were larger than this within the last 100 years. Tales (some with accompanying photos) have come from homes in the Oregon coast range telling of giants that exceed dimensions of any tree known to be living today. Some of these make it plausible that the largest Sitka spruce may have been larger than the largest Douglas fir. In any case, these two close rivals of the pine family are awesome spectacles from any perspective. ▲

The Queets Spruce lays claim to being the world's largest spruce of any kind, and can be seen here vaulting out of the Olympic rain forest.

San Juan Spruce

Volume	11,780 ft³	333 m³
DBH	12.2 ft	371 cm
Height	205 ft	62.5 m
AF Points	683	

The San Juan Spruce is in British Columbia, only a few air miles from the Red Creek Tree, the largest known Douglas fir. Located on the shores of the San Juan River about 15 miles from where it flows into the ocean at Port Renfrew, the San Juan Spruce is the largest known spruce in Canada. This tree is briefly mentioned in Randy Stoltmann's *Hiking Guide to the Big Trees of Southwestern British Columbia*. I did not see this tree until December of 1998 and even then, if it hadn't been close to the Red Creek Tree I probably still would not have made the trip. The description in Randy's book is of an unremarkable tree with a large diameter below a broken top. Diameter is less closely linked to stem volume in Sitka spruce than in most other trees, so I did not expect it to approach champion size.

The San Juan Spruce is very prominent when seen from the bridge over the San Juan River. It looks at first like a small grove of spruce trees—the main trunk is nearly obscured by several large reiterations —but is in fact one tree. The lowest reiteration starts at 14 feet off the ground and is nearly the tallest part of the tree. Some of the other reiterations are nearly as impressive. What is most impressive about this tree, however, is the main trunk. Even though it has broken off at 178 feet , it is still one of the largest known spruce trunks. While the 12.2-foot DBH is fairly unremarkable, the trunk has very little taper above the largest, lowest reiteration, does not fall below the 10-foot-diameter mark until 55 feet off the ground, and is the thickest spruce stem known from 60 to 112 feet, above which point the Queets Spruce is thicker. This very impressive tree with very ordinary diameter and height is a perfect example of how a really big tree can go unnoticed for a long time. How many others like this are waiting out there? ▲

The San Juan Spruce has a most unusual lower trunk. What this tree lacks in the buttressing common in many rain-forest spruces, it makes up for with a slow taper and several reiterated trunks. Chris Earle provides a perspective on the scale of the tree.

Quinault Lake Spruce

Volume	10,540 ft³	298 m³
DBH	17.7 ft	539 cm
Height	191 ft	58.2 m
AF Points	882	

The Quinault Lake Spruce is another giant tree that began its public life steeped in controversy. It is located on the south shore of Quinault Lake, on the western side of the Olympic Peninsula, and is well known to local residents. I stopped in at the Ranger Station there to ask where I might find big trees, and I was directed to this tree. My first reading, which was based on 4.5 feet above what I thought was average ground level, gave a circumference of 63'1". I sent in the nomination and was soon notified that this was a new champion. Maynard Drawson had been the nominator of the Klootchy Creek Giant in Oregon, which had been the champion since 1974. He had seen the Quinault Lake Spruce, but felt he could not nominate it because of the giant root on one side that inflates the circumference reading. On this point he was right, yet similar buttresses are found on most giant spruces, including the Oregon tree. Most rain-forest spruces grow on nurse logs and/or on floodplains that have shallow soils. In such settings a flared

In 1986 I stood for one elated moment high up on the slopes of the Quinault Lake Spruce. I had just completed measurements for what was at the time the new world champion for this species.

root system, or buttresses, will render a tree more stable against the winter winds that blow onto the Oregon and Washington coasts. Arthur Lee Jacobson, who had also measured the tree, suggested that a group be formed, including the nominators of both trees, to go out and remeasure them both with the same equipment on the same weekend. At the end of a very rainy weekend, the Oregon tree turned out to be 56'3" in girth and 206 feet tall to a dead top, for a total of 902 points. The Washington tree was 58'11" in girth and 191 feet tall, for a total of 922 points. The AFA wisely declared that for these two really giant trees, co-champion status would be declared. This was a wise move as 20 points is only 2 percent of the point total. Even so, the Oregonians still felt gypped, and their tree still has the "world's largest" sign on it. On the other hand, so does the Washington tree. ▲

Klootchy Creek Giant

Volume	10,450 ft³	296 m³
DBH	16.7 ft	508 cm
Height	204 ft	62.1 m
AF Points	855	

The history of the Quinault Lake Spruce, described above, already covers part of the controversy surrounding this tree. In 1974, when the Klootchy Creek Spruce first earned its title, it was in a battle for size with another Washington tree—the longtime title-holder from Washington known as the Helen Clapp Tree. The Clapp tree has a large basal swell, and never had nearly as much wood as the Klootchy Creek Giant. I speak in the past tense here, as the Helen Clapp Tree broke up in a storm in the early 1980s, leaving only a 100-foot-tall relic of its former self. Even if it had not broken, several larger spruces have since been discovered that would have dropped it out of the Top Ten in terms of volume. The Klootchy Creek Giant is a very impressive tree, and perhaps most impressive

The Klootchy Creek Giant is the largest tree in Oregon, and has been the national champion since the early 1970s. This spectacular tree can easily be seen in a small wayside park near Seaside.

because of its very heavy lower trunk. While the Queets Spruce has a much larger upper trunk, and the Quinault Lake Spruce a larger base, from 10 to 18 feet off the ground the Klootchy Creek Giant has the largest trunk of any spruce. This is also the portion of the tree that is most noticed as people approach the tree. Both the Klootchy Creek Giant and the Quinault Lake Spruce are what I call "sacrificial trees." Such trees are in highly public places, easy to find, and really big. Most people's curiosity about seeing the giant trees of the Pacific Northwest will be satisfied by these trees, and that will leave the remaining giants a little less visited, and so perhaps leave their root systems— the most vital and fragile part of a tree—a little less trampled. The Klootchy Creek Giant is located in a small park on US Highway 26, just a few miles east of Seaside, Oregon. In 1995, money was donated for the construction of a walkway around the tree to protect the giant's delicate root system. A storm whipped up only a week after the dedication and knocked off a huge branch, shattering the walkway, but it was then repaired. While I continue to feel that heavily visited trees should have walkways or fences like this to help minimize the damage, I also appreciate the concept of sacrificial trees that provide protection to many other trees by drawing attention to themselves. ▲

Rector Ridge Spruce

Volume	9,870 ft³	280 m³
DBH	14.2 ft	432 cm
Height	185 ft	56.4 m
AF Points	740	

A close runner-up to Oregon's largest tree, the Rector Ridge Spruce is unique in that it is not growing on a floodplain, but high on a ridge overlooking Gods Valley in the Coast Range.

Brian O'Brian is a writer who lives in Salem, Oregon. He is also a tree detective who has written a very exciting account of how he tracked down the largest spruce ever recorded, published in *Forest World* in Summer 1988. It all started when he was browsing through a copy of *The Trees of Great Britain and Ireland* (Elwes and Henry, 1906) and stumbled upon a description of the Gods Valley Spruce. After months of tracking down leads he uncovered some photos and the dimensions of this mighty tree. The diameter of the tree was a phenomenal 24 feet, a number that literally dwarfs the spruces listed in this book, and even though it had a large basal root-flare, the photo shows that at 30 feet up the tree was still nearly 14 feet thick. The tree was redwood-sized! Although Brian later learned of the tree's demise, he had often thought it might still be out there in the heavy growth in the forests along the Oregon Coast. After talking with some old-timers who lived in the Gods Valley area he was eventually taken up Rector Ridge, adjacent to Gods Valley, to a giant tree that the locals had known about. It wasn't the tree he was seeking, but it was nevertheless an enormous spruce. Brian gave me a copy of his article and directions to the Rector Ridge Spruce during the fall of 1999 and I finally made it out to the tree in late January of 2000. In fact, this was the final tree visited for the making of this book. His directions were excellent and we easily found the tree—the snag top he described was readily visible above the surrounding forest. Approaching the tree I was stunned at how heavy the trunk appeared. Not smooth and round as in many giant spruces I have seen, but bumpy and warty and spiraled and swollen. As Brian had indicated, this tree had very little taper and even though the top was dead the tree had many large branches and reiterations that gave it plenty of foliage. What was most odd to me, however, was that this was the only giant spruce I had ever seen that was not growing along a floodplain. This tree is up on a ridge. To be fair, however, it is in the saddle of the ridge and immediately adjacent to a spring. As I was measuring this tree I kept thinking that this might make the 10K cubic foot mark. It didn't quite, but for most of the distance from 18 to 60 feet off the ground, this tree has the thickest trunk of any known spruce. ▲

Preston Macy Tree

Volume	9,600 ft³	272 m³
DBH	13.1 ft	399 cm
Height	257 ft	78.3 m
AF Points	768	

This tree is a longtime champion, originally noted in the early 1940s by Preston Macy, first superintendent of Olympic National Park. Among the several trees Macy nominated when the National Big Tree Program was first started were the Queets Fir, the Quinault Lake Cedar, and the Enchanted Valley Hemlock, all of which are still among the largest known. The Preston Macy Tree has been seen by millions, as it is at a wayside along the route to the Hoh Rain Forest Visitor Center in Olympic National Park. Ever since I first drove up the Hoh Valley in 1985, this drive has been among my favorites. The 8-mile stretch of road from the park boundary to the Hoh Visitor Center is one of the most magnificent sections of forest I have ever seen. With mile after mile of towering spruces and hemlocks and the occasional grove of Douglas fir, this is truly one of the nicest pieces of road one could drive. This is the place to drive with the sunroof open, the better to marvel at the living skyscrapers that line the roadway.

The largest tree along this scenic drive is the Preston Macy Tree. Labeled "Big Tree," the perfectly formed spruce is a show-stopper. While the trunk is massive, the tree never loses its beauty and still retains the appearance of youth, fitting in nicely with its giant rain-forest denizens. At first glance the tree even seems to be like many of the other giants that line both sides of the roadway. It is not until one gets out of the car and approaches the tree that its truly immense stature becomes apparent. The flaring roots around the ample base quickly coalesce to form a smooth-tapering column. The massive shaft is 10 feet thick at 19 feet off the ground, and by 100 feet up it is still 7 feet thick. The lowest branches extend skyward, like a glorious ladder, up the bole of the tree. ▲

The Preston Macy Tree is a famous wayside attraction along the road in the Hoh Rain Forest in Olympic National Park. It is named for the park's first superintendent.

Maxine's Tree

Volume	9,410 ft³	266 m³
DBH	13.2 ft	403 cm
Height	265 ft	80.8 m
AF Points	778	

The west coast of Vancouver Island is a land of extremes. Rugged and remote to a high degree, the area contains some of the finest forests as well as some of the most devastated landscapes one would ever want to see. Maxine's Tree is a gorgeous spruce growing in the Walbran Valley, deep in the coastal rain forest. The more famous Carmanah Valley is adjacent to the Walbran, and although the lower reaches of both valleys are in Pacific Rim National Park, the main sections of the valleys were not. Recent clearcutting in the upper reaches of these valleys, and the discovery of the Carmanah Giant which at 315 feet was, at the time, the world's tallest spruce, prompted an environmental outcry that ultimately led to the formation of Carmanah Walbran Provincial Park. The nearly 40,000 acres (16,450 hectares) preserved in these two valleys contain some of the finest cedar-spruce rain forest in existence. Randy Stoltmann had much to do with these valleys being set aside, as he used to make long treks to these valleys before there were established trails. He discovered and wrote about some of the giant trees here, and was a major inspiration for the installation of a canopy research site there.

I have been unable to locate the Maxine this tree is named for, but one story about the tree has been made into a children's book. To quote the jacket, "Maxine's father is a volunteer who builds trails in the Carmanah Valley to raise public awareness of the beauty and value of the ancient rain forest. Maxine often plays among the giant trees while her father works. She does her best to save her favorite Sitka spruce from logging by making a sign that says 'Maxine' and putting it on the tree. She figures that nobody would hurt someone's favorite tree." The little girl no longer has to worry about this particular tree, which is now within the Provincial Park. The tree is also among the most beautiful spruces I have ever laid eyes on. The tree is nearly

Maxine's Tree, the largest tree in the Carmanah Walbran Provincial Park, stands just a few yards from West Walbran Creek. The trek out to make a visit is well worth it; the wilderness here is as wild as it gets.

identical in shape, size, and form to the Preston Macy Tree, although it is in a much more remote location. ▲

Cougar Flat Sentinel

Volume	9,150 ft³	259 m³
DBH	13.6 ft	416 cm
Height	202 ft	61.6 m
AF Points	731	

The main trail up the Hoh Valley is one of the world's greatest trails. A 45-mile round-trip hike can take you on a spectacular rain-forest walk with towering trees along the Hoh River, to the summit of glacier-clad Mount Olympus, and back through the forest. I have climbed Mount Olympus via this trail, and the splendor of the trip still amazes me. It sums up, in one hike, all that is magic about the Olympic Mountains. The first 12 miles of the Hoh River Trail are along the river through the lofty spruce rain forest. Robert Wood, author of the *Olympic Mountains Trail Guide,* found a champion spruce in the area near Cougar Creek way back in 1951. He also noted two other giants in the vicinity. One of them was the Cougar Flat Sentinel, described here. The other, the Schenk Tree, blew down in a storm in 1953, and the log was measured at 302 feet. In the late 1960s, soon after the Helen Clapp Spruce was declared national champion, the Cougar Creek Tree also blew over, having no doubt died of a broken heart. In 1987, I found a giant western hemlock near Cougar Creek that, thanks to its lofty 241-foot top, became the national champion. The Sentinel is also mentioned in Randy Stoltmann's book, *Hiking the Ancient Forests of British Columbia and Washington.*

The Cougar Flat Sentinel is located in a large, grassy meadow with a sparse scattering of trees. The tree itself is huge—the main trunk comparing favorably with the others listed here. At a height of 80 feet, it is still 8 feet thick and it does not drop below 6 feet thick until 130 feet up. This, unfortunately, is where the trunk is snapped. What the top of the tree once looked like is impossible to know. Since then, new leaders, resprouting from several of the branches, have regenerated much of the lost crown. The tallest of these now measures 117 feet, and brings the top of the tree back up to 202 feet. ▲

The main route to Mount Olympus includes a 12-mile hike along the Hoh River Trail through lush rain forests of giant spruces, hemlocks, and firs. The Cougar Flat Sentinel is its largest known inhabitant.

Big Flat Tree

Volume	9,080 ft³	257 m³
DBH	13.5 ft	410 cm
Height	189 ft	57.6 m
AF Points	708	

The South Fork of the Hoh River is a great gem of a rain-forest valley. The endless throngs that visit the main Hoh Valley are not here, for several reasons: there are no tourist facilities; there is only one path and it is a short, dead-end trail; and it's a long drive along logging roads to get to the trailhead. Yet the valley has the same spectacular rain-forest formations of giant moss-draped spruce and hemlock that attract so many visitors to the mainstem Hoh. Two former champions—a Douglas fir and a vine maple—grow along the trail. Annual field trips from the University of Washington come up this valley in Olympic National Park to learn about rain-forest ecology.

The trail starts out in an area that had been previously logged by railroad and is now covered in a dense, dark, young spruce forest, and shortly enters the national park along a wonderful Douglas fir–covered glacial terrace. One of these firs was briefly the national co-champion, but is not listed in this book because it does not measure up against the plethora of other giant trees that have been found in the Quinault area. Big Flat is a large terrace along the South Fork Hoh whose entrance is marked by a monstrous spruce snag next to the trail. The Big Flat tree is a short distance beyond, flanked by two smaller yet taller spruces. It sits on the lower terrace of the South Fork Hoh River, surrounded by a sea of vine maples, some alders, and a few other spruces. This forest

The peaceful and secluded South Fork Hoh Trail is just as spectacular as its big sister along the main Hoh, but without the crowds. The hugely grotesque Big Flat Tree is the largest tree as yet discovered in the valley.

stands in stark contrast to the dark, dense, conifer forests of the upper terraces and lower slopes. Sections of these lower terraces are hardwood dominated with the odd spruce towering above.

The thick shaft of the Big Flat Tree is easily visible from the trail, the thin, flaky bark barely concealing the giant column of wood underneath. Ravaged by time and the elements, its snapped top and huge, sheared limbs attest to former glory. One giant limb remains, supporting a rapidly growing new top that may soon become the tallest part of the tree. ▲

Cape Meares Giant

Volume	9,030 ft³	256 m³
DBH	15.4 ft	470 cm
Height	182 ft	55.5 m
AF Points	781	

Brian O'Brian has long been interested in big trees and the controversies that surround them. While I was describing to him the location of Oregon's largest western red cedar, discovered by Frank Callahan, he mentioned that he had seen some ancient cedar trees there in the past. I questioned him on other areas along the Oregon coast where one might have a chance of finding some big trees—not an easy task in such a heavily logged area—and he mentioned Cape Meares State Park. Currently, the most famous tree along the Oregon coast (perhaps the most famous tree in Oregon) is the Octopus Tree, which is at Cape Meares. This gnarly, grotesque tree sits a few feet from the bluff overlooking the ocean, sculpted by centuries of constant wind. The tree's namesake

Cape Meares State Park is the location of the Octopus Tree, probably Oregon's most famous tree. Overlooking the Pacific from not far away, however, is the true behemoth of the park—the lonely Cape Meares Giant.

feature, possibly due to some freak accident when the tree was young, are its lowest branches, which have turned upright and become trunks. A half-dozen of these trunks, all about equal in size to the main trunk, radiate out as much as 30 feet from the center. Considering the surrounding forest of smallish spruce and pine, this tree is well worth a visit. However, knowing that the forest at Cape Meares might contain something besides the Octopus Tree, I was skimming a book at the library on the state parks of Oregon that happened to show a map of Cape Meares with the Octopus Tree and another, labeled "Big Tree." Curious, I questioned Brian if he had seen this tree. He hadn't. The next time I traveled south I stopped by and first saw the Cape Meares Giant.

After a short walk on a spur trail, I encountered a gigantic spruce. I instantly knew this tree was worth measuring because of the massive, slow-tapering trunk. The huge reiterations off to one side gave it its own unique presence in the wind-blasted, old growth spruce forest. The huge, buttressed base quickly tapers to 11 feet at 12.5 feet up, but then becomes columnar. At 70 feet above the ground the main trunk is still over 9 feet thick, which is larger than most of the other giant spruces listed here. The main trunk has succumbed to the constant ocean winds but is valiantly working on replacing its broken top. The Cape Meares Giant is now the third-largest measured tree in Oregon and a worthy companion to the overvisited Klootchy Creek Giant. ▲

SUGAR PINE *Pinus lambertiana*

This is the noblest pine ever yet discovered in the forests of the world, surpassing all others, not merely in size but also in kingly beauty and majesty.
—*John Muir, 1881*

Sugar pine has been called the most majestic of all pines, a statement I must agree with. Thick maroon shafts lift the massive, graceful crowns above the surrounding fir forest, providing the splendor that accompanies a walk in an ancient Sierran forest. Unlike many of its associates, including other pine species, the sugar pine develops an individuality at maturity like no other. The long branches snake their way for 30 or 40 feet before the tips are reached, each one adorned with the long, pendant cone that is this species' trademark. Ancient sugar-pine boles launch themselves through the canopy of lesser trees and spread out their branches over the top of the canopy—each emergent pine a unique statement of majesty as it surveys the sea of fir and cedar spread out below.

Although I have heard the account several times, I would be remiss not to include the story of the first western description of sugar pine in a book on forest giants, as it is a classic plant-hunter's tale. It was spring of 1826 when David Douglas, the now famous Scottish botanist, set out from Portland in search of the legendary pine with giant cones. On March 25, he came across a fallen specimen of sugar pine that is still the largest ever recorded. The trunk was 57'9" in circumference at a point 3 feet above the root system, and was still 17'5" in circumference at a point 134 feet along the bole. The total height was 215 feet. The trunk circumference of that tree is 20 feet greater than any known sugar pine. John Muir, who knew of this description and had himself seen a lot of ancient pine forests, thought that the 57'9" was a typographical error and should have been 37'9". If true, it would fit the other measurements better. This is my judgment as well, since our largest pine (the Whelan Tree) does not taper to 17'5" in circumference until 155 feet up the stem.

The high quality of sugar pine lumber was quickly recognized and thus these great pines have been the staple of the timber industry in the California mountains for the past 15 decades. As a result, the old-growth mixed-conifer forests that once cloaked the mid-elevation, western front of the Sierras are largely gone. The only places where large patches of old growth remain in the Sierras are in reserves (national or state parks), and even these bear the scars of early logging. One remarkable sugar pine forest may be seen on the ridge north of the South Calaveras grove of giant sequoias, and exceptionally fine groves of this species are easily visible at various places along the drives into or out of Yosemite Valley. The western half of Yosemite National Park, dominated by sugar, ponderosa, and Jeffrey pines, represents the finest pine forest on the planet. ▲

Sugar Pine

Forest

Woodland

Non-forest

Water

Tree Locations

Left: The best spots for sugar pines are the mid-elevations in the Sierras and the mountains of southern Oregon and northern California. The wet meadows sprinkled throughout this area are especially nice, providing lovely flower displays and enough water to keep the pines happy.

Right: This sugar pine found a lonely spot on Moro Rock in Giant Forest, close to where many of its relatives tower to 250 feet.

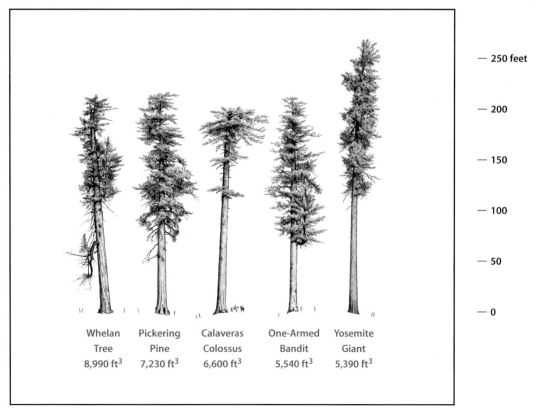

Whelan Tree	Pickering Pine	Calaveras Colossus	One-Armed Bandit	Yosemite Giant
8,990 ft³	7,230 ft³	6,600 ft³	5,540 ft³	5,390 ft³

— 250 feet

— 200

— 150

— 100

— 50

— 0

Whelan Tree

Volume	8,990 ft³	255 m³
DBH	11.0 ft	334 cm
Height	206 ft	62.8 m
AF Points	636	

Dorrington, California, is a small timber town located near Calaveras Big Trees State Park. This small area is the sugar pine nexus—the site of some of the largest sugar pines—and thus most of this area was brought into private ownership long before the formation of the Forest Reserve System in 1889. Consequently, the largest sugar pines are on private land, not federal land. The town consists of a few buildings, several houses, a famous Girl Scout camp, and a general store—the site of the most activity. From the parking lot of the store, stand at the side of the building and peer across the meadow to the forest beyond. Several large trees will be visible emerging above the forest canopy. These are ponderosa pines, except for the broken-topped tree on the right. This is the Whelan Tree. This sugar pine was first recognized as being the largest in 1937, when it was measured after the land it is on had been purchased by the San Francisco Girl Scouts. The tree was deposed in the mid-1960s when a tree called the Pickering Pine was discovered growing nearby. My measurements indicate that while the Whelan Tree may not be the point champion, it is the largest by volume. Indeed, it is the world's largest known member of the genus *Pinus,* the true pines.

The tree is named for Maude Whelan, whose contributions over the years have kept the Girl Scout camp well equipped with up-to-date facilities. The tree was mentioned in an *American Forests* article for 1941, when the Champ was first purchased by a chapter of the San Francisco Girl Scouts. It has been one of only three champion sugar pine trees to appear on the National Register. One of these, the tall tree from Yosemite (see below), was in for only a few months. The other two, the Whelan and the Pickering Pine, have shared the list during its nearly 60-year history. ▲

The great shaft of the Whelan Tree over-shadows Morgan Dutton. Famous for over 50 years, the world's largest pine has watched over the local Girl Scout camp throughout its reign.

Pickering Pine

Volume	7,230 ft³	205 m³
DBH	11.5 ft	352 cm
Height	209 ft	63.7 m
AF Points	659	

The Pickering Pine sits on the canyon rim of California's North Fork Stanislaus River near Board's Crossing. Named after the lumber company that owned the land when the tree was discovered, and currently the national champion, it is the largest tree in a grove of giant trees. The 10-acre grove is in a draw surrounded by dry, oak–conifer woodland. White fir and incense cedar make up the majority of the company, but they are overtopped by an emergent canopy of ponderosa and sugar pines. When I first entered the grove in 1996, I descended through the forest and spied a large pine down-slope. Arriving at that tree, I spied yet another one. As I descended further, finally the massive bole of the One-Armed Bandit loomed into view. After wrapping my tape around it and seeing it was still not the tree I was looking for, I saw the enormous upper crown of a tree still lower down, and knew I had found the Pickering Pine.

The Pickering Pine has a large basal swell which, at 11.5 feet in diameter, gives it the largest diameter known for a living sugar pine. This has kept it in the champion spot since it first appeared in 1967. The tree supports a large and very healthy crown despite two large fire scars that adorn its base, one of which punches right through the trunk to the other side. Even though it is both larger in diameter and taller than the Whelan Tree, which gives it an extra 23 AF points, it has only 80 percent of the wood volume. The stem tapers more rapidly than that of the Whelan tree, and is substantially smaller for most of its length. Nevertheless, the tree is extremely impressive, and, unlike its larger rival, the Pickering Pine is in an old-growth forest setting. ▲

The Pickering Pine has been the national champion for much of the last 40 years. This awesome tree sits in a fine 10-acre grove of giants overlooking the North Fork Stanislaus River in the Sierras.

Calaveras Colossus

Volume	6,600 ft³	187 m³
DBH	9.8 ft	300 cm
Height	202 ft	61.6 m
AF Points	587	

The Calaveras groves of giant sequoia have a long and colorful history. The first Euro-American sighting of these giant trees occurred when A. T. Dowd stumbled into the North Grove while bear hunting in 1847. This area was made a California state park in 1931 and has since been a major destination for millions of people from the San Francisco/Sacramento area. While the sequoias here are worth a visit, the really large sequoias are located 200 miles farther south, in the Kings and Kaweah drainages. Calaveras has some of the finest mixed-conifer forest in existence, so timber companies had already privatized much of the area before the formation of the Forest Reserves in the 1890s. Yet right in the heart of this private ownership area and adjacent to the original state park sat the nation's smallest national forest, the Calaveras Bigtrees National Forest. This national forest was unique in that its goal was simply to preserve the sequoias. True, a few sequoias of the South Grove spilled over the ridge into this area, but the real treasure, in my mind, is the fantastic sugar pine forest it contained. In 1994 , this 340-acre national forest was turned over to the much larger adjacent state park to manage as a unit. This was a wise move, because the park has one of the best prescribed-burning programs I have seen any-where—a procedure absolutely essential to maintaining such pine forests.

During the summer of 1998, I organized an expedition to explore the Calaveras area for tall giant sequoias and to try to find the largest pine in the park. Between the ten of us we had three lasers. We measured more than 200 sequoias in both the North and South Groves, and found several trees in each grove that were over 280 feet, with the tallest being 283 feet (some of these trees had previously been claimed as over 300 feet tall). Another day was spent searching for big pines in the former national forest, and the Calaveras Colossus was our largest discovery. The Colossus has a very slow taper and a very interesting top—the trunk is over a yard wide within a few feet of the top, and the bole is clear for most of the tree's overall height. The top is also extremely flat, with some of the topmost branches reaching out over 40 feet. ▲

The Calaveras Colossus stands out as the largest sugar pine in one of the finest sugar pine forests remaining. Nevertheless, as with all giants, a still larger one may yet be found around the next ridge.

One-Armed Bandit

The One-Armed Bandit first came into view when I was looking in California's North Fork Stanislaus River canyon for the Pickering Pine in 1996. I kept noticing larger and larger trees as I descended into the grove. The Bandit caught my eye as I came to a terrace in the hillside. Judging by its size, I figured that I had found the national champion I was looking for. It was certainly the largest pine I had ever seen at the time. As I wrapped my tape around the trunk and read only 28'9", I realized that this was not the champion, but a very noteworthy contender. Nearby I did find the national champion, which I then measured. All the while I kept peering over at this tree thinking that it was very big. I took full measurements of the tree that day, and in several years of further looking I have seen only three others that exceed it in size. Normally, I like to include notable trees from different locations, but in this case two of the five largest sugar pines are nearly adjacent to each other.

The namesake feature of this tree is an enormous lower limb that bends skyward, forming a giant arm. The trunk has a rather modest 9.1-foot DBH, but its slow taper keeps it above 7 feet thick for the first 70 feet, comparable to the big boys listed above. Its wonderful location, along with its beautiful purple bark, make this tree well worth a stop before proceeding on down to the Pickering Pine. ▲

Volume	5,540 ft^3	157 m^3
DBH	9.1 ft	278 cm
Height	209 ft	63.7 m
AF Points	568	

A junior partner to the Pickering Pine, the One-Armed Bandit is a giant in its own right. As I measured it, I thought I'd eventually find a bigger tree. Indeed, I have measured plenty since then, yet this tree remains the world's fourth largest pine.

Yosemite Giant

Volume	5,390 ft³	153 m³
DBH	9.2 ft	281 cm
Height	268 ft	81.7 m
AF Points	633	

Yosemite is world famous for its glacially sculptured landscapes, granite cliffs, and plunging waterfalls. The Yosemite Valley is certainly one of the most spectacular places I have ever seen. On my frequent trips to this area, however, I rarely go into the valley. Why? Not because of the formidable crowds, but because 98 percent of Yosemite National Park is outside the valley, and the park contains the finest remaining Sierra Nevada mixed-conifer forests. Several hundred thousand acres of contiguous forest blanket the mountains in the western portion of the park, easily earning the title of the world's finest pine forest. In the middle of this outsized landscape stands the Yosemite Giant. Of the 110 or so species of pines throughout the world, this is the world's tallest. Curiously, the only other species of pine to grow over 250 feet, the ponderosa pine, has several trees of nearly this height in the vicinity. This tree was first noted in the early 1990s by Paul Dettman and Chris Collacott, two park employees who live near Hodgdon Meadow, and the tree.

Five separate trips were needed to find this tree, with my repeated failures mostly due to bad directions. I finally saw the Yosemite Giant in the summer of 1998. I was with Rand Knight and Morgan Dutton doing some fieldwork in the Sierras, and we hooked up with Brian Mattos, park forester, who had seen the tree before. When Rand called out that he had found the tree, I skirted a ridge and peered down, and *boom*—there it was. This was easily the finest-looking pine I had ever seen. As it turned out, on one of my previous attempts I had passed within about 50 yards of the tree. Not only was it tall, but it was healthy, with the top alive, pointy, and still growing. Even though this is the tallest known living pine, it does not appear to be at its limit of growth—so I guess I'll have to come back and get a new record every few years. And beyond all this, the Yosemite Giant is colossal enough to be the fifth-largest known pine in the world! ▲

The Yosemite Giant is the world's tallest known pine. It seems particularly fitting that this tree, the ultimate expression of its genus, stands in the middle of the largest old-growth pine forest on earth.

INCENSE CEDAR *Calocedrus decurrens*

The cinnamon-colored boles of the old trees are without limbs as they make striking pillars in the woods where the sun chances to shine on them—a worthy companion to the kingly sugar and yellow pines.
—*John Muir, 1869*

Incense cedar is another of our four West Coast "cedars," all members of the cypress family. True cedars, in the genus *Cedrus,* are members of the pine family, inhabit the Old World, and were named for their fragrant wood. Similarly, our western cedars have decay-resistant, aromatic wood, and can live to great ages to develop very interesting character.

People often visit parks in the Sierras, such as Calaveras, Yosemite, or Sequoia/Kings Canyon at least in part to see the giant sequoias. Incense cedars have often been mistaken for young sequoias, since they

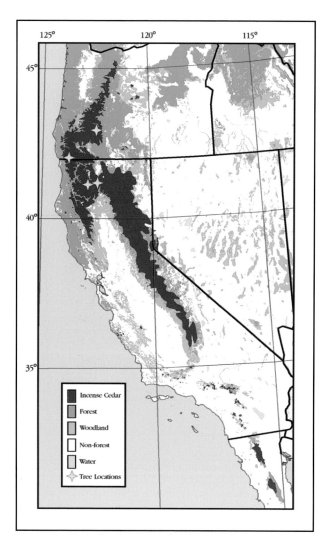

Incense Cedar

Forest

Woodland

Non-forest

Water

Tree Locations

often grow nearby and have a similar orangy bark. The foliage of the two species can also appear similar at first glance. Sequoia foliage is covered with sharp, scalelike leaves and tends to have a bluish cast. Incense cedar has similar scalelike leaves, but they are blunter and a bright, grass-green color. In addition, and this is a useful metaphor to help people distinguish the two, the incense cedar leaves appear as if someone had taken a giant sequoia twig and ironed it flat. That distinctive flattening to the leaf arrangement, once recognized, makes it easily differentiated from its companions.

The ecology of incense cedar, like the other cedars listed in these pages, is a good deal more complex than many of its associates. The species can be strongly bimodal in its habitat distribution. I have seen it growing out of recent lava flows—an extremely harsh, hot, and dry environment—but it also grows in floodplains where its roots are constantly washed by water. At first these may seem like two environments that couldn't be more different, yet both have something in common. In one situation the tree is starving for water, and in the other the tree is starving for air. Both are stressful environments, and this is a tree that can tolerate stress. Incense cedar is not, however, restricted to stressful environments. It is common in forests with productive soils from the mountains of southern Oregon down through California and on into northern Baja. While almost never dominant in the forests where it is found, it is usually at least present in small numbers.

One thing that really hit home for me while collecting information (and trees) for this book was the importance of the north-facing cirque basins of the Siskiyou and Klamath Mountains. These ranges are uniquely situated in having been far enough north to have had glaciers during the Ice Age, far enough south so that these glaciers were small, and low enough to now have productive forests nearly up to the major ridgelines. During the peak of the last glaciation some 25,000 years ago, small glaciers carved out amphitheater-like bowls on the north sides of many of the major peaks in the Siskiyou/Klamath complex of mountains. Today, these steep, north-facing cirque-basins are the sites of abundant headwater springs, lakes, wet meadows, and, quite often, impressive stands of incense cedar. These

basins have all of the ingredients to grow record-sized cedar: abundant moisture; low tree competition (due to soggy soils and/or shrub dominance); and protection from fire (even the thick-barked incense cedar can eventually be consumed by repeated fires). The most recent incense cedar discovery is on the north slopes of Condrey Mountain in a large amphitheater known as Alex Hole. Frank Callahan came across this tree in early 2000, right before a major storm sealed off the area for the next several months. I was not able to get out to the tree before this book went to press, but the 15-foot diameter he measured is certain to draw me up there before long. ▲

Incense cedar has a great ability to grow in extremely dry places such as this lava flow in central Oregon. However, perpetually wet areas can also supply the trees with everything they need to grow large—all four trees featured in this section grow in such sites.

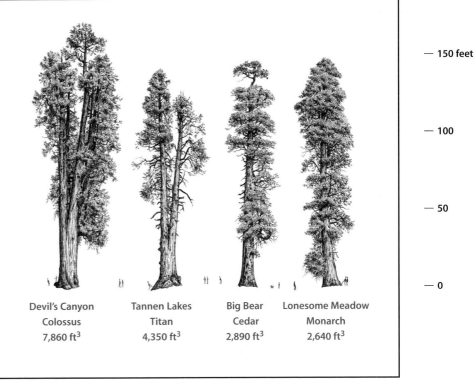

Devil's Canyon Colossus	Tannen Lakes Titan	Big Bear Cedar	Lonesome Meadow Monarch
7,860 ft³	4,350 ft³	2,890 ft³	2,640 ft³

— 150 feet

— 100

— 50

— 0

Devil's Canyon Colossus

Volume	7,860 ft³	223 m³
DBH	12.4 ft	378 cm
Height	165 ft	50.3 m
AF Points	645	

The champion incense cedar was first nominated in 1969 by a group of foresters from the local ranger station who discovered it in the Marble Mountain Wilderness of northwestern California. While the Devil's Canyon Colossus is one of the largest trees in the country in terms of AF points (it has ranked anywhere from seventh to eleventh among all species through the years of its reign), very few people have visited it. In the summer of 1997, Al Gronki and I, along with several friends, hiked out to see this tree. Al was the district ranger at Sawyer's Bar, the district of the Shasta-Trinity National Forest containing the tree, when it was first nominated. The trail up Devil's Canyon travels through wonderful mixed conifer forests of sugar pine, Douglas fir, white fir, and incense cedar. Al had peered down into this basin nearly 30 years earlier and remembered the open nature of the forest at the head of the valley and the massive crowns of the cedars visible there. Upon reaching the upper valley, we saw openings of Sitka alder begin to carve their sinuous paths through the conifer forest. As the openings increased their aerial extent, large cedars began to appear, then massive, deeply furrowed orange trunks of cedar, armed with upright, thick, twisted branches clothed in verdant green foliage. At a point when I thought we had reached our target, the huge crown of the champion appeared across the next meadow. An old sign proclaiming our champion's dimensions assured us we had reached the appropriate tree.

The tree showed multiple reiterations of the stem, a new character I had not observed before in this species. In fact the branching pattern reminded me of some of the giant coastal red cedars from Washington or British Columbia. But unlike many of the red cedars that share this architecture, each reiteration on this tree was alive and supporting a healthy mass of foliage. The tree was a giant, although it was probably not as old as many others I have seen. It had no fire scars, being surrounded by wet meadows that would also allow it to grow very fast. It also had no neighbors competing with it for light. As a result is it has a full crown and no water limitations—ideal growing conditions. This champion is probably no more than 400 years old. ▲

The Devil's Canyon Colossus is nearly too big for words. Having almost twice the volume of its closest rival, this cedar completely changed my thinking about this species—both as to its ecology, and as one of the world's arboreal wonders.

Tannen Lakes Titan

Volume	4,350 ft^3	123 m^3
DBH	12.9 ft	394 cm
Height	137 ft	41.8 m
AF Points	633	

The Tannen Lakes Titan sits near the shore of the lakes of the same name in the Red Buttes Wilderness of Oregon and California. It grows in a location similar to that preferred by many other giants of this species, the bowl of a north-facing cirque basin.

The Tannen Lakes Titan is a cedar that was discovered by Frank Callahan, an expert botanist and tree hunter from the Medford, Oregon, area. Frank spotted this tree while scouting for Brewer's spruce—one of our rarest conifers. The Siskiyou/Klamath region is the native range of the Brewer's spruce, which is found in rocky areas protected from fire. The Tannen Lakes are a pair of lakes just on the Oregon side of the Oregon–California border, a stone's throw from the Red Buttes Wilderness. Callahan discovered a new national champion Brewer's spruce at West Tannen Lake—a huge, ancient tree growing among the talus in the cirque basin holding the lake. There are many large cedars in the area, including some very tall, forest-growth specimens along the northeast-facing slopes below the lakes. The largest cedar he has seen, however, is the one growing at the forest edge in a seep near East Tannen Lake.

The Tannen Lakes Titan has an enormous lower bole that is made even larger by several burl formations near the base. At a little over 20 feet up, the main stem splits into two, one of which rises to nearly 140 feet. Although the vigor of this tree indicates the tree is in decline, it is nonetheless a spectacular sight. ▲

Big Bear Cedar

Volume	2,890 ft³	82 m³
DBH	9.1 ft	277 cm
Height	141 ft	43.0 m
AF Points	495	

Most people do not think of California as a lonely place. With 35 million people within its borders, it's not hard to see why. But there is one part of the state that is different. It's an area in excess of 15,000 square miles with a population density of only five people per square mile, and not a single town with a population over 4,000. No, it is not the Mojave Desert. It is the Siskiyou/Klamath Mountain complex in northwestern California (and southwestern Oregon). This remote and densely mountainous region is too rugged for most agricultural or urban developments, and lacks the big peaks to draw most of the outdoor adventurers, winter or summer. As a result, over 2,000 square miles of this area, or about 1.3 million acres, have been set aside as wilderness. Because many California newcomers are drawn to the more famous wilderness areas of the Sierras, the Siskiyou/ Klamath wilderness areas are mostly sought out by local adventurers. Fisherman here like to hike up into the Trinity Alps Wilderness to Big Bear Lake, a beautiful timberline lake near the eastern edge of the Wilderness. Little do they know, however, that the short, 4-mile hike up to the lake passes by two trees featured in this book.

I first spotted the Big Bear Cedar a few minutes before arriving at the Bear Creek Twin ponderosa pine. I was hiking up the trail to see the pine that Al Gronki had seen a few years earlier, when an immense, bright-orange trunk came looming into view upslope from the trail. At the time I had not seen the other cedars listed above, and so I was duly impressed by what was then the biggest incense cedar I had ever seen. The massive, bell-bottomed base was much larger than what I was accustomed to seeing on large trees of this species from the Sierras. The 12-foot-thick base quickly tapers down to 7 feet thick by 15 feet up, but then becomes more columnar. It is still 5 feet thick 65 feet up, and that allows it to accumulate nearly 3,000 cubic feet of wood before reaching its 141-foot top. ▲

The Big Bear Cedar, with its beautiful orangy trunk, was an accidental discovery that came to light as I hiked past it on my way to the giant Bear Creek Twin ponderosa pine, located only a few hundred yards away.

Lonesome Meadow Monarch

Volume	2,640 ft³	75 m³
DBH	9.3 ft	284 cm
Height	143 ft	43.6 m
AF Points	504	

The great trees in and around Lonesome Meadow have been known about for decades. The Forest Service map for the Umpqua National Forest mentions the giant cedars in and around these meadows. I first visited this area in 1989 while working on a university forest sampling crew, and stopped by these meadows to see what large incense cedars looked like. What struck me was how brightly colored these trees were—orange bark with bright green foliage. I returned in the fall of 1997 to measure a tree for this book. While there are many giant trees in this area, I did not see any to compare with the Devil's Canyon Colossus. Later, after searching high and low for other contenders,

I realized that the trees I was seeing were actually quite large for the species. Then Brian O'Brian, a writer and big-tree enthusiast from Salem, told of some giants he'd measured around there. I returned again in the fall of 1999, determined to find the largest tree and measure it. By now I had talked to several people familiar with the area and learned that the largest trees were in a particular meadow. The centerpiece of the meadow is a huge cedar with a massive burl about 13 feet in diameter at its base, and emerging out of the top are twin cedars. While this may be one tree, the two individual stems caused me to discount the tree. Even so, the two trees growing out of the burl are not particularly large. Nearby, however, was a giant single-stemmed tree, easily the largest tree I had seen in the area—the Lonesome Meadow Monarch.

The tree is very healthy—the many branches and eight or so reiterations support a dense crown of foliage. As with many incense cedars, the huge base quickly tapers down to a tree of modest proportions. Indeed, 75 percent of the wood volume in this tree is in the first 50 feet. While the Monarch is not in the same class as the Devil's Canyon Colossus, the extensive meadows where it grows surrounded by giant cedars are well worth a visit. Who knows, larger ones may still be lurking in the shadows of Lonesome Meadows. ▲

Lonesome Meadow is the site of a large and glorious cedar grove along the Rogue-Umpqua Divide in southern Oregon. Its largest known inhabitant is the Lonesome Meadow Monarch, a lovely and very healthy specimen found in the lower grove.

Its strippy, whitish bark is truly the garb of nobility. Its shape and form are proud testimonials of its adaptation to this austere high-elevation environment. Here the growing season is brief; the cedar's immensity is clearly the result of centuries of growth.
—William Moir, 1989

This book will forever change the way a great many people think of this species. The largest yellow cedars have been discovered only within the last several years. Among these are the largest and tallest ever recorded for the species—trees that rank among the largest of our western trees. A close cousin of the Port Orford cedar, yellow cedar was formerly considered a much smaller relative. Now, whether because of intensive logging of Port Orford cedar, or because the U.S. populations of yellow cedar tend to be restricted to small trees at high elevation, or because of new finds in British Columbia, the largest living yellow cedars are larger than the largest Port Orfords. At present, trees of this species rank eighth largest by wood volume, right behind the Big Five, sugar pine, and incense cedar.

Yellow cedar is very picturesque, and includes probably the oldest-growing trees in the Pacific Northwest. Ages over 2,000 years are very likely, as dozens of specimens have been cross-dated and verified at ages between 1,500 and 1,834 years. Wood samples from old-growth yellow cedar often have paper-thin rings, making it is easy to imagine a 12-foot-diameter tree being over 2,000 years in age. The wood of old-growth trees has always fetched a very high price in lumber markets, although very little of this wood is cut anymore in Washington. Alaska and British Columbia, however, still have unprotected areas of old-growth yellow cedar that are still being logged. The Japanese have two related species of *Chamaecyparis* that are considered sacred and are highly valued woods for use in temples. A very high price is often paid for old-growth logs of yellow cedar and Port Orford cedar, which are of the same genus.

Yellow cedar is also known as Alaska cedar, Alaska yellow cedar, yellow cypress, or Nootka cypress. Yellow cedar is a subalpine tree throughout much of the Pacific Northwest. It is not usually dominant, but commonly occurs in association with Pacific silver fir or mountain hemlock in forests of the Cascades, Olympics, and Vancouver Island. Although it can be found east of the Cascade crest with such unlikely associates as grand fir or ponderosa pine, it achieves its best development in cool, wet sites such as are found on Vancouver Island and adjacent areas, and Vancouver Island is where the latest discoveries of giant trees have been made. ▲

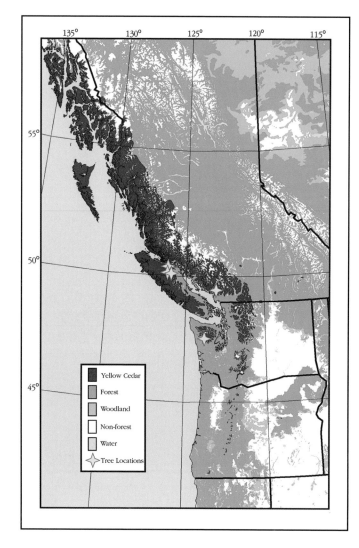

Yellow Cedar
Forest
Woodland
Non-forest
Water
Tree Locations

Yellow cedars lay claim to being the oldest trees in the Pacific Northwest, with many individuals dated at over 1,500 years. While never dominant, these trees do provide a welcome component within the subalpine forests of western Washington and British Columbia.

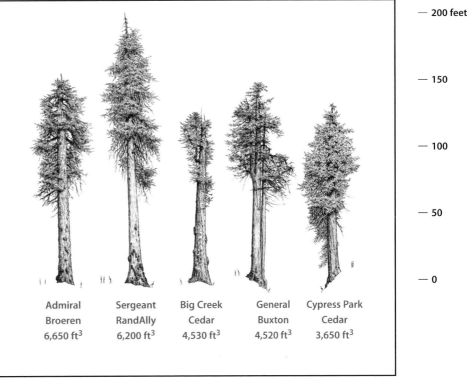

	— 200 feet
	— 150
	— 100
	— 50
	— 0

Admiral Broeren	Sergeant RandAlly	Big Creek Cedar	General Buxton	Cypress Park Cedar
6,650 ft³	6,200 ft³	4,530 ft³	4,520 ft³	3,650 ft³

Admiral Broeren

Volume	6,650 ft³	188 m³
DBH	10.9 ft	331 cm
Height	154 ft	46.9 m
AF Points	575	

Admiral Broeren was discovered before the Sergeant RandAlly but after the General Buxton Trees listed below. While it does not have the impressive circumference or height of the RandAlly, its stovepipe trunk gives it a greater volume. With over 6,600 cubic feet of trunk volume it stands as the world's largest known *Chamaecyparis*. The day I saw this tree was a 16-hour marathon during which three giant yellow cedars were measured. The Admiral was the last of the three and the most difficult to get to. Erik Piikilla, Bill Beese, their friend Buck, and I started out for this tree at the end of the day when we were already tired, and to top it off it had just started raining. Bill, ecologist for MacMillan Bloedel (now Weyerhaeuser), was the only one of us who had been to the tree before. When Bill first saw this tree in the Memekay River valley of Vancouver Island, he had hiked about 200 yards up from the lower road. He said that because the lower slopes were about a 100 percent grade, it would be better to drop down from above. He was wrong. The slopes were at least as steep from above and from a direction that he hadn't been over before. After scrambling down a couple hundred yards of incredibly steep slopes we were losing confidence of locating the tree, and I for one (who was packing the laser and tripod) was not looking forward to the hike back up the cliff. Luckily for us, Bill was determined. He scrambled down ahead of us and was able to find the tree.

The Admiral Broeren is growing on a level bench about equidistant between the two roads on this nearly vertical hillside. In fact, the bench was so small it did not even show up on our detailed topographic map. But the tree was unmistakable, and the stovepipe description Bill used was totally appropriate. While the tree had the smallest DBH of any of the trees we had measured that day, its lack of taper erased any doubt that this was the most voluminous of the trees measured that day. The tree was originally named the General Broeren after longtime Menzies Bay forester Martin Broeren, but later changed to Admiral in order to reflect his passion for boating. After we took the measurements, we had just enough time for a couple of photos before darkness began closing in around us. On our way up and out, we traded off carrying the equipment, which was a great relief to me. ▲

Few tree experiences I have had can compare to the day I first saw the Admiral Broeren. Until we were almost next to it, the steep slopes and constant rain hid this tree well. While it is not the tallest nor the thickest, its stovepipe-shaped trunk contains the most wood of any yellow cedar.

Sergeant RandAlly

Volume	6,200 ft³	175 m³
DBH	13.7 ft	416 cm
Height	200 ft	61.0 m
AF Points	728	

The Sargeant RandAlly Tree owes its life to ecologist Bill Beese (center), as he rerouted a road cut that was slated to pass through where the tree now stands. If the picture does not do this tree full justice, it will at least record one of the most spectacular trees I have ever seen.

This tree shattered all my preconceptions about the size a tree of this species can attain. In one tree we have the thickest ever recorded, the tallest ever recorded, and the first *Chamaecyparis* that measures larger than 6,000 cubic feet in volume. Discovered on Crown land north of Campbell River on Vancouver Island in 1993 by road engineers for MacMillan Bloedel, this tree would normally have been cut to make way for the logging road. I say normally, because Bill Beese, ecologist for MB, had earlier started a conservation program designed to protect giant or unusual trees uncovered during the company's timber surveying or cruising. The program had already located two other giant yellow cedars, and this one had dimensions that were substantially larger than the other trees. This time, the road design was changed to accommodate a 400-foot buffer around the tree. The road engineers who first came upon the tree were Randall Dayton and Ally Gibson, hence the name RandAlly. "Let it be known that we found it absolutely together, at the exact same moment in time," says Ally Gibson. "We both looked up and said, 'Look at that tree!'" agrees Randall Dayton. The "sergeant" in the name comes from their desire to call it after the highest enlisted rank, as they were engineers and not management.

I first saw the RandAlly tree during a Vancouver Island Big Tree Tour in 1997 with Erik Piikilla, Bill, and their friend Buck, a three-day period in which several of Canada's largest trees were visited and measured. That particular day was jam-packed—three giant yellow cedars were measured. This tree was located inside the bends of a giant hairpin turn in a logging road, so we parked in the bend and hiked into the stand. The stand was composed of western red cedar, western hemlock, and Pacific silver fir, so when the yellow cedar was spied within them it stood out dramatically. Not only was the silvery, shaggy trunk of the cedar in stark contrast to the other trees, but the RandAlly dwarfed all of the others, including the red cedars. Even though I was familiar with the rough dimensions of this tree from measurements Bill had taken earlier, I was astounded by how truly huge this tree was. I couldn't believe that what I was seeing was real. At that instant this tree became the world's largest known *Chamaecyparis,* eclipsing the champion Port Orford cedar in Oregon. ▲

Big Creek Cedar

This yellow cedar is the current National Record tree, and had the largest trunk diameter ever recorded until the Sergeant RandAlly was discovered. It grows along the Big Creek Trail high on the slopes above Quinault Lake in Olympic National Park, an area that receives 200 inches of precipitation annually, and has a mystic aura of great age and nobility.

Volume	4,530 ft³	128 m³
DBH	12.0 ft	365 cm
Height	129 ft	39.3 m
AF Points	587	

My first visit to this tree was on a weekend excursion with my friend Arthur Lee Jacobson. Over the previous several years we had taken similar hikes to remeasure or discover new record trees. Our first event was a four-day trek to remeasure the champion alpine fir, to update measurements last taken in 1963. Our second trip was to remeasure the 1945 record Enchanted Valley Hemlock and to measure a potential champion mountain hemlock that Robert Wood found while out hiking some years ago. This time out we had company—four others who all had an interest in trees, and one of whom had access to a cabin on the shores of Quinault Lake. After a night in the cabin and a peaceful morning, we were ready. It was raining now, with no sign of a letup—raingear would be useless. With rain like that, raingear only adds discomfort to the inevitable wetness. My raingear was off after the first ten minutes and stayed off.

After hiking through the spruce rain forest we gradually ascended into montane forest. The Big Creek Cedar was easily visible from the trail—an enormous burly trunk, festooned with moss, rising about 120 feet to a large, snapped-off top. After lunch we took some group photos, trying to keep the cameras as dry as possible. We also remeasured the tree, and found it had not grown since first measured in 1982. The height measurement was confounded by the humidity fogging up my clinometer after only one quick reading. Luckily Arthur also had his clinometer along, and I was able to get a good reading this time before it too fogged up. ▲

When Arthur Lee Jacobson and I made our trip to the Big Creek Cedar, the largest yellow cedar in the United States, we made an event out of it. We also found out the hard way what it is like to be in an area that receives 200 inches of rain annually.

General Buxton

The General Buxton was the first giant yellow cedar found and protected by ecologist Bill Beese. He first saw it in December of 1989 and saved it literally hours before the tree would have been cut down. The tree now stands on the edge of a giant clearcut in the upper drainage of Big Tree Creek, north of Campbell River on Vancouver Island. It grows on Crown land within an area called TFL (tree farm license) 39, leased to MacMillan Bloedel for timber harvesting. Once the tree was saved, Bill approached his supervisors with a management plan for protecting giant trees like this found during surveying or cruising. Now, if anything large or unusual is located while the field personnel are out doing what they do, it is reported to Bill, who evaluates whether special protection is warranted. The General is visible from the clearcut, and now grows only a few yards from the forest edge. The base consists of a large burly pedestal with a small cave in one side. From this expanded base emerges the main trunk, which divides about 30 feet up into two main leaders. The twin trunks give it an inflated circumference value but cost it in the volume department. Even so, this tree is a gigantic specimen that, when discovered, was the largest known of the species. ▲

Volume	4,520 ft³	128 m³
DBH	10.9 ft *	332 cm *
Height	148 ft	45.1 m
AF Points	572	* Measured at 6'7"

This giant cedar was the first of three immense trees discovered in the Kelsey Bay area on Vancouver Island. Saved only minutes before it was going to be felled, the General Buxton Tree now sits just a few feet from a large clearcut.

Cypress Park Cedar

Volume	3,650 ft³	103 m³
DBH	7.5 ft *	228 cm *
Height	130 ft	39.6 m
AF Points	421	* Measured at 7'

Vancouver, British Columbia, is blessed with spectacular mountains rising up right outside of town. Clothing these mountains are equally spectacular forests. Even though the logging history of Vancouver is similar to many western locations, and nearly all of the low-elevation forests were logged years ago, the steepness of the terrain here has meant that trees at many of the higher elevations have been left intact. Their condition may also be due to the peculiar fire history (or lack thereof) in these mountains. Most of the upper forests in the mountains north of Vancouver have not had any fires for several thousand years. The Douglas firs that were probably present in the past are long gone, leaving a climax forest of hemlock, fir, and cedar. The historic logging pattern basically was for crews to follow the Douglas fir up the river valleys until it was exhausted, and then shift elsewhere. Cypress Provincial Park, just above West Vancouver, is an area representative of these ancient, subalpine forests—in fact, this is where Ken Lertzman of Simon Fraser University did the first studies demonstrating the great age of these upper-slope forests. The largest known tree in the park is the Cypress Park Cedar, which grows along the road to the Cypress Bowl recreation area.

Randy Stoltmann first publicized this tree by nominating it as the BC champion in 1988. He showed me the tree in 1989. At that time, although we were not too impressed with the lower trunk, a modest 7.5 feet thick, the tree actually appeared to increase in diameter higher up the bole. This, in fact, is a feature I've noted in many subalpine forests. Growing seasons are short at these elevations, and wood is deposited from the top down as trees grow. In some years when the snowpack is late in melting or early to arrive in fall, wood may not be deposited along the trunk near the base of the tree. Over the centuries, this can lead to a thicker stem higher up the tree (and more growth rings inside the tree at that height as well). Even though the diameter near the ground is only 7.5 feet, the tree does not drop below 7 feet thick until 28 feet up. A partial core from this tree reveals that it is at least 1,200 years old—not bad for an almost urban tree. ▲

Certainly the easiest of the giant yellow cedars to visit, the Cypress Park Cedar is a roadside tree in Cypress Provincial Park near Vancouver, British Columbia. Exceeded in diameter by a great many other cedars, its inclusion in this book was assured by the volume of its huge, slow-tapering trunk.

NOBLE FIR *Abies procera*

Noble fir displays the beauty and vigor which makes this fir tree one of the stateliest and most splendid inhabitants of the forests of the northwestern states.
—*Charles Sprague Sargent, 1901*

Noble fir is a beautiful subalpine tree from the Cascades and Coast Ranges of Oregon and Washington. In Washington the tree is found from the vicinity of Stevens Pass southward in the Cascades, and there is a population in the Willapa Hills of southwestern Washington. In Oregon the tree occurs on the highest peaks of the Coast Ranges and in the subalpine forests of the Cascades south to the McKenzie River.

Technically, the range extends south toward Crater Lake, where it grades into the Shasta red fir, but the area between the McKenzie River and Crater Lake has surprisingly sparse populations. This is interesting because north of the McKenzie River the tree is continuously distributed north to the Columbia River.

Noble fir is the largest of all the world's *Abies,* with specimens that have reached over 300 feet in height and nearly 6,000 cubic feet of stemwood volume. Unlike many others of its genus, noble fir is often a pioneer tree that comes in aggressively after disturbance. Many young and mature stands in the Cascades are often pure noble fir, which does not regenerate under its own shade, but old-growth stands eventually give way to shade-tolerant species such as Pacific silver fir or western hemlock. Noble fir does not have the longevity or decay resistance of Douglas fir, so that once a forest gets to be 300 to 400 years old, the noble fir component quickly begins to decline. On a good site, however, noble fir can grow quickly, outgrowing even its Douglas fir associates. An old-growth noble fir tree can have up to 30 percent more wood volume than a Douglas fir of the same height and diameter, because of its thinner bark and a slower stem taper.

The ultimate development of this species seems to be near Mount St. Helens, as all the largest ones are found here. A beautiful grove grew near Harmony Falls, northeast of the mountain, before being destroyed by the 1980 eruption. This grove contained an individual that was measured as having a height of 325 feet. Although not a laser-based measurement, this is the tallest known specimen of any *Abies* ever recorded, and only two western species have been measured taller, one a coast redwood, the other a Douglas fir. Southwest of the mountain and not affected by the events of 1980 is another beautiful grove, which not only contains the tallest known living *Abies,* but also has the Pacific Northwest biomass record—44,584 cubic feet per acre or 3,120 cubic meters per hectare—excluding coast redwood stands. ▲

Legend:
- Noble Fir
- Hybrids with California Red Fir
- Forest
- Woodland
- Non-forest
- Water
- Tree Locations

Noble fir is a subalpine tree with a relatively small range in the Cascades and Coast Ranges of Washington and Oregon. It shares many traits with its lower-elevation rival, Douglas fir, particularly in being a long-lived pioneer species. Its ability to tolerate heavy snow while young, however, gives it an advantage at higher elevations.

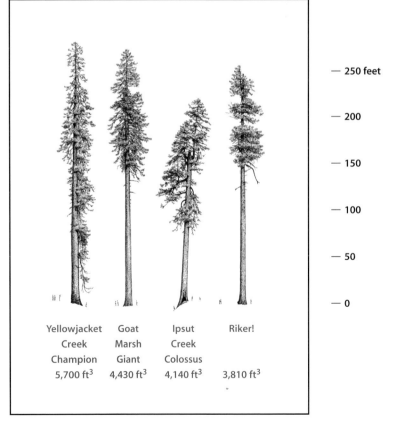

				— 250 feet
				— 200
				— 150
				— 100
				— 50
				— 0
Yellowjacket Creek Champion	Goat Marsh Giant	Ipsut Creek Colossus	Riker!	
5,700 ft³	4,430 ft³	4,140 ft³	3,810 ft³	

Yellowjacket Creek Champion

The Yellowjacket Creek Champion is the world's largest known *Abies*. It was discovered in 1964 when the area was being logged. The tree was part of an exceptional grove of noble firs that had been designated a Botanical Area. Old maps of Washington's Gifford Pinchot National Forest show the Noble Fir Botanical Area on upper Yellowjacket Creek. I guess the high value of the protected trees was too much temptation for the Forest Service, as the entire grove, save two trees, was logged in the mid-1960s. This left the champion and its neighbor completely exposed to the clearcut, as clearly shown in old photos. The tree has been slowly declining since then. I was first shown the tree in the late 1980s by Jim Riley, a longtime ranger at the local Randle District Ranger Station who had an interest in big trees. By that time the top 30 feet had blown off the tree. The tree has declined even more since then. The top is now at 227 feet, and the upper foliage is thinning. My drawing relies on earlier photos for the topmost piece, since I have never seen that part intact.

The trunk of the Yellowjacket Creek Champion, however, has no peer within the genus *Abies*. The second-largest known fir is the Goat Marsh Giant (below), which has only 78 percent as much wood volume. The Yellowjacket's DBH is slightly over 9.5 feet and the trunk is still 7 feet thick at 54 feet up. The part of the trunk above 130 feet is fairly similar to some other trees, but the size of the lower section is astounding. ▲

Volume	5,700 ft³	161 m³
DBH	9.5 ft	290 cm
Height	278 ft *	84.7 m *
AF Points	647	* Original; now 227' tall

The Yellowjacket Creek Champion is the world's largest *Abies*, or true fir. Once the pride of a great noble fir grove, this lonely tree now sits at the edge of a clearcut, its top 50 feet gone.

Goat Marsh Giant

Volume	4,430 ft³	126 m³
DBH	8.3 ft	253 cm
Height	272 ft	82.9 m
AF Points	597	

I first saw the Goat Marsh Giant in the spring of 1985, on my way to work at Lake Crescent Lodge in Olympic National Park. I had already read *Natural Vegetation of Oregon and Washington* by Jerry Franklin and Ted Dyrness, which mentions the giant trees at Goat Marsh. By 1989 I was a student of Dr. Franklin's, and was part of the crew that remeasured a 4-hectare plot at Goat Marsh that contains this tree. Goat Marsh is on the southwest slopes of Mount St. Helens and fortunately remained unscathed by the 1980 eruption. The marsh was set aside as a Research Natural Area in the early 1970s after a Weyerhaeuser timber cruiser (it was Weyerhaeuser land at the time) came across the grove and thought it the finest he'd ever seen. The land was traded to the Forest Service, who then created the Research Natural Area out of it. One plot was put in this grove in 1972, followed by a permanent research plot in 1977. The plot has the largest wood volume per unit area of all of our research plots, and it is not even dominated by Douglas fir. Nearly 450,000 board feet per acre is found in this stand, of which almost two-thirds is noble fir.

The Goat Marsh Giant is the largest tree in a stand of giant trees. It grows at the bottom of the grove, surrounded by the purple columns of its siblings. Dr. Franklin had not been to many of the giants with me, but this tree was well known to him. Noble fir is his favorite species, and he is at least partly responsible for this grove having been designated a Research Natural Area. Above the 8.3-foot DBH, the tree is a perfect, smooth-tapering cone that rises up to its 272-foot top. Truly an awesome tree in a most awesome grove. ▲

The Goat Marsh Giant is the largest tree in a grove of giant trees that holds the height and biomass records for any *Abies* forest, and that Jerry Franklin helped protect. Now he can stand back and admire.

Ipsut Creek Colossus

Volume	4,140 ft³	117 m³
DBH	8.9 ft	272 cm
Height	217 ft	66.1 m
AF Points	564	

Ipsut Creek is a drainage in Mount Rainier National Park. Like many of the drainages around this massive volcano, it is short and steep. At the top of the drainage are subalpine meadows and alder-choked avalanche chutes, while the base is in low-elevation rain forest along the Carbon River. Ipsut Creek is well known to the scientific community, for the subalpine forests in the upper Ipsut have the oldest trees in the park. Yellow cedars are consistently the oldest known trees in the Pacific Northwest, and trees along Ipsut Creek have been aged at over 1,200 years. One of these, almost large enough to be listed in this book, is just shy of 12 feet in diameter and 133 feet tall, and was once the national champion. Most of the subalpine forests of upper Ipsut Creek are thought to have gone thousands of years without a fire and are now composed only of shade-tolerant trees like the hemlocks, Pacific silver fir, and yellow cedar. There is one exception, however. Along the trail at the 4,000-foot elevation stands a lone noble fir. The Colossus is visible from near Ipsut Pass, 1,000 feet above and a quarter mile beyond the tree, appearing as a towering blue crown emerging above the dark green hemlock-fir canopy.

The nearly 9-foot-diameter trunk is quite out of place at this elevation, and the multiple reiterations that make up the top give the tree a spectacular gnarl that its companions lack. The main trunk, broken off at 162 feet, is a near twin to the Goat Marsh Giant, as both have 4,000 cubic feet in the first 162 feet. While the reiterations make up most of the lost volume, the intact top of the Goat Marsh Giant gives it the edge in total volume. ▲

The forests along Ipsut Creek stand within a drainage that contains the oldest known trees in Mount Rainier National Park, as well as this giant noble fir, the Ipsut Creek Colossus.

Riker!

Volume	3,810 ft^3	108 m^3
DBH	7.3 ft	222 cm
Height	253 ft	77.1 m
AF Points	539	

One descends into the colossal Goat Marsh forest at Mount St. Helens conscious of an unparalleled atmosphere. Huge columns of trees tower all around, yet because there is a very sparse understory, carpeted mostly by small herbs and ferns, a visitor can see far into the grove. The Goat Marsh forest has many of the largest known noble firs. In addition to the Goat Marsh Giant, the tallest known noble fir, its spike top piercing the canopy at 295 feet, grows here. Of the ten largest known noble firs, eight grow in this grove. The second-largest tree at Goat Marsh (affec-tionately named Riker! and familiar to *Star Trek* fans as the second-in-command), is barely larger than the third largest. I hope this book will inspire more eyes to search, and subsequently to find new, even larger trees. However, I can give you a long list of places where I have looked and not found them.

Riker! is not a tree that jumps out at you like the Goat Marsh Giant. I found out about it while examining the plot records. I noted several of the trees with the largest diameters in the stand and individually searched them out. The one having the second-largest diameter in the grove is, unfortunately, rather short and in decline. Riker! was third based on diameter, and is almost hidden by a large log on one side and some small hemlocks that have sprouted up near its base. The heavy shade cast by the hemlocks gives the tree a black, mysterious look as one approaches. Riker! has a trunk that tapers slowly and evenly, like that of the Goat Marsh Giant, but is slightly smaller. For its first 150 feet, this tree is decidedly smaller than the others listed here, even though the upper trunk compares favorably with the other giants. At 161 feet up, where it is 3.8 feet diameter, this tree is larger than any other known noble fir. ▲

Riker! is the second largest of dozens of huge noble firs at Mount St. Helens. Because the 1980 blast from the mountain was directed to the north, some of the nicest forests in the area, to the south and southwest, luckily escaped damage.

PORT ORFORD CEDAR *Chamaecyparis lawsoniana*

White cedar possesses the finest qualities commercially of any timber tree known to commerce. Oregon may well feel proud that she has among her timber family the stately and valuable white cedar, the equal of which as a lumber tree is not extant.
—Timberman, *1908*

Port Orford cedar has had a rich and interesting history. During the early part of the twentieth century, it was considered the most valuable timber tree of the West. The fragrant, clear wood is very strong yet lightweight and easily worked. Descriptions of this tree from old lumber journals are overflowing with flattering adjectives, and hail the Port Orford cedar as the greatest of all western woods. The Japanese have long considered their own species of *Chamaecyparis (C. obtusa* and *C. pisifera—* called Hinoki and Sawara) to be superior and often reserved them for use in temples. Once old-growth sources of the Japanese species were depleted, the Port Orford and yellow cedars were found to have the same desirable qualities. Port Orford cedar has been heavily logged for the last hundred years, and for these reasons premium prices are still fetched by old-growth logs.

Port Orford cedar is distributed over a fairly wide gradient of elevations and climatological conditions, yet has a very small geographic range. The Siskiyou Mountains are the place this tree calls home. When seeds of this species were sent back to England and grown, unusual varieties began to appear among the seedlings as early as 1855. Since then, more than 200 cultivated varieties, showing variations in foliage color, texture, and growth form, have been developed. Many of these cultivars are trees, but the majority are shrubs or ground cover forms. The cultivated plants are collectively known as Lawson cypresses after the Lawson Nurseries in Scotland, which first introduced the ornamental conifers. Lawson cypresses have been very common ornamental plants in the Pacific Northwest and Great Britain for the last hundred years.

An introduced root-decay fungus *(Phytophthora lateralis)* has decimated many of the native stands of Port Orford cedar. The fungus is lethal—once infection occurs, infected trees usually die within about a year. The disease is easily transported by water and can be carried into new areas by cars or even on hikers' feet. Certain stands are in areas that seem susceptible, yet the disease has not taken hold. Such is the case with the national champion Port Orford cedar south of Powers, in Oregon. This tree, the biggest in terms of points, diameter, and wood volume, seems to be in ideal conditions for root disease, yet remains healthy (its dead top is not related to the disease). Other areas in remote valleys near the southern end of its range in California are luckily still free of the disease. ▲

Legend:
- Port Orford Cedar
- Forest
- Woodland
- Non-forest
- Water
- Tree Locations

Port Orford cedar is one of the most unusual of our western conifers in having a fairly wide ecological amplitude, yet growing in a small geographic range. A beautiful species, it has many ornamental varieties that have been widely planted in the United States and Europe. Sadly, an introduced root rot has made scenes such a this one common in many of our urban landscapes.

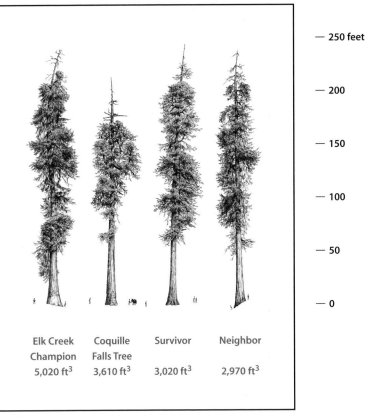

				250 feet
				200
				150
				100
				50
				0
Elk Creek Champion	Coquille Falls Tree	Survivor	Neighbor	
5,020 ft³	3,610 ft³	3,020 ft³	2,970 ft³	

Elk Creek Champion

Volume	5,020 ft³	142 m³
DBH	12.0 ft	365 cm
Height	229 ft	69.8 m
AF Points	690	

The quote from the timber journal at the opening of this chapter sums up the fate of Port Orford cedars during the twentieth century. With a wood so valuable and a geographic range so small, this species did not stand much of a chance. Add to that a fatal root rot, and you are not left with much. Most of the giants of this species were felled long before the start of the Big Tree Program in 1940. Stumps up to 17 feet in diameter have been recorded from the northern end of Port Orford cedar's range. Oregon's Coquille River Valley is home to all of the Port Orford cedars listed here, and to several historic records as well, although only two trees have been listed during the last 60 years. The giant along Elk Creek has been in the record books since its discovery in 1971. From the moment it was found it easily became the national champion, as the previous record holder was far smaller.

I first saw the Elk Creek Champion during the summer of 1989. Although the top is dead, the tree does not have the root rot. Top dieback is common with this species, as it is with all of our cedars, as it is related to drought stress during hot spells, not to the fungal disease. Some of the earlier measurements of this tree indicate the tree is 239 feet tall, a number that I have seen reprinted in a number of places. This is unfortunate, as the top is still intact on this tree, and it is 10 feet shorter than originally claimed. Nevertheless, the huge trunk has a 12-foot DBH, and it is still 5 feet thick at 90 feet. That gives it what is needed to maintain the largest known diameter for this species for the entire length of the tree. ▲

The Elk Creek Champion is the undisputed giant among Port Orford cedars. Although larger trees have been reported from the past, this tree has been the largest recorded since record-keeping began in 1940.

Coquille Falls Tree

Volume	3,610 ft³	102 m³
DBH	9.0 ft	275 cm
Height	206 ft	62.8 m
AF Points	556	

In doing research for this book, I remembered a Forest Service publication on the ecology of Port Orford cedar, because its cover photo showed a very impressive tree. Jerry Franklin, with whom I studied at the University of Washington, had taken hundreds of large-format black-and-white photos during his more than 30-year tenure with the Forest Service. I came across some photos of this same tree in his files, and asked him to recall the tree. He stated that it was within the Coquille River Falls Research Natural Area. This was a place I had visited previously and where I found the lovely forests very impressive. Some of the moist benches within this area contain beautiful Port Orford cedars, along with some of the largest Douglas firs remaining in Oregon. Ten-foot-thick, slow-tapering monsters tickle the sky 280 feet above your head as you wander through the groves. Dr. Franklin's description of the cedar, combined with the distinctive scarring on its bark, made the tree relatively easy to find. Even though the photos were over 30 years old, the tree was still healthy when Chris Earle and I relocated it in 1998. The proximity of a logging road and nearby young trees dying from the root-rot apparently do not faze this cedar. The Coquille Falls Tree is an example of a tree located in what should be an ideal spot to contract the disease, yet it has not. Our initial nickname for this tree was the "Road Warrior," as it has apparently battled the disease for decades and lives on.

The 9-foot-thick trunk of the Coquille Falls Tree is clothed in thick bark, replete with charcoal patches attesting to previous bouts with fire. The trunk is still 6 feet thick at 40 feet up, and at that height is nearly as thick as the Champion. The upper crown is very densely covered with foliage, and supports a number of healthy, reiterated trunks. This well-formed, very healthy tree gives every indication that it can survive for several centuries more. ▲

The Coquille Falls Tree is the largest known cedar in the Coquille River Falls Research Natural Area in southwestern Oregon. Photos of this tree taken during the 1970s have appeared in several books and research publications about Port Orford cedar.

Survivor

Volume	3,020 ft³	86 m³
DBH	8.5 ft	260 cm
Height	235 ft	71.6 m
AF Points	564	

In the middle of the beautiful Coquille Falls Research Natural Area (RNA) in southwest Oregon stands the Survivor. We named it so because all around it are giant snags of cedars that have been slain by *Phytophthora* root rot, the most lethal disease known to this species. The steep slopes of the RNA straddle a section of the Coquille River that contains the namesake falls. While much of the RNA is composed of Douglas fir/hemlock/tanoak forest, certain moist benches found throughout the area support some of the finest surviving groves of Port Orford cedar. Sadly, root rot has reduced many of these groves to towering clusters of cedar skeletons, although other groves have gone unscathed, and still others have some dead and some living trees. This strange pattern leads me to think that the natural population of Port Orford cedar has some trees that are resistant to the disease. Once the disease strikes, trees usually die within a year. As noted above, the disease is very easily transported by tires, feet, or through the water table. It seems that with the disease so widespread in this area, if trees were going to die, they would already be dead. Most of the current mortality I noted in the area is found among young trees growing along roadsides. The Survivor is the only living cedar tree in a grove of skeletons.

When it was first measured, the Survivor became the tallest Port Orford cedar ever recorded. This may sound more impressive than it actually is, for records on the historic sizes for this species are poor, and even these tend to emphasize the trunk dimensions rather than height. The Survivor's reign was short-lived, however, as a few hours later we found a slightly smaller tree that measured 3 feet taller. However, these are still the only two trees of this species I know of that exceed 230 feet in height. Its swollen base, great height, and hefty upper trunk give the Survivor the extra wood volume needed to make it a giant of its species. ▲

The Survivor is so named because it is the lone living tree in what once was a fantastic grove of Port Orford cedars. The root disease affecting this species has resulted in a forest of skeletons here, leaving just this one living (and surprisingly healthy) tree.

Neighbor

Volume	2,970 ft³	84 m³
DBH	8.4 ft	256 cm
Height	228 ft	69.5 m
AF Points	553	

Neighbor is a nearby companion to the Elk Creek Champion that impressed me as I was taking the Champion's measurements. The entire drive through the "working forest" south of Powers, Oregon, on my way to visit the largest known Port Orford cedar, makes its way through young forests with the occasional big tree emergent above. Why these were not cut with the rest of the trees, I am not sure—it could be they were left as seed trees. In any case the drive is dotted with the occasional towering tree of either Douglas fir, or, as one gets closer to the Champion, Port Orford cedar. The dense brush in the area does not allow much of a view in to where the trees are, so you see just their tops poking out above the young canopy. The largest ones all appear to be in the vicinity of the Champion, with the Neighbor the largest I have yet seen.

Although the Neighbor is decidedly smaller than the Champion, it has similar proportions and is a very large tree in its own right. The nearly 8.5-foot-thick trunk has a gentle, sweeping spiral bark pattern that erupts from the ground as it spins its way up to its 228-foot top. The trunk is still over a yard wide at 130 feet up, which compares favorably to the other Port Orfords I have measured. My expeditions have not thoroughly exhausted the areas of surviving Port Orford cedars, so there is still the possibility of finding still larger ones in the misty rain forests of coastal southern Oregon. The extremely rugged Port Orford Cedar Research Natural Area also has very large trees that have yet to be explored. ▲

The Neighbor takes its name because of its proximity to the Elk Creek Champion. In my search for large Port Orford cedars, I at first thought that I would find many larger trees, but this tree, spiraling its way out of the Siskiyou rain forest, remains the fourth largest I have found.

Jeffrey pine develops a stout trunk not so tall as ponderosa, but with a big-limbed, spreading crown. This is the pine most often seen clinging to stark granite domes and gleaming rock slopes overlooking major Sierra canyons.
—Stephen Arno, 1973

Jeffrey pine is a close cousin to the ponderosa pine, but was found to be a distinct species by the Scottish botanical explorer John Jeffrey, after whom the tree is named, way back in the 1850s. Jeffrey is credited with discovering a number of California plants, including the foxtail pine. His sudden disappearance in 1853–54 in the desert of southern California remains one of the great mysteries of botanical exploration. Jeffrey pine, mainly a California species, barely strays across the border into Oregon (in the Siskiyou Mountains), Nevada (near Lake Tahoe), and Mexico (the San Pedro Martir Mountains in northern Baja). Generally found in upper montane or even subalpine forests, these trees are often found in open forests or even on exposed rock surfaces. Rarely outfitted with the long, slow-tapering stems and tall, narrow crowns of ponderosas, Jeffreys more than compensate with their enormous crowns of wide-reaching branches. While young trees are very similar in appearance to ponderosa, and the wood volumes of the largest are comparable, the giants of the two species are worlds apart in appearance.

The unusual fragrance of Jeffrey pine bark is often used in its identification. In California, the bark of ponderosa pine has a slightly piney smell. The Jeffrey pine, particularly when warmed by the sun, can be quite fragrant. I have heard the smell likened to vanilla, chocolate, or even pineapples, but my son put it best for me—cream soda. The scent comes from different chemicals found in the resin, one of which is the hydrocarbon heptane. Nearly pure heptane is in fact obtainable from Jeffrey pine, and was used in the development of the octane rating for gasoline. One of the early uses for ponderosa pine was collecting the sap for making turpentine. When one turpentiner from Butte County made the mistake of collecting from a Jeffrey, an explosion destroyed his still. ▲

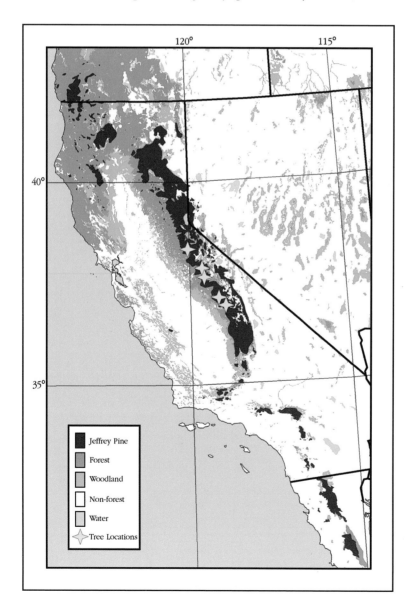

Jeffrey Pine
Forest
Woodland
Non-forest
Water
Tree Locations

Jeffrey pine is certainly most famous for the picturesque, windswept forms it takes on the exposed granite domes and cliffs of the Sierras. It is also, as of this writing, the second largest species of pine in the world.

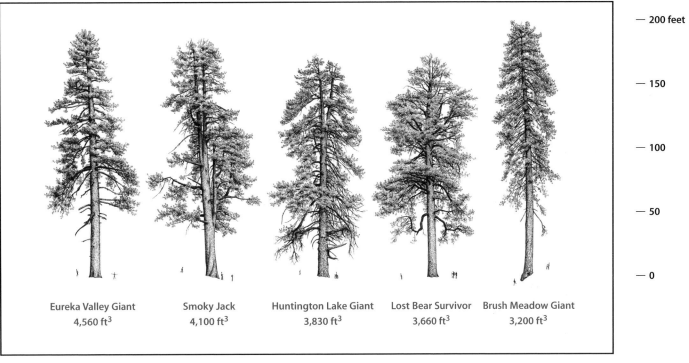

Eureka Valley Giant	Smoky Jack	Huntington Lake Giant	Lost Bear Survivor	Brush Meadow Giant
4,560 ft³	4,100 ft³	3,830 ft³	3,660 ft³	3,200 ft³

— 200 feet
— 150
— 100
— 50
— 0

Eureka Valley Giant

Volume	4,560 ft³		129 m³
DBH	8.1 ft		247 cm
Height	192 ft		58.5 m
AF Points	521		

The Sonora Pass highway travels through some wonderful stands of Jeffrey pine in California's Stanislaus National Forest before climbing the last few miles up to the 9,600-foot pass. This area contains a former champion and the current champion (since 1984). I searched for and found the former champion with a group of friends during the summer of 1998. Unfortunately, the tree appears to have fallen soon after it was discovered in 1969, leaving behind an enormous pine log. From the looks of the log it was clear that it would have ranked as one of the largest pines in volume. The Eureka Valley Giant is the current champion and is farther up the valley near the Columns of the Giants lava formation.

The Eureka Valley Giant has planted its roots in the moist soil adjoining a wet meadow, one of the many tricks trees use to get themselves into the record books. Even though most people consider the Jeffrey a smaller tree than its cousin the ponderosa pine, this specimen has a greater wood volume than any ponderosa that I have yet measured. In fact, it is the world's largest known hard pine (*Pinus* subgenus *Pinus*). While the architecture of this tree is similar to that of the much smaller Jeffreys, the proportions have been expanded, although this tree is probably not as old as the next three trees listed here. Rand Knight, a friend who has accompanied me on several big-tree excursions, including a visit to the largest sugar pine, felt this to be the most impressive pine he had ever seen. Seven-foot-diameter Jeffrey pines are a rare sight—I know only of a half dozen or so—but this tree is still 7 feet thick at 47 feet off the ground. ▲

When I first saw the Eureka Valley Giant in 1996, I was amazed that a Jeffrey could get so big. Since then, after seeing and finding the trees listed below, I have come to realize that this is indeed one of the world's truly giant pine species.

Smoky Jack

Volume	4,100 ft³	116 m³
DBH	7.5 ft	227 cm
Height	186 ft	56.7 m
AF Points	485	

More than once while driving along a magnificent stretch of forest highway, I've spied a giant off in the distance. Occa-sionally the tree is not all that far off the road. Smoky Jack is such a tree. In plain sight about 50 feet from the Tioga Pass Road in Yosemite National Park, the second-largest Jeffrey pine was probably overlooked by a million people before being singled out as a legitimate giant. Perhaps the general magnificence of the forest along this entire stretch of road is so impressive as to make the exceptional seem ordinary, because this gigantic tree has been ignored for decades. While smaller than the current record holder, Smoky Jack outpoints all of the previous champions. Possibly its unusual shape obscured this tree's great size. Smoky Jack's nearly 7.5-foot-thick trunk tapers to 6 feet at 33 feet, just before the first of several reiterations peels off. The trunk then holds its diameter from this point up to 100 feet, where the second major split occurs. At that point the trunk is still over 5.5 feet thick. This is also a tree that leans, so the bark is smooth on the top curve of the trunk, having been brushed smooth over the centuries by falling twigs and bark. The tree has several reiterations 2.5 to 4 feet in diameter.

The largest of these measures over 350 cubic feet, and all told the reiterations contribute over 1,000 cubic feet of wood to the total volume. By all accounts Smoky Jack is an unusual tree, and in my mind the most amazing Jeffrey of them all. ▲

Smoky Jack, its massive trunk spiraling up, is the largest known Jeffrey in Yosemite. Until I measured it in 1998, its size went unnoticed, even though tens of thousands of people see this tree every year as they drive the Tioga Pass Road. Here Brian Mattos marvels at the tree.

Huntington Lake Giant

Volume	3,830 ft³	109 m³
DBH	7.6 ft	231 cm
Height	173 ft	52.7 m
AF Points	476	

The Huntington Lake Giant reigned briefly as national champion during the 1970s. Fortunately, American Forests still had the records on this tree, whose impressive dimensions, like many other previous champions, still make it one of the largest trees known.

The National Big Tree Program was started in 1940. Since then, and for many species, a number of trees have occupied the list through the decades. In some cases a tree was cut or otherwise had died or fallen and was replaced. But in many cases the tree was simply outpointed. This is the case with the largest Jeffrey pines. When I began doing research for this book, I wrote to Bill Cannon at American Forests, and he came up with three former record-holding Jeffreys. One of them was the Huntington Lake Giant. I had the legal description of where the tree was, and after a short search I found it near Huntington Lake in the Sierras.

I was blown away when I first saw this tree. It had a completely different architecture from Jeffreys I had seen before, and some of the limbs were enormous. The tree obviously had spent most of its long life in an open-grown situation—a situation it desperately needs to regain, because it is being smothered by a dense forest of young pines. These small trees shade its lower branches, killing them, and also compete with the larger tree for soil nutrients. Even worse, these little pines pose a fire hazard that could easily allow the entire tree to die from some ordinarily mild fire. Some judicious thinning of the surrounding forest could keep the Huntington Lake Giant safe and alive for decades to come. Despite its crowded setting, the tree is still a spectacular sight. Its lower trunk is massive. Above that, the 7.6-foot DBH tapers only slightly, so that at 45 feet up the stem is still 7 feet thick. ▲

Lost Bear Survivor

Volume	3,660 ft³	104 m³
DBH	7.3 ft	222 cm
Height	173 ft	52.7 m
AF Points	462	

While scouting the Yosemite area on an unrelated project, I spied some fantastic red fir and Jeffrey pine forests along the 18-mile road out to Glacier Point. I came back when I had more time to explore and found a grove of giant Jeffreys high on a knoll above the road. The grove contains about a dozen huge pines, several of which are dead, scattered over an area of about 3-acres. The king of the grove is the Lost Bear Survivor, which I measured on the spot, certain of its tremendous size. My impression of Jeffrey pine was rapidly changing, since I had first laid eyes on the Huntington Lake Giant just the day before. The Giant and the Lost Bear are very different from the largest examples of their close relative, ponderosa pine. They are shorter and far more gnarly than giant ponderosas. The massive, long-reaching branches of these giants also set them apart from other pines (including other Jeffreys). Later, I showed the tree to Brian Mattos, park forester at Yosemite, who informed me that these trees were survivors from the Lost Bear Fire of 1992. This tree is very similar in size and proportion to the Huntington

The Lost Bear Survivor was spotted while I was scouting the Glacier Point area for big firs. Sitting in a fine grove of huge Jeffreys, several of which were killed in the Lost Bear Fire, this tree is the patriarch of the grove.

Lake Giant. While the Huntington tree is larger for the first 60 feet, the Lost Bear Survivor is larger from that point up. In fact, at 110 feet above the ground it is still over 5 feet thick—larger than any other Jeffrey. ▲

Brush Meadow Giant

Volume	3,200 ft³	91 m³
DBH	6.9 ft	210 cm
Height	200 ft	61.0 m
AF Points	473	

In the fall of 1997 I was searching the Teakettle area of the Sierra National Forest for a former champion Jeffrey pine. The long, winding road from Shaver Lake out to the Wishon and Courtright Reservoirs travels through some magnificent forest—especially in the area around the McKinley Grove of giant sequoias. I found the old champion in an area between the two reservoirs on a short road leading out to some power lines. The tree is a handsome, perfectly formed specimen nearly 7 feet thick and 195 feet tall. At the time I measured it I had only measured one larger Jeffrey, the Eureka Valley Giant. Since then I have found and measured

The Brush Meadow Giant was found by chance as I was returning from measuring a previous national champion Jeffrey pine near the Teakettle Experimental Forest in the Sierras. This new find ended up being both taller and thicker than the old champion, not to mention easier to spot from the road.

the larger trees featured in this book. On my drive out that day, however, I spied an even more massive Jeffrey below the road near the sequoia grove. I stopped and measured it and was surprised to find it larger than the tree I had just checked out—in all dimensions. Here was a tree, easily visible from the road, that was larger than one that had once been a national champion. Sometimes I think that when people come upon giant trees in their travels they don't realize they are seeing a record-setting tree just because they are not familiar with what the record is. Or perhaps they think a record tree would not be in plain sight, or figure someone else would have surely seen it and measured it. I think the reason I have been able to locate so many of these giants is simply because I know the dimensions of the champs, and can judge size fairly well.

The Brush Meadow Giant rises a full 200 feet to its bent-over top, making it one of the taller Jeffreys I have measured. The nearly 7-foot-thick base keeps its diameter fairly well, as the tree is still 5 feet across at 80 feet up. Its shape is more reminiscent of the ponderosa-like Jeffreys that I originally was much more familiar with. This tree will probably eventually be replaced as the fifth largest of this species by some giant with an architecture more in line with the other giants listed above. ▲

PONDEROSA PINE *Pinus ponderosa*

Ponderosa pine surpasses all its race in the majesty of its port and the splendor of its vitality; and, an emblem of strength, it appears as enduring as the rocks, above which it raises its noble shafts and stately crowns.
—Charles Sprague Sargent, 1901

Ponderosa pine is the most widespread of our western conifers. Common in every western state, from British Columbia down to the border with Mexico, ponderosa pines are often the first trees encountered as one approaches the mountains when traveling from the Great Plains to the West. No other tree can capture the essence of the great American West like the ponderosa pine. When set against an azure western sky, the bright orangy trunk, supporting its verdant, airy canopy, is a vision few people forget. Ponderosas are part of the first forest formations encountered when travelers leave California's Central Valley and head up into the mountains, and they form the lower timberline throughout the Rockies and on to the eastern slopes of the Cascades.

As common as ponderosas are throughout the Rockies, the Rocky Mountain form (var. *scopulorum*) is not featured in this book. It is the much less widespread coastal form, described here, that greatly exceeds its inland cousins in size to become a true forest giant, and the mid-elevation forests in the mountain ranges of California are home to the largest ponderosas. The eastern slopes of the Cascades of Washington and Oregon grow some mighty examples, but the Sierra Nevada and adjacent Klamath/Siskiyou Mountains are where the species achieves its best development.

As is the case with most of our important timber trees, the largest ponderosas are long gone, although several extremely impressive giants remain. Because there are many trees with similar dimensions out there, it's no surprise that eight different trees have graced the pages of *American Forests'* National Register of Big Trees over the years. Indeed one of these, the La Pine Giant, has held the title four separate times over the last 50 years. The dimensions of the champions listed in this book are fairly similar, and are matched or nearly matched by many trees, over two dozen of which I have measured as contenders in the last several years. ▲

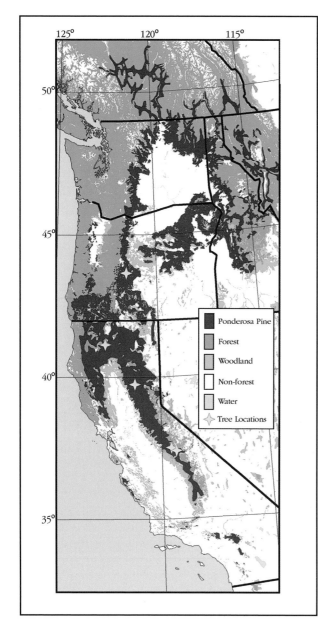

Ponderosa Pine
Forest
Woodland
Non-forest
Water
✧ Tree Locations

Ponderosa pine is without question the most abundant as well as one of the most easily recognized trees in the West. Often it is the first tree encountered as one ascends from the plains or deserts into the mountains, and most people don't realize that the Pacific Coast race of this species has individuals that can reach 8 feet in diameter and 259 feet in height.

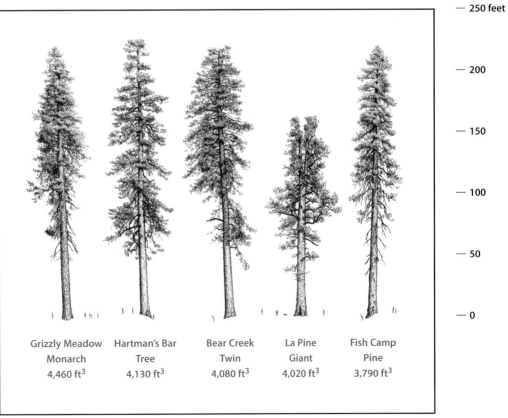

| | | | | | — 250 feet |
| Grizzly Meadow Monarch 4,460 ft³ | Hartman's Bar Tree 4,130 ft³ | Bear Creek Twin 4,080 ft³ | La Pine Giant 4,020 ft³ | Fish Camp Pine 3,790 ft³ | |

Grizzly Meadow Monarch

In 1973 the world's largest known ponderosa pine was briefly the national champion. The tree first caught my attention when I noticed mention of it while looking at back issues of the National Register of Big Trees to see if I could find any trees that were outpointed by new champions, but perhaps still alive. I wrote to Bill Cannon at American Forests to see if he could locate any of the old records on these trees. After a bit of digging, he came up with correspondence concerning four previous record ponderosas, two in the Sierra National Forest and two in the Shasta-Trinity National Forest. Located just south of Yosemite National Park near Grizzly Meadows, this was the first of these I visited, on a trip with some students. When we drove up, the corral built around the tree during its reign was still partly present.

Although slightly more slender than the ponderosas mentioned below, the Monarch has very little taper as it shoots skyward for well over 200 feet. While taking its measurements, I knew it would make the Top Five, but I had no idea it would surpass all others. Indeed, this tree is smaller than the other four for the first 55 feet, which is where nearly 40 percent of the volume occurs. But for the next 155 feet, the tree is consistently larger than its rivals, and that more than makes up for its slender lower stem. Its diameter drops below 7 feet thick right above the basal root swell, but it does not drop below 6 feet thick until 75 feet up. Indeed, at 160 feet the trunk is still 4 feet thick—a full 8 inches thicker than its closest rival. ▲

Volume	4,460 ft³	126 m³
DBH	7.3 ft	222 cm
Height	223 ft	68.0 m
AF Points	511	

A small contingent from a forestry field trip stopped to pay homage to the Grizzly Meadow Monarch, the world champion ponderosa pine. Briefly the national champion during the 1970s, it was put in the shade by trees with larger bases, but has returned in force. This tree is a rocket!

Hartman's Bar Tree

Volume	4,130 ft³	117 m³
DBH	7.8 ft	237 cm
Height	227 ft	69.2 m
AF Points	537	

The Hartman's Bar Tree was discovered deep in the canyon of the Middle Fork of the Feather River in the Plumas National Forest of California. The national champion since 1976, this tree is a fantastic specimen. During the early seventies there were five national champion ponderosa pines; two each from the Sierra National Forest and Shasta-Trinity National Forest, as well as the La Pine Giant, for its second reign. One of the Sierra National Forest trees died and was cut, and the other is the Grizzly Meadow Monarch, listed above. I tried to locate the two Shasta-Trinity trees in 1997 but both had been logged; I found young plantations where they were supposed to be. The Shasta-Trinity trees were both over 250 feet tall—one measured at 262 feet was the tallest ponderosa ever recorded.

I first hiked down to see the Hartman's Bar Tree in the summer of 1996, before I saw the other California giants listed here. It was a sunny summer day and the hike down to the tree was occasionally blessed by a cool breeze flowing down one of the few creek crossings along the trail. The tree grows in a canyon-slope forest of pine and black oak, and is visible from high above because it is growing past one of the long switchbacks that traverse down the canyon. There was no mistaking it, even though several other large pines are in the vicinity—its 227-foot top towers above the surrounding hardwood canopy. My first reaction was one of childish giddiness; this tree was far more impressive than any pine I had seen before. While I now know that the Grizzly Meadow Monarch and Bear Creek Twin are both very similar in dimensions, the Hartman's Bar Tree stands out particularly well because of the way it dominates its small, hardwood neighbors. ▲

The unusual appearance of trees sloping toward each other is caused by the giant pine. The Hartman's Bar Tree leans uphill, amid a forest of oaks that are leaning downhill. Seeing the tree in the company of surrounding forest canopy that is only a third of its height is well worth a visit.

Bear Creek Twin

Volume	4,080 ft³	115 m³
DBH	7.8 ft	238 cm
Height	223 ft	68.0 m
AF Points	532	

The Trinity Alps Wilderness Area in northern California is home to the Bear Creek Twin. The mountains are significantly lower in the Klamath/Siskiyou province than in the Sierras, and thus the wilderness areas include proportionally more mid-elevation mixed-conifer forests than the alpine-rich Sierra wilderness does. So it is no surprise to find giants like this tree living there. The Bear Creek Twin was discovered by Al Gronki, retired Forest Service District Ranger (and an excellent woodcarver) while on one of his many hikes in the region. I initially became aware of the tree through the first edition of the California Register of Big Trees, where it was listed as being slightly smaller than the Hartman's Bar Tree. The trunk was recorded as being larger, however, and the similarity in dimensions led me to believe this could be one of the big ones. Contact with the California program put me in touch with Mr. Gronki, who told me about his discovery.

The tree is growing near a wet meadow, which may partly explain its size and lack of fire scars. I call it the Bear Creek Twin because a nearly identical tree (just slightly smaller) stands about 10 feet from it. Together the two trees form an imposing spectacle. The Twin is also nearly identical in every respect to the Hartman's Bar Tree, located several hundred miles away in the Plumas National Forest. The two trees are within 1 percent of each other both in diameter and wood volume, and 4 feet is all that separates them in height. ▲

These are the "Twins" of Bear Creek. The two giants, the Bear Creek Twin (the larger pine in the foreground), and its unnamed companion, are found in a grove of pole-sized white firs within California's Trinity Alps Wilderness. Here I am standing in the narrow space between them.

La Pine Giant

Volume	4,020 ft³	114 m³
DBH	9.1 ft	277 cm
Height	166 ft	50.6 m
AF Points	519	

Only a stone's throw from the banks of the Deschutes River in central Oregon stands the fattest ponderosa pine on record. This tree has been known for a long time and first appeared on the Big Tree Register in 1945 when Donald MacKay nominated it to oust a Washington champion that appeared on the first list, in 1941. The La Pine Giant has been on and off the list several times over the decades, periodically replacing a number of tall California trees; at present several trees with impressive point totals are known. While large in diameter, the La Pine Giant is not particularly tall, and is growing in an area of lodgepole and ponderosa pines that are subject to frequent burning and insect attacks. Perhaps its proximity to the river has allowed this tree to survive the severe fires that eliminated its original companions. Even so, several large fire scars adorn its impressive base. Unlike the other giant ponderosas I have seen, often very cylindrical of bole, tall, and clothed with long, sweeping branches, this squat tree has an open crown with short, stout branches, and is covered with lumps and bumps.

The drawing shows the tree as it appeared in 1989, when I first measured and photographed it. Sadly, the 1990s were not kind to the Giant, as the left leader has snapped off. The tree is now in a general state of decline, as evidenced by an overall loss of foliage. A fence around the tree (which has been there for several years) has protected the tree's root system, but it appears that bark beetles have begun to take their toll on this aged tree.

The enormous, swollen base of the La Pine Giant gives some indication of its great age. Sadly, the combination of huge burn wounds and recent beetle attacks has greatly reduced the tree's vigor.

I hope it can recover from this setback and remain the diameter champion for decades to come. ▲

Fish Camp Pine

Volume	3,790 ft³	107 m³
DBH	7.4 ft	226 cm
Height	223 ft	68.0 m
AF Points	514	

The ponderosa pine at Fish Camp is well known to the US Geological Survey, but practically unknown to everyone else. Yet it is seen by tens of thousands of people every year, because the road into the Mariposa entrance to Yosemite National Park goes right by it—actually touching the tree—conveying perhaps a thousand cars per day.

The Fish Camp Pine is a witness tree, used as a benchmark by surveyors. A plaque on the tree states: "Do Not Disturb—Land Survey Marker." The tree shows up as BM 3423, which is the benchmark elevation (in feet) used as a reference to calculate all other elevations for features covered by every USGS topographic map for the area.

When I first noticed the Fish Camp Pine I was going into the park on my way north to do some research fieldwork in the Sierras. I didn't pause, but I remembered seeing this huge pine. The next time I came through the area was on a field trip, and I made a point of stopping to check out the tree. Although it is not in a convenient place to pull over, the town of Fish Camp is only a couple of hundred yards away.

In the early twentieth century Fish Camp was one of the largest railroad logging camps. This tree and a couple of giant neighbors must have been local favorites, because every other tree had been logged for miles around except for these few giants close to their camp. Possibly its benchmark status protected this tree through all the subsequent decades of logging in the area. However it happened, a tree once surely recognized as special enjoyed several decades of obscurity before being thrust into the limelight again. ▲

The Fish Camp Pine is the most famous tree that nobody seems to know about. A witness tree for over a century, this pine is located right in the middle of what was once the largest railroad logging camp in the Sierras. Morgan Dutton and Rand Knight give an idea of the size of its base.

WESTERN HEMLOCK *Tsuga heterophylla*

The noblest of hemlocks, Tsuga heterophylla *surpasses all its associates in the forests of northwestern America in the graceful sweep of its long and drooping branches and in its delicate lustrous foliage.*
—*Charles Sprague Sargent, 1901*

Western hemlock is considered the largest growing of the world's 10 species of hemlock, though I recently saw a photo of a *Tsuga dumosa* from southern China that was truly enormous. One of the most shade-tolerant trees in the Pacific Northwest, western hemlock dominates forests throughout the low-elevation coastal areas in southeastern Alaska, British Columbia, Washington, coastal Oregon, and into the redwood region of California. The graceful, weeping nature of this tree makes it highly prized as an ornamental, as well as making it a wonderful contrast to the firs and cedars in our native woods. Western hemlock is often not thought of as a big tree, in part because it is often found growing with much larger species such as Douglas fir, Sitka spruce, western red cedar, or coast redwood. In addition, since it is a shade-tolerant tree, in old-growth forests it is found in all size classes, the majority of these being small, understory trees. While often overlooked in our old-growth forests due to the large sizes of its companions, the amount of foliage maintained by western hemlocks is impressive. Even though a stand might be only 40 percent hemlock by wood volume, the foliage in the same stand can be as high as 80 percent hemlock. What impresses me is not only the huge volume of needles maintained by hemlocks, but also the massive and often very deep crowns these trees possess. No other western tree casts a shade as deep as the western hemlock.

Despite these general observations, western hemlock can grow to great sizes and ages. The largest specimens are usually found in cool, moist, mid-elevation forests dominated by Pacific silver fir. These forests have very little moisture stress, even during the summer months, and the decay organisms that usually kill western hemlocks in warmer forests are not as aggressive. The Olympics have had four champion hemlocks since 1947, when the Enchanted Valley Tree was first nominated by Olympic National Park superintendent Preston Macy. A co-champion was briefly listed during the 1980s on Crown Zellerbach land near Tillamook, Oregon. I tried to relocate this co-champion when preparing this book, but discovered it had blown down only a year earlier. In 1987 I nominated one giant I found growing in the Hoh Valley, which racked up points due to its intact top, 241 feet high, but this tree was too slender to have the volume needed to be included in this book. ▲

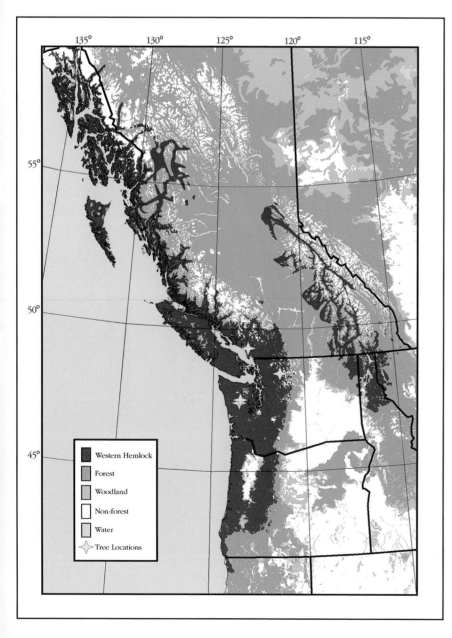

Western Hemlock
Forest
Woodland
Non-forest
Water
✦ Tree Locations

Western hemlock is at home in the rain forests of the West Coast. Often overlooked, perhaps owing to comparisons with this tree's even larger kin—Sitka spruce, Douglas fir, and western red cedar —hemlocks are the most numerous of these conifers, and dominate at all levels of the canopy.

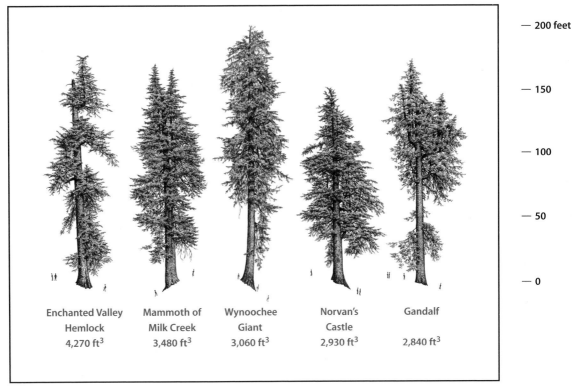

						— 200 feet
						— 150
						— 100
						— 50
						— 0

Enchanted Valley Hemlock	Mammoth of Milk Creek	Wynoochee Giant	Norvan's Castle	Gandalf
4,270 ft³	3,480 ft³	3,060 ft³	2,930 ft³	2,840 ft³

Enchanted Valley Hemlock

Volume	4,270 ft³	121 m³
DBH	8.9 ft	271 cm
Height	172 ft	52.4 m
AF Points	523	

The world champion western hemlock can be found at the east end of the Enchanted Valley in Olympic National Park. This tree has been on the record books since 1947, when Preston Macy, then superintendent of Olympic National Park, notified *American Forests* of its size. In the late 1970s a tree in northwest Oregon shared the record as national co-champion. The Enchanted Valley tree was briefly dethroned in the late 1980s by two other Olympic National Park hemlocks, which are still co-champions, but after being remeasured in 1993 was reinstated.

The first time I saw the tree was in 1986, and I noticed that its broken top had a new, rapidly growing leader. Since its previous measurement had been in 1972, I figured it might have regrown enough to regain its throne as the national champion. In addition, Bob Wood, author of *The Olympic Mountains Trail Guide,* found in his notes a large mountain hemlock growing nearby on the O'Neill Pass Trail. So in the fall of 1993 Arthur Lee Jacobson and I took two days and hiked 36 miles to measure the two hemlocks—one a remeasurement, and the other a potential new champion. The Enchanted Valley Hemlock had indeed regained enough points to share the title as western hemlock co-champion, and the O'Neill Pass hemlock became a new national co-champion.

In 1999 Arthur and I again did the very long overnight hike into the Enchanted Valley, this time to measure the hemlock's volume. Even though it has an 8.9-foot DBH—one of the largest diameters recorded for a living western hemlock—it rapidly tapers to 7 feet thick at 11 feet off the ground. At that point the taper then slows dramatically, and the diameter does not drop below 6 feet thick until 80 feet up,

The Enchanted Valley Hemlock is no stranger to the record books, having been on the list for nearly all of the last 60 years. Its major status was reaffirmed when I was able to measure the volume of this slow-tapering monster.

making it by far the largest tree in this category. The tree is located in a fantastic stand of ancient silver fir–hemlock forest at the head of the valley. Many other giant hemlocks surround this tree, the king of its species. It sits a few feet from an open river channel and has a great view of West Peak and its glaciers—the hydrographic center of the Olympics. ▲

Mammoth of Milk Creek

Volume	3,480 ft³	99 m³
DBH	8.9 ft *	271 cm *
Height	167 ft	50.9 m
AF Points	516	* Measured at 5'3"

Another Randy Stoltmann discovery, this is the only giant hemlock we know of from the Cascades. All other known hemlocks over 8 feet thick are much closer to the coast. Spotted while Randy was scouting for his Pacific Northwest hiking guide (published posthumously as *Hiking in the Ancient Forests of British Columbia and Washington)*, the

The Mammoth of Milk Creek was discovered by the late Randy Stoltmann while he was doing research for one of his excellent hiking guides—it was an unusual find in being so far from the ocean. This huge specimen stands at the headwaters of Milk Creek, home to many other thousand-year-old trees.

Mammoth is on the Pacific Crest Trail near its junction with the Milk Creek Trail in the Glacier Peak Wilderness.

In 1998, Arthur Lee Jacobson and I hiked out to see this tree during the early fall. The 15-mile hike passes through some fine forests as it ascends to the alpine country surrounding the Glacier Peak volcano, including a Douglas fir stand with trees that have been aged at 1,000 years. As one approaches the headwall of the valley and the Pacific Crest Trail, the forest gives way to meadows that alternate with swaths of forest. The Mammoth is located in one such swath, along with several other giant western hemlocks, some Pacific silver firs, and a few mountain hemlocks. The top of the tree, as has happened with many ancient giants, blew out in some storm long ago, yet its huge trunk surpasses all others for the first 50 feet of its height. At 20 feet off the ground the trunk is still 7.5 feet thick, far larger than any other known hemlock. Although the main stem is broken off at just over 140 feet, where it is still 2.5 feet thick, two reiterations continue on for another 20 to 25 feet. These make up some of the lost volume and add greatly to the character of the tree. ▲

Wynoochee Giant

The third-largest known western hemlock grows along the upper Wynoochee Trail in Olympic National Park. The Wynoochee Valley once contained some of the finest forest anywhere in the Pacific Northwest. Early reconnaissance timber surveys in this region found higher volume-per-acre totals for Douglas fir here than anywhere else in its range. Sadly, all but the uppermost section of this valley is outside of the park and has been logged. The upper valley is extremely wet, and well over a thousand years have elapsed since the last fire. As a result the Douglas fir are long gone, but a climax forest of hemlock and Pacific silver fir has developed.

The Wynoochee Giant was first noticed by Bob Wood when he was scouting the region for his book on trails in the Olympic Mountains. The tree grows on a side slope and the trail passes right above it. Bob notified me about it in 1988, and it became a new national record once I measured it. The tree measures over 9 feet in diameter where the base emerges from the slope and reaches 195 feet to its topmost sprig, which is now dead. The massive crown crowds neighboring trees and towers above the surrounding forest. While the base measurement is inflated due to the steep slope, the stem does not drop below 6 feet thick until 20 feet up, helping it to amass nearly 3,100 cubic feet of trunk volume. The surrounding forest has many extremely large western and mountain hemlocks, even though the majority of the forest is composed of smallish Pacific silver fir. Altogether, this drainage holds the finest hemlock forest I have ever seen—the 10 acres or so surrounding this tree contain a dozen hemlocks over 6 feet in diameter, including the nearby Gandalf, described below. ▲

Volume	3,060 ft³	87 m³
DBH	9.1 ft *	276 cm *
Height	195 ft	59.4 m
AF Points	549	* Measured at 5'6"

The Wynoochee Giant receives an upper tape measurement by Steve Sillett. Several measurements are taken with the tape to augment the laser measurements; they are particularly useful in situations like this, when the trunk is not round.

Norvan's Castle

Volume	2,930 ft³	83 m³
DBH	9.5 ft	290 cm
Height	149 ft	45.3 m
AF Points	525	

The largest hemlock in Canada grows in the upper reaches of the Lynn Valley along Norvan Creek in a wonderful stand of ancient hemlocks, firs, and cedars. The lower Lynn Valley is well known for having once been home to a Douglas fir measuring over 400 feet tall (cut, then measured on the ground), and many other Douglas firs in the 14- to 16-foot DBH range. The entire lower valley has been logged and is now in second growth. The upper reaches are very remote, and it required 13 miles of hiking one fall to get into and out of the old-growth forests up there. The mid-November days in British Columbia are short, and the last 4 miles of hiking out was accomplished with the aid of moonlight. The upper elevations in this area contain very wet forests that have gone for several thousand years since the last fire. All of the giant western hemlocks I have measured are at their upper elevational limits, and are commonly mixed with mountain hemlocks, Pacific silver firs, and yellow cedars. This tree had previously been seen by the late Randy Stoltmann, who has found many record trees in the Vancouver area. Ralf Kelman led me to the tree, which is surrounded by several hemlocks in the 6- to 7.5-foot diameter range. The big tree, now named Norvan's Castle, has the largest base ever recorded for a western hemlock. The DBH measures 9.5 feet and the height to the top of the uppermost foliage is 149 feet, despite the fact that the main trunk is broken off at 116 feet, where it is still 2.8 feet thick. The tree has six major reiterations that range from 1 foot thick to a little over 2 feet in diameter. The multiple tops and overall very complex architecture inspired the tree's name. The trunk is massive, maintaining a thick stalk across a great height. At 45 feet off the ground, the main trunk is still 6 feet in diameter, although the massive reiterations obviously account for the rapid taper above that point. Overall, the tree has a trunk volume of 2,930 cubic feet, ranking it fourth among our giants of this species. ▲

Norvan's Castle is a recent find in the old-growth upper Lynn Valley watershed of Vancouver, British Columbia, an area that holds the first of what I expect to be many future tree records in this area.

Gandalf

Volume	2,840 ft³	81 m³
DBH	7.1 ft	215 cm
Height	168 ft	51.2 m
AF Points	447	

Gandalf (shown here) and the Wynoochee Giant are the largest inhabitants of the finest hemlock forest I have yet seen. This area of the Olympics offers the ultimate expression of forest succession, since there have been no recorded fires in several thousand years.

The upper Wynoochee Valley in Olympic National Park is home to the finest hemlock forests I have seen. These are also among the oldest forests in the Pacific Northwest. The cool, moist summers here combine with 200 inches of precipitation (much of it as snow) to make this area nearly fireproof. Extremely wet valleys such as this can go several millennia between fires, and the individual trees reach ages approaching (or exceeding) 1,000 years. The Wynoochee Giant has many rivals sharing its valley, the gnarliest of which is this second-largest, Gandalf. Gandalf is found only a few hundred yards inside the park boundary, just below the Wynoochee trail near a slide area. When I was showing off the Wynoochee Giant to Steve Sillett in March of 1999, we spent some time exploring the off-trail areas to see if we could find some additional giants. On our return hike, Gandalf's huge trunk and gnarly crown loomed large through the trees.

Gandalf has at least four main reiterations between 1 and 2 feet thick, which were branches that turned vertical in response to the main stem being snapped centuries ago. While the main trunk is only 136 feet tall to the break, the great shaft is impressive. In the section from 10 to 120 feet, Gandalf has a volume of 2,310 cubic feet, which is slightly more than the Wynoochee Giant for the equivalent section. It is amazing to observe how different these subalpine trees can be from their relatives of the same species lower down in the coastal rain forest. ▲

This is the most exactly beautiful tree in the Sierra woods, far surpassing its companion species in every respect.
—*John Muir, 1881*

The California red fir is the primary subalpine forest tree species from Crater Lake south through the entire length of the Sierras. It has been separated into varieties based on the appearance of the cones, but ecologically the whole complex is very similar. The cone of the Shasta red fir (*A. magnifica* var. *shastensis*) is distinguished by its reflexed bracts, which protrude past the cone scales. While this may seem a small difference, it has been used to suggest a gradient of species from noble fir in the north, to Shasta fir in the middle, and California red fir in the south. For the most part, this key works, even though the southernmost populations of this gradient (in the vicinity of Sequoia National Park) also have exposed bracts. Because this aberration seems a minor one to me when compared to the ecological similarity between the Shasta and California red varieties, I've lumped them together in this treatment.

The ecology and appearance of noble fir is so different from that of the red firs that this lumping seems justified. Conveniently, there's also a geographical separation between the two groups. Noble fir forms extensive stands in subalpine forests from Stevens Pass in Washington to the McKenzie River in the central Oregon Cascades. Throughout its range, noble fir is a pioneer species that is replaced by Pacific silver fir as the stands age. Similarly, the red firs form extensive subalpine forests from Crater Lake in the southern Oregon Cascades through to the southern Sierra subalpine forests. Throughout this range, red fir is the shade-tolerant climax species, and typically forms nearly pure stands or shares dominance with mountain hemlock (northern stands) or western white pine (southern stands). The hundred or so miles between continuous populations of noble fir north of the McKenzie River, and the continuous populations of Shasta fir from Crater Lake south, contain a few scattered populations that exhibit characteristics of one or the other or both species. In any case, the trees called California red fir in this book include basically everything from Crater Lake south to the southern Sierras.

The California red fir is an intensely beautiful tree whose scientific name is as fitting as any I know. The sharp contrast between the delicate turquoise to aquamarine foliage and the rugged cinnamon bark offers a delightful reprieve from the more common greens and browns of the sierran forests, and the ever-present summer sun bakes the bark to a delicious brick red. A different mood envelops the visitor to a red fir forest. The forest floor is often very open, with few shrubs or herbs to block the way. Frequently, red fir forests consist of a

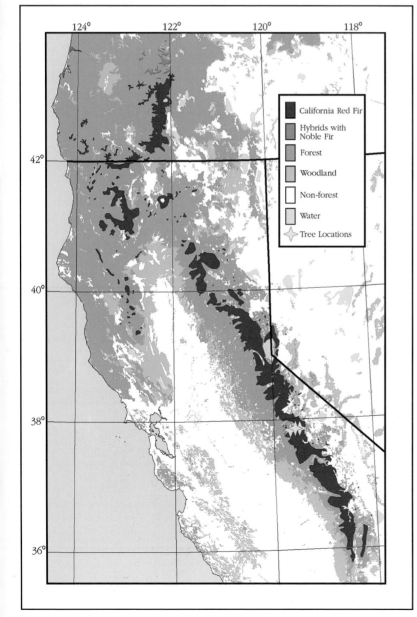

California Red Fir
Hybrids with Noble Fir
Forest
Woodland
Non-forest
Water
Tree Locations

single tree species. Since fire is not a major factor in these forests, the Jeffrey, lodgepole, and western white pines that would otherwise generally be associates are often absent. ▲

The species name magnifica is an excellent epithet for the California red fir. The term comes to mind every time I gaze up at these beautiful trees with their unique combination of maroon bark and turquoise foliage.

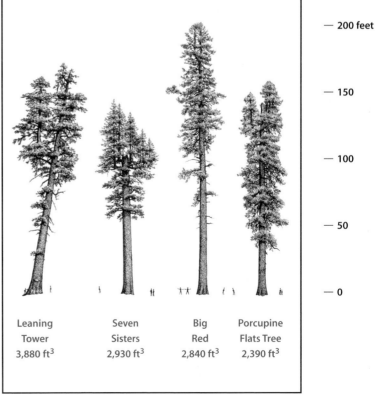

Leaning Tower	Seven Sisters	Big Red	Porcupine Flats Tree
3,880 ft³	2,930 ft³	2,840 ft³	2,390 ft³

— 200 feet
— 150
— 100
— 50
— 0

Leaning Tower

The Leaning Tower was first noticed during a working trip to Sequoia National Park, where I went to install some permanent plots, areas that are used to track a population of trees through time. As I was driving my crew through Yosemite along the Tioga Pass Road to show them what I thought were some of the finest red fir stands I had seen, we saw the Seven Sisters Tree. Later, after looking for another tree, we stopped at a turnout to examine a large fallen red fir that had been cleared off the road. Out of the corner of my eye I noticed a large leaning red fir off through the woods. My first impression was that this was another 7-plus footer (we had measured a few others of this size a little earlier). Upon closer inspection, I realized that this tree was really big. I called the crew over and as they arrived they first saw it with me standing at the base to give it some scale. We all gathered around and were amazed at the first measurement—the trunk circumference was 30'5"! This dimension pretty much guaranteed that it was a new record, but beyond that it also made it the largest known trunk measurement for any living *Abies*.

The true firs generally have little of what I call character, a term I usually reserve for trees like western red cedar, coast redwood, or giant sequoia that develop bizarre forms after a millennium or two of surviving the elements. Even so, with its strong lean and codominant branch this tree has about as much character as I have seen in an *Abies*. The diameter is a real record for the genus, although this measurement is due in part to its lean, which causes excessive growth near the base of the tree. With all of that said, the trunk is massive—still nearly 6 feet thick at 50 feet. ▲

Volume	3,880 ft³	110 m³
DBH	9.7 ft	295 cm
Height	172 ft	52.4 m
AF Points	547	

As I was showing off the great California red fir forests of Yosemite to some of my colleagues, we discovered the Leaning Tower. This huge tree has the largest base of any known *Abies*.

Seven Sisters

Volume	2,930 ft³	83 m³
DBH	8.1 ft	246 cm
Height	148 ft	45.1 m
AF Points	462	

Throughout the Sierras, the best forests occur on plateaus. Giant Forest, the gem of Sequoia National Park, occurs on a broad plateau with steep mountain slopes both above and below it. The plateau is situated at the perfect elevation for the development of a wonderful mixed-conifer forest. The transition forest below and the red fir forest above are reduced to fairly narrow areas on the fringe of this vast plateau. At Yosemite, the broad plateau on the western edge of the park also supports a wonderful mixed-conifer forest. Yosemite Canyon, however, is nearly 4,000 feet deep, stretching from the transition forest right on up through the mixed-conifer forest to the red fir forest on top. The valley floor supports unusually productive ponderosa pine–incense cedar forests, and the rim supports red fir. Both the south rim along the Glacier Point Road and the north rim along the Tioga Pass Road travel through marvelous red fir forests.

Seven Sisters was discovered about an hour before the Leaning Tower described above. As the crew was driving up the Tioga Pass Road admiring the beauty of the surrounding red fir stand, this huge trunk appeared through the woods. We quickly pulled over and walked to the tree. The forest in this vicinity was almost all red fir, with many individuals in the 5- to 6-foot diameter range. When we spied this tree, however, we knew that it was much larger. Not only did it have a large lower trunk, it had a thick stem with little taper. We were disappointed when we looked up and saw that the top had been blown out years earlier at slightly over 100 feet. The seven leaders sprouting from the top give the tree its name, and are quickly replacing the lost upper crown. The tallest of these is already 45 feet above the missing top. The laser confirmed that although the tree is snapped, the main trunk is very respectable—maintaining a 5-foot diameter to 100 feet off the ground. Had the upper trunk been intact, this tree would have been a close rival to the Leaning Tower. Even so, from 83 feet to the break at 103 feet, it is the thickest known red fir. ▲

Like the Leaning Tower, the Seven Sisters Tree is located near the Tioga Pass Road in Yosemite. Finding these two giants just a few minutes away from each other—and located so close to the road—makes one wonder what lies in store deeper into these fantastic forests.

Big Red

If there is a match for the groves of red fir in Yosemite along the Tioga Pass Road, the only contenders are the groves just across Yosemite Valley, accessible from the Glacier Point Road. The very pleasing combination of maroon trunk and aqua foliage makes these easily some of the most attractive forests in existence. The bark, unlike that of noble fir, a close relative, develops into very thick, flat plates that are baked to a dark, rich maroon in the ever-present California sun. Chunks of this bark, converted into glowing embers by huge bonfires, were formerly used to make the nightly "firefall" when dumped over the cliffs above Yosemite Valley. Though it was a spectacle that titillated thousands of tourists, the Park Service has since found more constructive uses for their red fir forests. Curiously, the extensive red fir forests of central Yosemite National Park are still largely unexplored for giant trees. The giants I have listed here are just a few I happened to find while doing some minor exploring. The forests are vast, however, and chances are good that several of these trees will be replaced by larger trees in years to come.

Big Red dominates a very fine grove located well off the road in an area of Yosemite near the headwaters of the South Fork Tuolumne River. I stumbled upon it after having stopped to get a better look at Smoky Jack, the second-largest known Jeffrey pine. Big Red is what I call a "specimen tree," the kind that is nearly perfect—the archetypal form of that species. Specimen trees are not necessarily big, just perfect. While the lower trunk of Big Red is no match for the Leaning Tower, its thick, intact top compensates, giving it a volume of over 2,800 cubic feet. At 170 feet up, above the tops of most of the trees in this forest, the trunk is still over 2 feet thick. ▲

Volume	2,840 ft³	80 m³
DBH	7.4 ft	226 cm
Height	203 ft	61.9 m
AF Points	491	

Big Red, in its Yosemite home, is a perfect specimen of California red fir. "Specimen trees" like this can be near-perfect examples of a tree species at maturity, but are not generally giants. In this case, the tree measures up to both qualifications.

Porcupine Flats Tree

Volume	2,390 ft³	68 m³	
DBH	7.2 ft	220 cm	
Height	159 ft	48.5 m	
AF Points	442		

Porcupine Flats is located several miles from the other red fir forests along Yosemite's Tioga Pass Road. The road traverses large expanses of granite with their forest component of western junipers and Jeffrey pines. Alternating with these, and in the deeper soils between ridges, it crosses red fir country. These are some of the most attractive forests in the Sierras. While the forests often develop an open, bare understory, it is not generally due to fire, as except for the rare conflagration that devastates the whole landscape, fire is not a major player in these forests. What does help provide this interesting feature are the dense shade and the litter

these trees create. Some of the red fir forests contain no other tree species. On toward thinner soils, Jeffrey pines become a forest component. Likewise, near wet spots or cold-air drainages Sierra lodgepoles are encountered and can become dominant. Such is the case in Porcupine Flats. Porcupine Flats is a broad, shallow valley at the headwaters of Porcupine Creek, just east of Yosemite Creek, and both creeks sport spectacular falls that plummet down to Yosemite Valley. The broad swale of Porcupine Flats is pure Sierra lodgepole pine forest. Flanking this area to the west is a fine, nearly pure stand of red fir.

It is said that an 8-foot-thick western white pine once grew in the red fir forest west of Porcupine Flats. While scouring the area for this (perhaps legendary) pine, I came across two red firs over 7 feet in diameter and several others over 6 feet thick. I never did locate the pine. The largest of these red firs is what I call the Porcupine Flats Tree. Its trunk is very much like that of Big Red, a beautiful, bright maroon with thick, chunky-flat plates of bark protecting the living stem inside. Even though the top was blown out centuries ago at 143 feet, the trunk is still a respectable 3 feet wide at 125 feet up. ▲

I came upon the Porcupine Flats Tree as I was searching the forest for a legendary giant western white pine near a campground in Yosemite National Park. In its place, I was pleased to find this giant California red fir among several other immense trees.

But throughout all the vicissitudes of its life on the mountains, come what may, the noble grandeur of the species is patent to every eye.
—John Muir, 1881

White fir is the main shade-tolerant tree of the mixed-conifer forests of the Sierras, and as such is probably the most numerous tree in the sierran forests. Many think them too numerous, as fire suppression has greatly benefited white fir at the expense of the pines. Also, firs in general do not have the longevity of many of their associated conifers, and many of the champions are old and do not stay champions for long. During 1995, for example, the official champion white fir, Shasta fir, and California red fir trees were all found to be dead. While the replacement national champions I have found are quite impressive trees, some of the runners-up I have included in this book are by comparison in many respects lacking. I have tried to fill out this list with very large trees, yet I fully realize that with some trained eyes and serious searching several of the trees included here could be bested. Although the trees I have listed for California red fir and California white fir are in Yosemite, I have not searched there exclusively. On the contrary, I have looked throughout the Sierras (and Klamath Mountains) for large firs. The Yosemite area just has so many large firs that I have not found another area with trees nearly as large to match it. I hope this book will inspire others to search these out. The Sierras are vast and there are a lot of large firs out there.

For years the champion California white fir was a giant, nearly 9 feet in diameter. According to the last several big tree lists, this tree was growing in Meridian, California. However, there is no place called Meridian in the state. Puzzled, I went back into some older issues of *American Forests* to look at the description of the tree when it first appeared, in 1972. At that time, *American Forests* gave the legal description, followed by "Mt. Diablo Base Meridian"—the name of the meridian on which surveys for the townships and ranges in California are based. Over the years this description had been abbreviated until finally it was pruned down simply to "Meridian, CA," which is meaningless. Anyway, after phoning the district where the tree was, and having a friend do some poking around, we finally found someone who knew of the tree and could draw us a map. According to *American Forests,* the tree was reported dead in 1991. I still wanted to see it, however, especially if it was still standing. We found it after a short search—fallen. The trunk was enormous—it was by far the largest white fir trunk I had ever seen. The 27'11" circumference dimension was impressive, but just as impressive was the bole of this giant, which had very little taper. I quickly realized that if I was going to find a suitable replacement, I would need to search pretty hard. ▲

Map legend:
- California White Fir
- Colorado White Fir
- Hybrids with Grand Fir
- Forest
- Woodland
- Non-forest
- Water
- Tree Locations

Probably the most numerous trees in the Sierras, California white firs are even more common now than in the past. Ferociously aggressive, as well as shade tolerant, these trees were once kept in check by the frequent fires occurring in the pre-twentieth-century environment. Their present status threatens many of the other species they grow with, not just by their competition, but by shifting the fire regime to one that could be more catastrophic.

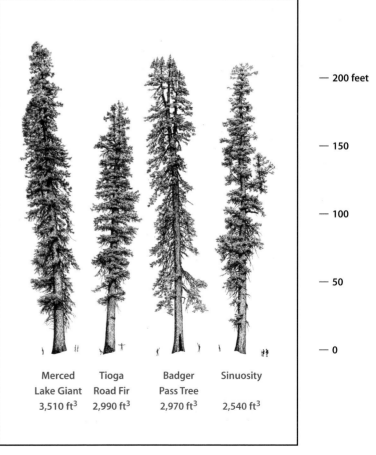

Merced Lake Giant	Tioga Road Fir	Badger Pass Tree	Sinuosity
3,510 ft^3	2,990 ft^3	2,970 ft^3	2,540 ft^3

Merced Lake Giant

In *Discovering Sierra Trees,* by Steven Arno, mention is made of large white firs growing near Merced Lake. *Tree Adventures in Yosemite Valley,* by Rod Haulenbeek, mentions a tree 8.3 feet in diameter growing near the lake. Although both of these references were fairly old by the time I came to the area, I had to see for myself. Yosemite Valley, as you may know, is one BIG, yet spectacular, hole, and Merced Lake requires a 30-mile hike to get into and back, so I had to plan for an overnight trip. The occasion arose when I was there in early November of 1997. The weather was gorgeous, and the valley crowds had greatly thinned. I started at dawn, to make full use of the short days and get to the tree and perhaps even partway back on the first day. This might have been a bit optimistic, since in addition to my regular backpacking gear I was lugging the survey laser, tripod, and batteries, which add an additional 35 pounds! I reached the lake in early afternoon and proceeded to the east shore, where the fertile soils appeared to be. One of the first trees I encountered at the far end was the Merced Lake Giant—a towering monster over 7 feet in diameter. The valley-floor soils there had grown some amazing trees, including several other white firs between 6 and 7 feet in diameter, as well as many large Jeffrey pines. From the looks of the area it appeared to be a bustling High Sierra camp and ranger station during the summer months. I saw not a soul.

The Merced Lake Giant stands right by the trail near a large snag, a tall Jeffrey pine, and an enormous log that must have been the 8.3-foot-diameter white fir I had read about. Considering the exposed location of this grove near the lake, I was very impressed with the heights of the firs—several were over 200 feet. After taking the measurements I calculated that the Merced Lake Giant broke the 500-point barrier, only the third white fir to do so, the others being the nearby log and a former champ that I had seen dead a year earlier. ▲

Volume	3,510 ft³	99 m³
DBH	7.3 ft	223 cm
Height	217 ft	66.1 m
AF Points	503	

The long hike out to Merced Lake in Yosemite National Park not only shows one the full splendor of the geological and waterfall features of the park, but the forest around the lake also has many huge Jeffrey pines and California white firs. Among these is the Merced Lake Giant, the largest known white fir.

Tioga Road Fir

Volume	2,990 ft³	85 m³
DBH	7.2 ft	218 cm
Height	176 ft	53.6 m
AF Points	456	

The largest old-growth mixed-conifer forest on the planet may be found in the western reaches of Yosemite National Park. At over 100,000 acres, this contiguous, pine-dominated forest ranks (in my opinion) as one of the wonders of the botanical world. While it is the pines (ponderosa, sugar, and Jeffrey) that dominate, the white fir is the shade-tolerant species that makes up the middle canopy and understory of these forests. This vast area probably contains individuals, white fir as well as the pines, that will grace the pages of future editions of this book. For now we will settle for the world's tallest pine, two Jeffrey pines, a few red firs, and two white firs.

After I had seen its massive trunk prostrate during the summer of 1996, the long-time white fir champion left a strong impression on me. Once I knew what to look for, the first candidate for replacement was a tree I spotted while driving up the Tioga Pass Road in Yosemite National Park. The Tioga Road Fir looms over the road about a mile past the parking lot for the Tuolumne Grove of giant sequoias. While the tree has probably been seen by millions of people, it is one of those species that tends to be ignored. The much more dramatic and colorful pines, including the often much larger sugar pine, are more likely to attract attention than the smaller yet far more numerous white firs. This giant fir is 7.2 feet in diameter and was even larger—a fire scar on one side reduces the measurement. In addition, the top has blown off at least once, as the multiple reiterations indicate. Even so, this tree has a very heavy main trunk, and the 60-foot section from 83 to 143 feet is thicker than all of the other trees listed in this section. ▲

The huge trunk of the Tioga Road Fir actually leans out over the Tioga Pass Road in Yosemite. Many such giants lie hidden in these fantastic forests, attracting much less attention than the larger and more showy sugar, ponderosa, and Jeffrey pines.

Badger Pass Tree

Volume	2,970 ft³	84 m³
DBH	7.3 ft	223 cm
Height	207 ft	63.1 m
AF Points	492	

On a trip through Yosemite to show my friend Steve Sillett the Lost Bear Survivor Jeffrey pine, I was keeping a special eye out for firs, as the Glacier Point road travels through some particularly fine fir forests. I was fully expecting to find a red fir to put in this book, feeling that only the forests along the Tioga Pass Road were as nice. After watching some hang gliders launch themselves over the Yosemite Canyon rim, we were driving back slowly and I was showing Steve areas that I had not yet explored. After pointing out one particular ravine that had some tall trees, Steve blurted out "Uh-oh, we're going to have to turn around." There was a monster crown just visible across the valley. When I finally parked the car he jumped out with his compass, got a bearing, and made a beeline for the tree.

The forest at this elevation 7,400 feet—is mostly red fir, but on this south-facing slope there were also several white firs, as this one turned out to be. The massive, reiterated crown Steve had spotted from the road made the tree easy to locate. As I approached, I realized that it was substantially larger than its neighbors. The bottom 10 feet of the tree includes a huge burn cavity, and the tree has compensated for this by growing an excessive swell on the opposite side. Above the basal swelling, the Badger Pass Tree is quite columnar—there is a 40-foot section that only tapers 5 inches, from 63 inches at the base to 58 inches at the top. At 150 feet, just below an old break where several reiterations emerge, the trunk is still nearly 3.5 feet thick, thicker than any other known white fir. And while I was setting up the laser equipment for measuring, Steve explored another section of the slope and found a still taller tree that was nearly as large. ▲

This immense California white fir, the Badger Pass Tree, takes its name from the Badger Pass ski area in Yosemite, not far from the ravine where it stands. The tree's complex and gnarly crown was spotted from a great distance, welcoming closer inspection.

Sinuosity

Volume	2,540 ft^3	72 m^3
DBH	6.4 ft	194 cm
Height	202 ft	61.6 m
AF Points	451	

In preparing for this book, I spent a great deal of time trying to resurrect what was currently known about the giant trees of the Pacific Coast. I knew of the current national champions, generally one tree per species. I also had information on previous national champs that were outpointed yet (I hoped) still around. This strategy worked well for ponderosa and Jeffrey pines, as some of the former champs were indeed quite impressive. I also knew of many state champions, which in many cases were nearly as large as the national champs. Then I had numerous leads from my big-tree friends, Forest Service rangers, and many people generally interested in trees. But for certain species, such as the two Sierra firs, I did not have much initial information. At that time, both the current and all former record-holders of these two species were dead. While the two new champions I have found are awesome trees, I fully realize some of these runners-up are going to be place-holders until new giants are found. One of my hopes is that this book will convince more people to hunt down these trees and to lend a hand in making the next edition more complete.

On my return trip after measuring the Merced Lake Giant, I was impressed by other white firs and stopped in the Little Yosemite Valley to measure an exceptionally large one. Sinuosity has a large diameter and a bole that did not lean, yet gracefully snaked its way into the sky for over 200 feet. This was again in an exposed area where the tree towered over its neighbors. While it didn't have the volume of the other white firs I have listed, the tree has character, and will make a fine member of the champion club until other, larger trees are discovered. ▲

Sinuosity is yet another giant white fir from Yosemite, located in Little Yosemite Valley, a lovely glen tucked in behind the famous Vernal and Nevada Falls of the Merced River.

The heavy forests of northwestern Montana and the adjacent mountains of Idaho, constitute one of the most important bodies of timber in the United States; here the western white pine reaches its greatest development, which spread in great luxuriance over the mountains.
—*Charles Sprague Sargent, 1884*

The western white pine is a widespread western conifer that grows over a great variety of habitats throughout its range. Its place in history is secure, for it provided a transitional link in our logging history from the great pine forests of the eastern United States to the Douglas fir forests of the Pacific Northwest. The most valuable wood in the East was eastern white pine *(Pinus strobus),* a close cousin to our western white pine. When the great forests of New England were cut, the timber industry moved on to the fantastic pine forests of the Great Lakes. By the time these forests were gone, a new species of white pine was discovered—a tree even larger than the eastern white pine. For a few short decades, the great pine forests of western Montana, northern Idaho, and northeastern Washington, collectively known as the Inland Empire, provided the wood for this country's expansion. Enter John Muir, Gifford Pinchot, Teddy Roosevelt, and an age of conservation. Before the western forests had been completely leveled, like the preceding areas, the National Forest system was set up to control the depletion of our timber resources.

Although the western white pine grows throughout Washington, Oregon, and California, in none of these locations does it achieve the dominance it once had in the Inland Empire. The introduction of white pine blister rust *(Cronartium ribicola)* in British Columbia in 1910 permanently changed the nature of our western white pine forests. No other conifer disease has caused more damage or costs as much to control as this rust introduced from Asia. When the effects of the rust are combined with those of the mountain pine beetle *(Dendroctonus ponderosae),* the result is that we have nearly lost the western white pine component from many of our forest lands. The proportion of western white pine regeneration in the Inland Empire had already shrunk from 44 percent in 1941 to 5 percent by 1979. The attempt to liquidate the alternate host of the rust, a gooseberry (millions of dollars were pumped into a program that had field crews cut every gooseberry from British Columbia to California), has been a complete failure. For about 20 or 30 years it seemed as if

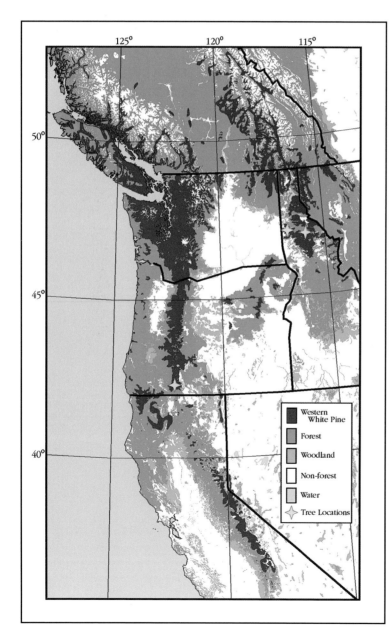

Western White Pine

Forest

Woodland

Non-forest

Water

Tree Locations

Western white pine is an accommodating tree that can grow in swamps near the ocean, at timberline in the Sierras, and just about every place in between. Here a young tree is seen sprouting from the base of an ancient incense cedar.

western white pine would never again be a part of our reforestation efforts. The breeding programs, however, have had some success, and are at the point now where resistant strains of pines are again being planted.

The character and ecology of western white pine varies greatly depending on where it is located within its range. The Inland Empire is the only place where nearly pure stands of white pine can be found. Throughout most of its range, the pine occurs as a minor component in the Cascade, Olympic, and Sierra forests it inhabits. Western white pine can grow at near sea-level in the wetlands of the Olympics, Cascades, and on Vancouver Island, and on up to high mountain forests in the same ranges. It is common in the gravelly soils of the Puget Sound Basin, and as scattered individuals throughout the Cascades. It becomes a subalpine tree as it moves south into the Sierras of California, and can even be found as timberline krummholz at 11,000 feet in the southern Sierras. Tall, forest-grown pines may be found in all but the California populations. While the largest trees have long since been logged or have succumbed to rust or beetles, we still have a few mighty specimens left to remind us of what once was. ▲

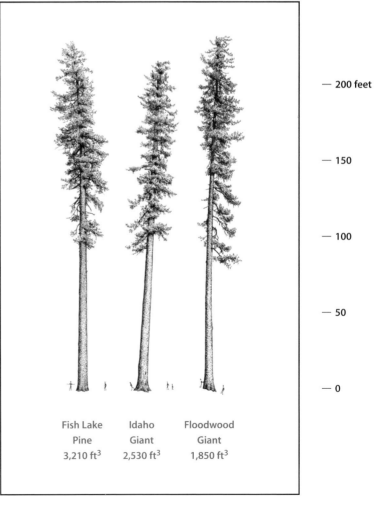

Fish Lake Pine 3,210 ft³ | Idaho Giant 2,530 ft³ | Floodwood Giant 1,850 ft³

Fish Lake Pine

The largest known western white pine is a giant growing near Fish Lake, east of Medford, Oregon. Holding the national record from 1973 to 1986, this tree was out-pointed by a double tree near Lake Tahoe—really two small trees fused at the base that when added together yield a huge diameter—which is smaller than many trees I have seen and not large enough to be in this book. The Fish Lake tree, however, is a giant reminiscent of the great pines that once clothed the Idaho Rockies. When first nominated, it replaced the Idaho Giant, a very similar tree, by out-pointing it 496 to 483. It turns out that both trees' heights were overestimated at the time, the Fish Lake Pine by 17 feet. When I first saw this tree, in 1989, I was mainly interested in its height, since it was no longer the national champion, and it was close to the record height for the species. An earlier record of a white pine cut in Idaho that yielded fifteen 16-foot-long logs (for a total length of more than 240 feet) is the all-time height record. Naturally, I was a bit dis-

Volume	3,210 ft^3	91 m^3
DBH	6.7 ft	205 cm
Height	222 ft	67.7 m
AF Points	484	

appointed to find the tree was not 239 feet as had been long claimed, yet was stunned with how huge this tree really was. It is truly a spectacular pine.

The Fish Lake Pine is much larger than the dimensions would indicate. Western white pines are noted for slow taper, but this tree epitomizes that quality. Because it has only a very small basal buttress, the 6.7-foot DBH is a real reflection of its size. It drops to 6 feet thick at 12 feet up, but then does not fall below 5 feet thick until 74 feet up the stem. At 50 feet up this tree is a full 10 inches thicker than its closest rival, the Idaho Giant, which has only 79 percent of the wood volume of the Fish Lake Pine. ▲

The matchless shaft of the Fish Lake Pine can be seen by making a short jaunt out of Medford, Oregon. Reminding one of the now only legendary forests of northern Idaho, this towering monster has been on the books for nearly 30 years.

Idaho Giant

Idaho has the well-deserved reputation of being white pine country. When loggers came across the mountains of northern Idaho, then thickly blanketed with white pine forests, dozens of giant trees were photographed or written about before being cut. The first tree on the national list was an 8-foot-thick giant from northern Idaho. By 1945, an even larger tree, 8.5 feet by 207 feet, was found near Bovill, and stayed on the list for a decade. But by 1955 that tree was either cut or (more likely) died from bark beetles or blister rust, because the Idaho Giant then appeared on the record books. Its reign lasted until the Fish Lake Pine was nominated in 1973. For another 24 years the Giant remained Idaho's largest pine. As its reputation grew over the years, the nearby campground came to be called Giant White Pine Campground, and the stretch of Highway 103 travelling through Clearwater National Forest in this section of Idaho was named White Pine Drive. Meanwhile, the Idaho Giant was surrounded by a beautiful stand of old-growth mixed-conifer forest composed of western red cedar, Douglas fir, grand fir, and western hemlock, along with a smattering of ponderosa and lodgepole pine.

White pine blister rust, a disease introduced from Europe, reached these mountains in the 1930s (it had already reached Vancouver, British Columbia, in 1910) and caused incalculable damage to Idaho's white pines. The Idaho Giant, though, survived the epidemic and stood tall and healthy until 1997, when a bark beetle attack began on the tree. By the fall of 1997, when I measured the tree, it was dead. All of the foliage was still on the tree, but it had turned brown. In the spring of 1999, the tree was removed. To quote the Forest Service Web page on the tree, "Dozens of people gathered at the Giant White Pine Campground to witness the falling of the tree. Foresters, loggers, reporters, photographers, law enforcement officers, highway department personnel and others came to pay their respects. With a crash that shattered the rotten base of the tree, the title of 'Idaho State Record Western White Pine Tree' passed to a slightly taller but slightly smaller diameter tree in the Floodwood State Forest, 40 miles away." ▲

Volume	2,530 ft³	72 m³
DBH	6.8 ft	206 cm
Height	210 ft	64.0 m
AF Points	475	

The Idaho Giant was the last of the truly giant pines from the greatest white pine forest of the West. Eliminated by a devastating combination of bark beetles, an introduced disease called blister rust, and very aggressive overlogging, these great forests are now only a memory.

Floodwood Giant

Volume	1,850 ft³	52 m³
DBH	6.6 ft	201 cm
Height	227 ft	69.2 m
AF Points	481	

The Floodwood State Forest is a remote piece of the Idaho outback. Situated in the heart of the Idaho Panhandle, this is the area where western white pine reigns supreme. When I came across a big-tree list for Idaho on the Web, I was delighted to see several state champions listed in addition to the national record-holders I had already known about. Two white pines were listed; the

Idaho Giant, which was a former national champ, and the Floodwood Giant, which was new to me. I had heard the champ was in decline and wanted to see it before it was too late. It was October, and I knew the larches would be coloring, so it was a great time to head to the Inland Empire. I set aside several days and invited my friends Ron Brightman and Arthur Lee Jacobson to come along for a big tree trek to Idaho and Montana. Our quest was to locate two pines and three larches. We left Seattle early and made it to Idaho by mid-morning. Upon arriving at the Idaho Giant, we were saddened to see that it was already dead. The Floodwood Giant would now be the new state champion, by default. It looked like a short jaunt across the Panhandle to get to the tree, but the trip took most of the rest of the day on a seemingly endless series of logging roads. It was late in the afternoon when we arrived at the Floodwood State Forest. Fortunately, the directions I'd received from the state coordinator were excellent, and we soon found ourselves staring up at a towering grove of beautiful, healthy pines. We picked the thickest one, and its measurements closely matched those of the tree we were seeking.

The Floodwood Giant was a step down in size from the dead tree we had seen earlier in the day, but it made up for that with its vigor and the magnificence of its setting in a forest that had many lofty pines. By the time the measurements were complete, it was dusk, and I had just enough light to zap the heights on a few of its taller neighbors. Several trees in this area are over 220 feet, with at least one over 230 feet. This makes Floodwood the site of the world's tallest white pine forest, and has the look of a place that holds future discoveries. ▲

Some friends measure the Floodwood Giant. Although this tree is not nearly as big as the others mentioned here, it is still the third largest of many I have measured, and stands in a fantastic grove of tall trees, including at least one pine over 230 feet tall.

WESTERN LARCH *Larix occidentalis*

When you are calm enough for discriminating observation, you will find the king of the larches, one of the best of the Western giants, beautiful, picturesque, and regal in port, easily the grandest of all the larches in the world. To those who before have seen only the European larch or the Lyall species, or the little tamarack, this Western king must be a revelation.
—John Muir, 1891

Found along the eastern slopes of the Cascades from central Oregon north into British Columbia, this is a Pacific Coast species. The western larch also extends its range into the northern Rockies, like many of its conifer associates, but western larch is the only species in this book having featured trees as far inland as Montana. Unlike its associates, however, its best development seems to occur in the high, cool Rocky Mountain sites of the Inland Empire.

Of the 11 species of larch scattered over the Northern Hemisphere, the western larch is the only one whose primary habitat is not the subalpine, timberline, or boreal forest. Its deciduous nature helps allow the larch to thrive in an otherwise evergreen environment. The species is not tolerant of shade, so it has no need to carry the great volume of needles that a cedar or hemlock does. The species is also very well adapted to fire: the thick bark and high crown usually offer enough protection to carry an old larch through unscathed. The larch can tolerate some defoliation, whether by fire or insects, since it drops its needles at season end anyway. Along with all this, it has very rapid growth in height when young, which allows it to overtop its associates and maintain a dominant canopy position throughout its life.

As one of the few deciduous conifers, western larch provides visual treats throughout the year. In the spring, when the new needles are sprouting, the fresh, bright-green color makes a nice contrast with its darker evergreen associates. The fall, however, is when western larch really puts on a show. The golden foliage lights up the mountainsides, indicating the snows of winter will not be far behind.

Like most of our desirable lumber trees, the really big larches are gone. Even during the 50 years of the National Register, there are indications that there were once larger trees. The Wolf Valley Tree, pictured in the comparative drawing on the facing page, was a survivor on private land near Libby, Montana, until the late 1960s. When Charles Sprague Sargent and other botanical explorers traveled through this area during the 1800s, they told of very large trees. Western larch's highly valued wood and clear, relatively tall trunk made it a prime target during the massive lumber operations of the late nineteenth and early twentieth centuries. ▲

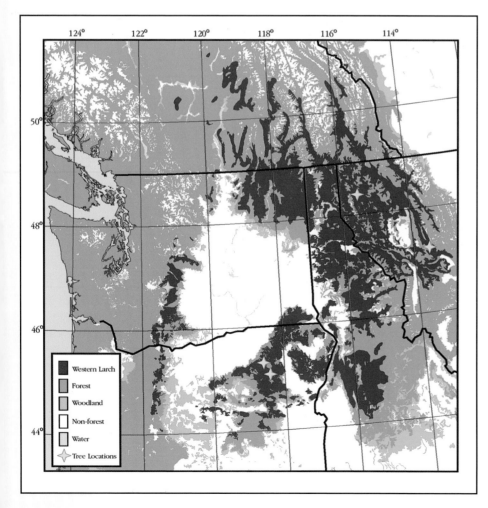

Western Larch
Forest
Woodland
Non-forest
Water
Tree Locations

The light green foliage of western larch stands out in this scene near Mount Stewart in the Washington Cascades. The western larch is one of our only deciduous conifers, and its golden fall color rivals that of the alpine larch, one of its kin native to high mountains such as the Enchantments, seen in the background here.

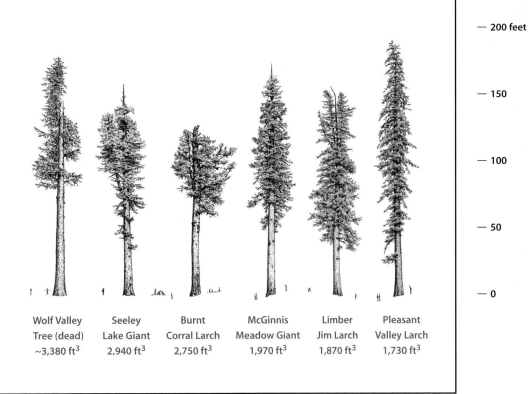

Wolf Valley Tree (dead) ~3,380 ft³	Seeley Lake Giant 2,940 ft³	Burnt Corral Larch 2,750 ft³	McGinnis Meadow Giant 1,970 ft³	Limber Jim Larch 1,870 ft³	Pleasant Valley Larch 1,730 ft³

— 200 feet

— 150

— 100

— 50

— 0

Seeley Lake Giant

I first read of the enormous larches growing at Montana's Seeley Lake in an *American Forests* article from 1927 titled "The Seeley Lake Tamaracks." The photo showed a nearly pure larch stand, something contrary to my understanding of how this early-successional tree behaves in an old-growth mixed-conifer forest. In addition to the large trees, the article also mentioned a stump aged at 911 years, which would place it among the oldest known western larches.

I visited the area in 1986, on my way to a hiking trip in Glacier National Park, when I convinced my hiking partner that a detour through the Seeley Lake area was in order. I believed then, as I still do, that visiting a stand like this will forever change your impression of the species. Seeing a species developed to its greatest potential puts a new perspective on all future encounters with it.

After a national co-champion was nominated from the Seeley Lake area in 1996, I returned with some friends in the fall of 1997, at the same time trying to time the peak of fall coloration. We received

Volume	2,940 ft³	83 m³
DBH	7.2 ft	221 cm
Height	162 ft	49.4 m
AF Points	444	

excellent directions from the Montana State Big Tree Program coordinator, and soon after arriving at the lake we found ourselves marveling at the Seeley Lake Giant. The tree is located in the Jim Girard Memorial Larch Grove, named for a Seeley Lake forester who developed a nationwide system of measuring timber for harvest. My first impression was that the measurements I had been given for the tree were wrong—this tree was no co-champ, it was much larger than I had expected. Because I had been the one to nominate the champion prior to this tree (the Pleasant Valley Larch), I knew what size to expect. Although my measurements varied only slightly from those of whoever else had measured the tree, the Seeley Lake Giant has much more wood than any other larch I know of. ▲

At the base of the Seeley Lake Giant, Rand Knight lends a sense of scale to the undisputed king of larches. The grove this tree stands in is well worth a visit, as the area has the only remaining old-growth forest completely dominated by western larch.

Burnt Corral Larch

Frank Callahan first mentioned this larch to me as he showed me a photo he had taken of it. The tree was enormous! It did not take me long to go down and visit it the next time I was in eastern Oregon. The tree grows near the Starkey Experimental Forest along the banks of Burnt Corral Creek. While surrounded by national forest, the tree is on a small parcel of private land, protected from the industrial logging that has denuded much of the national forest elsewhere. I later learned that both this tree and the Limber Jim Larch were on the Wallowa-Whitman National Forest big tree list. As I drove down the road I was directed to, I found it was easy to spot the tree across the creek; there's no mistaking this massive tree in its setting of young conifers. Frank told me that the top had sheared off in some ancient storm, so I had no idea that the trunk would be as large as it is. On one of his visits, Frank had spoken to an old-timer who had seen the tree in its prime, when it was over 200 feet tall! This is not a difficult height to believe, for at the height of its broken stem this tree is far larger than any other known larch, including the Seeley Lake Giant. The Seeley Lake Giant has a larger lower trunk for the first 52 feet. The Burnt Corral Larch has the largest trunk from there up to its 130-foot broken top. For the 30-foot section of the trunk from 80 to 110 feet, this tree is at least a foot larger than its closest contender. ▲

Volume	2,750 ft³	78 m³
DBH	6.9 ft	209 cm
Height	130 ft	39.6 m
AF Points	397	

The Burnt Corral Larch was at one time larger than the other trees listed here—probably over 200 feet tall—until an ancient storm sheared off the top. Fortunately the vigorous tree is rapidly replacing its lost crown.

McGinnis Meadow Giant

Volume	1,970 ft³	56 m³
DBH	6.3 ft	192 cm
Height	177 ft	54.0 m
AF Points	423	

The McGinnis Meadow Giant may be found in the lonely forest country south of Libby, Montana. If any area were to be called the western larch capital, it would be Libby. This is where, before loggers first came on the scene, the tree achieved its largest proportions and had the most dominance over the other species. More than a century and a half later, there is not much of this forest left to remind us of what once was. The giant Wolf Creek Tree and dozens more like it were reported from this area during the glory days of logging. Much of the best of the larch forest was privatized before the formation of the national forests, and the area around McGinnis Meadows is no different. When a tree was nominated in the late 1970s to replace the recently fallen Wolf Valley Tree, it came from this area.

The McGinnis Meadow Giant is located on private land in a selectively cut stand, on a slope above and overlooking the namesake meadow. I first saw this tree after the majority of larches had turned gold, in the waning hours of a fall day. But the McGinnis Meadow Giant was still green. I have noticed that deciduous trees larger than their neighbors often retain their leaves for slightly longer—thus extending their growing season by a week or two. This tree had been the national champion since 1980, but was dethroned by the Pleasant Valley Larch, below. Even so, this tree is slightly larger, by volume, than the Pleasant Valley tree, and appears to be far older, judging by the size and character of its crown. ▲

A former national champion, the McGinnis Meadow Giant is the largest remaining tree in the western larch nexus that is centered around Libby, Montana. The Giant stands in a partially cut woods on private land in the lonely landscapes of northwestern Montana.

Limber Jim Larch

As the Grand Ronde River filters its way out of the Elkhorn Mountains of northeast Oregon on its way to the Snake, it travels through some lovely mixed-conifer forests. In October, the abundant larches brighten up mountainsides, their glorious golden foliage shimmering in the breeze. Limber Jim Ridge is a spur of the Elkhorns, and way out on the end of this ridge, over-looking the Grand Ronde Valley, is an enormous larch. Towering above a canopy of lodgepole pine, this giant—along with a few other nearby larches and ponderosa pines—is a remnant of an ancient mixed-conifer forest. The old-growth larches and pines are now scarce in this area, their valuable wood having been exploited for the past century or more.

I first heard of the Limber Jim Larch when I obtained a copy of the big tree list from the Wallowa-Whitman National Forest and saw it listed along with the Burnt Corral Larch, a tree I had seen a couple of years earlier. Because it had similar dimensions I figured it must be worth a visit. It was. The glorious lower trunk is sheathed in thick, bright-orange bark, and the deep, full crown of light green foliage instantly made me think this the most attractive larch I have ever seen. The approach to this tree is cross-country, and the distinctive trident top is easily visible from a half-mile away, poking above the diminutive forest of lodgepole pines. I took several photos of the tree, both to aid me in making the drawing and in describing it for this page, but none of them really captures the beauty of the orange bark. The sunny fall day had produced a high-contrast, mottled light that my eye could see through, but that made photography difficult. One should preferably see this tree in person to fully appreciate its beauty—something I suppose is true for all the trees here. ▲

Volume	1,870 ft³	53 m³
DBH	6.4 ft	194 cm
Height	159 ft	48.5 m
AF Points	408	

The Limber Jim Larch is a fantastic specimen, found growing in Oregon's Elkhorn Mountains. The bright orangy bark of the tree makes it a standout, especially in contrast to the surrounding forest of smallish lodgepole pines.

Pleasant Valley Larch

Volume	1,730 ft³	49 m³
DBH	6.1 ft	186 cm
Height	189 ft	57.6 m
AF Points	428	

My wife, Kathy, and I stumbled across this tree on a Sunday drive over the mountains to Yakima. The drive up the American River, which takes us through part of Mount Rainier National Park, is always a treat. One stretch of the road runs through some particularly nice mixed-conifer forest, and that day I was noticing the fine specimens of western larch. The forests in the area have an unusu- ally high diversity of conifers. The typical eastside conifers are all there—ponderosa pine, Douglas fir, grand fir, western larch, western white pine, lodgepole pine, Engelmann spruce, and alpine fir. In addi- tion, because the road is close to the Cascade Crest, several westside species are there, including western red cedar, yellow cedar, western hemlock, noble fir, and Pacific silver fir. We pulled into the Pleasant Valley Campground to get out and walk along the river, and there it was, right in one of the campsites. I knew at once this tree would be a new state record, but I had no idea that its great height would give it enough points to become the national champion. Elsewhere in the area was a larch that was even taller.

While the Pleasant Valley Larch is tall, it is probably not as old as the giants listed above. Its location on the north bank of the American River provides it with full sun and rich soil. These factors have allowed it to develop a very deep crown, something that larches in dense forests, owing to their low tolerance of shade, are often not able to do. ▲

The Pleasant Valley Larch was a pleasant surprise for Kathy and me, as we happened upon the tree while on a Sunday drive near Mount Rainier. Its great height allowed it to became the national champion, although I now know of four trees that are larger.

Magnificent proportions and luxuriant growth ... make Abies grandis one of the stateliest and most splendid inhabitants of the forests of the northern hemisphere.
    —Charles Sprague Sargent, 1901

Grand fir is a shade-tolerant tree common throughout much of the intermountain west. Here it becomes the understory tree to overstory canopies of ponderosa pine, western larch, and Douglas fir. The best development of grand fir, however, occurs in low-elevation coastal river valleys from California to British Columbia. While considered shade-tolerant when compared with its intermountain associates, it is shade-intolerant when compared with western hemlock, western red cedar, or coast redwood. The big rivers of western Washington and coastal British Columbia tend to meander, providing continuing disturbances and opportunities for grand fir to become established. Once established, particularly on moist alluvial soils, grand fir can be one of the fastest growing tree species. In fact, on rich floodplain soils, grand fir can outgrow even Douglas fir, both in height and wood production.

Their glory is short-lived, however, because grand fir is the shortest-lived species of coniferous tree mentioned in this book. As of this writing, no individual is known to have lived for more than 300 years. The quality of the wood is what accounts for this, as grand fir is not equipped with the chemical extractives that make the wood of trees like red cedars or redwoods so resistant to decay. So the strategy of being very fast-growing has shortcomings.

Nevertheless, even though it doesn't achieve as great an age or even as large a diameter as other firs listed in this book, grand fir is one of the tallest tree species in the world—surprisingly, some specimens have been recorded reaching up to 300 feet. The tallest specimens known today are not that tall, as we know of only three individuals over 260 feet. Very tall trees, particularly short-lived species like this, seldom stay tall for long, as they either break or fall over. ▲

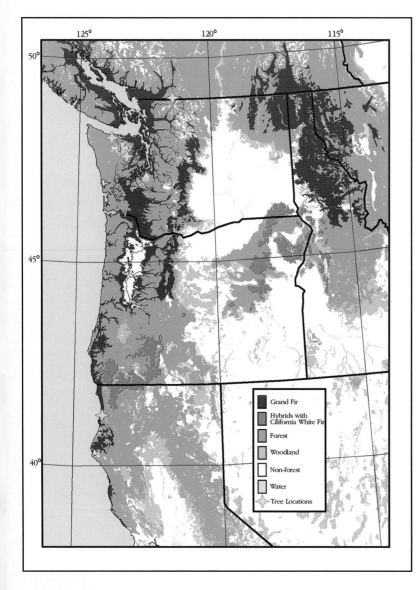

■	Grand Fir
■	Hybrids with California White Fir
■	Forest
■	Woodland
□	Non-forest
□	Water
✦	Tree Locations

Grand fir becomes the shade-tolerant species throughout many areas of the Pacific Northwest where western hemlock is absent. However, its favorite spots are rain-forest valleys such as this scene on the Suiattle River in Washington, where the meandering of the river provides the disturbance trees require in such sites.

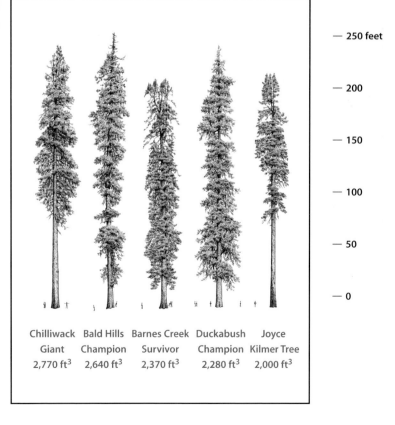

Chilliwack Giant	Bald Hills Champion	Barnes Creek Survivor	Duckabush Champion	Joyce Kilmer Tree
2,770 ft³	2,640 ft³	2,370 ft³	2,280 ft³	2,000 ft³

— 250 feet

— 200

— 150

— 100

— 50

— 0

Chilliwack Giant

Volume	2,770 ft³	78 m³
DBH	7.1 ft	216 cm
Height	246 ft	75.0 m
AF Points	522	

Grand fir is one of the few species whose world champion is found in Canada. The Chilliwack Giant was discovered by Randy Stoltmann, until 1994 the big-tree coordinator for British Columbia. His keen eye and robust constitution allowed him to discover a great many big trees while also writing several books on hiking trails through ancient forests. I first heard about this tree in 1987 when his Big Tree Program (like mine) was in its early stages. The early draft of his list was then one page long, typewritten, but it contained this tree. Now, as then, it scores higher than any other grand fir, past or present.

The Chilliwack Giant grows on the Canadian side of the Chilliwack River Trail, about a half-mile from the international border. Even though Randy discovered this tree in 1985, I wasn't able to see it for myself until 1997. The bottomland forest along the Chilliwack River is spectacular—groves of giant red cedars, together with spruce, hemlock, and grand fir, interspersed with shrub-scrub wetlands. The spruce in this area is a very rare hybrid between the coastal Sitka spruce and the Rocky Mountain Engelmann spruce. The valley is uniquely situated near the Fraser River, and almost at sea level, yet also runs deep into the heart of the North Cascades—conditions that provide opportunities for the two spruce species to come into contact. This hybrid may exist in a few other strategic valleys, but this valley is packed with them.

The Chilliwack Giant is unmistakable. Yet knowing the impressive dimensions doesn't prepare one for the moment when the perfectly formed gray shaft is spied 20 yards off the trail. The columnar bole extends nearly 100 feet to the base of the crown, and the uppermost branches tickle the sky a full 246 feet above the devil's club *(Oplopanax horridus)* understory. While it is not the tallest grand fir known, the full base and slow-tapering trunk make it the largest ever recorded. ▲

The perfect specimen that is the
Chilliwack Giant is a tribute to the species.
Towering above the surrounding forest,
the top of this tree surveys an old-growth
spruce–cedar–hemlock rain-forest canopy
at the base of the Cascades.

Bald Hills Champion

The Bald Hills Champion, first measured during the spring of 1997, bumped the first national champion I had nominated off the list. Although it is sad to see a tree dethroned, it is exciting to see larger and larger individuals represented. The Bald Hills Champion was the first grand fir in the history of the Big Tree Program to amass more than 500 AF points. It grows in a coast redwood stand in Redwood National Park with many tall grand firs that came in after a fire about 250 years ago. The Lady Bird Johnson Grove of coast redwoods is on the edge of this same burned area. Many coast redwoods survived the fire and form a tall overstory setting for the grand firs and Douglas firs that regenerated. Many of the grand firs have reached their height and age limits and are dropping out of the stand as they succumb to disease.

Forestry professor Dale Thornburgh of Humboldt State University often takes his classes to this stand to study species succession, and he told me of the great grand firs here. After hearing his tales of this unusual stand, Dale and I went there together to seek a new champion. The first tree we measured was 260 feet tall, one of the tallest known. Then, as we searched the stand for big trees, we found a snag that appeared to have been the largest tree until it had recently died. It wasn't until we were leaving that we spied the Bald Hill Champion not far from the road. The tree combines a large trunk with impressive height and is now the largest known grand fir in the United States. ▲

Volume	2,640 ft³	75 m³
DBH	6.5 ft	198 cm
Height	257 ft	78.3 m
AF Points	511	

The Bald Hills Champion was an unlikely find in the coastal redwood forests of California. The tree caught the attention of Humboldt State University professor Dale Thornburgh on one of his forestry field trips. The stand here also contains a grand fir 260 feet tall, the second tallest known.

Barnes Creek Survivor

Volume	2,370 ft³	67 m³
DBH	6.5 ft	197 cm
Height	218 ft	66.4 m
AF Points	474	

Here is a tree with nine lives. This tree was spared when Highway 101 was rerouted over Barnes Point near Lake Crescent Lodge in Olympic National Park. The old highway was noisy with logging trucks, and the delta of Barnes Creek was large enough to accommodate moving the highway farther inland. The new road cuts through some beautiful forest before crossing Barnes Creek, and the new bridge passes right next to an enormous grand fir, which I now call the Barnes Creek Survivor. The tree was located well within the construction zone and would normally have been removed, but someone must have realized that this tree was special. The workers fenced off the tree and construction went on around it. My friend Arthur Lee Jacobson was biking around the peninsula in 1984 when the construction was proceeding and photographed the Survivor with its fence, well out into the construction zone. I may never know who was ultimately responsible for saving this tree, but whoever it was—thanks!

Sixteen years after the construction, the tree looks as good as ever. While having one of the larger trunks known for a grand fir (6.5 feet), the tree is rather short (218 feet tall), having grown up in a large open area near the creek. No matter, since its 2,370 cubic feet of trunk wood volume is among the highest known. The Barnes Creek Survivor was briefly the national champion in 1986 when I discovered that the previous champion was dead, but soon after that I found the Duckabush Champion. ▲

The Barnes Creek Survivor stands proud near Lake Crescent in Olympic National Park, away from the forest, close to the road, and also luckily preserved from removal when Highway 101 was rerouted in 1984.

Duckabush Champion

Volume	2,280 ft³	65 m³
DBH	6.1 ft	185 cm
Height	246 ft	75.0 m
AF Points	486	

I found this tree during my first summer in the Olympics. I had just learned of the death of the champion grand fir on Lake Crescent (see the Preface of this book) and was actively looking for a new champion. I was hiking in the Duckabush Valley out on the east side of Olympic National Park when I came to an alluvial bench only a short way into the park that had some whoppers. The firs in that area are growing in shrub-filled wetlands with only the occasional western red cedar or grand fir towering above, conditions that are perfect for growing very large trees.

I tracked down the largest grand fir in the area, which happened to be right along the trail, and realized it was quite a contender. In fact it became the first of many nominations I have sent to *American Forests* over the years. Although I was looking for a suitable replacement for the fallen tree at Barnes Point, this tree had 491 points—the same as the fallen tree it was replacing. It held its record for 11 years, but was recently replaced by the Bald Hills Champion, described above. On my last visit to the tree, to measure the volume, I found it in a state of decline. Grand firs in general have the shortest lives of any species in this book, and they are very susceptible to disease, which often takes some of our very largest trees. In fact, most true firs grow very rapidly right up to the point when they die. Nearly all of our former record trees for these species were replaced—not necessarily because they were beaten, but because they ran out of time. ▲

This was the first tree I nominated as national champion back in 1986. Since then I have nominated dozens, but I'll always remember the excitement of finding the Duckabush Champion, which was at the time the largest specimen of this species in the country.

Joyce Kilmer Tree

Volume	2,000 ft³	57 m³
DBH	5.6 ft	170 cm
Height	219 ft	66.8 m
AF Points	439	

I first noticed the Joyce Kilmer Tree during my tenure as a cook at Lake Crescent Lodge in 1985. Across the creek from the lodge is a great grove of old growth, in which this fir is a standout. Joyce Kilmer was the man who wrote the poem "Trees" ("I think that I shall never see / A poem lovely as a tree . . . "), and who also has one of the finest stands of tulip trees (*Liriodendron tulipifera*) named after him (south of Great Smoky Mountains National Park in the Slickrock Wilderness). A sign that appears to have been there for a great many years names the tree for Kilmer. Mary Morgenroth, who also worked at the lodge that summer, told me that she lived on Barnes Point before the formation of Olympic National Park in 1938. Her father was Chris Morgenroth, an early pioneer and explorer. As first ranger of the Olympic Forest Reserve, he is credited with having shot one of the largest Roosevelt elk on record, a 17-pointer still on display above the fireplace at the lodge. Mary told me that Franklin Delano Roosevelt visited the area to see if it was worthy of national park status—obviously, he was convinced. Lake Crescent was one of the places where he was brought, to tour a trail with named trees, one of which was the Joyce Kilmer Tree. Although I have looked for other name signs, and know of at least two other trees that did have signs, as far as I know the Joyce Kilmer is the last one remaining. The tree is the most perfect specimen in a grove of large Douglas fir and grand fir near the mouth of Barnes Creek and is adjacent to a beautiful western red cedar grove. The upper portion of the fallen former champion grand fir lies next to the base of the Kilmer tree. ▲

The Joyce Kilmer Tree is one of a group of trees chosen to be part of a forest tour set up in the Olympics during the mid 1930s for a visit by President Franklin Delano Roosevelt. He made the trip to see if the area was worthy of national park status. The evidence that is now Olympic National Park convinced him.

PACIFIC SILVER FIR *Abies amabilis*

Unsurpassed among fir-trees in the beauty of its snowy bark, dark green lustrous foliage, and great purple cones, Abies amabilis *can never be forgotten by those who have seen it at midsummer towering high above alpine meadows clothed with lilies and great nodding dogtooth violets.*
—*Charles Sprague Sargent, 1901*

To me the Pacific silver fir, more than any other tree, defines the Pacific Northwest. It grows only in areas that are cool and wet, from the Coast Range in southern Oregon to southeast Alaska, and from the ocean to just beyond the Cascade crest. The sensitivity of this tree to drought conditions has led to its use by the scientific community as a marker of growing conditions for trees. The mere presence of naturally occurring Pacific silver firs indicates favorable moisture conditions. A quick comparison between the distribution map on this page with the map showing the distribution of Pacific Northwest rain forests (see fig. 11) will show some apparent similarities. These trees are normally found at 3,000 to 6,000 feet in the Cascades of Oregon and Washington, but they also occur near sea level in coastal Washington, British Columbia, and Alaska.

Pacific silver fir is as shade tolerant as any tree native to the West Coast. As such, it is often found as an understory tree in many of our coastal, montane, and subalpine forests. It is also the climax species in most of our wetter forest ecosystems. In fact, many of the Northwest's oldest forests are in high-rainfall environments with no recorded fires for the last several thousand years; these are usually dominated by Pacific silver fir. The scientific name, which means "lovely" or "beautiful," refers to the appearance of the tree and is certainly a fitting description, since its dark, glossy-green foliage with silver undersides makes such a striking impression, and the tree itself is often symmetrical and perfectly formed. The whitish, lichen-covered bark of young trees eventually breaks up into small flakes that turn purplish on trees of great age.

Although often thought of as a small, subalpine tree—which it is throughout most of its range—this conifer can get large and even approach ages of a thousand years in some of the cool, wet forests where it is found. In the coastal parts of the Olympic Peninsula, Vancouver Island, and the northern coastal mainland of British Columbia, the summers are cool enough to allow Pacific silver firs to grow very near sea level. These are the areas where the largest trees are found. The Bogachiel Valley on the Olympic Peninsula, another home of Pacific silver fir, has had a very different fire history from its neighboring rain-forest valleys, resulting in vast areas of thousand-year-old forests at low-elevation. ▲

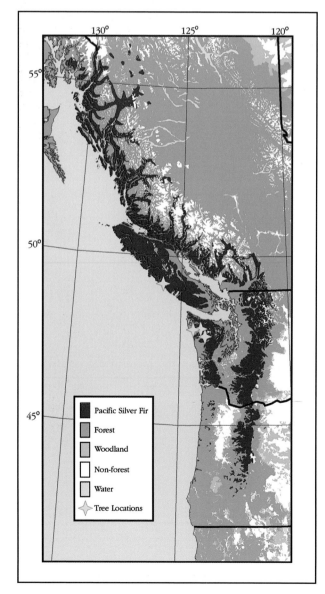

Pacific Silver Fir
Forest
Woodland
Non-forest
Water
Tree Locations

Pacific silver fir is our most shade-tolerant tree. It is also probably the least tolerant of drought. Therefore, it grows only in the wettest and coolest of our western forests.

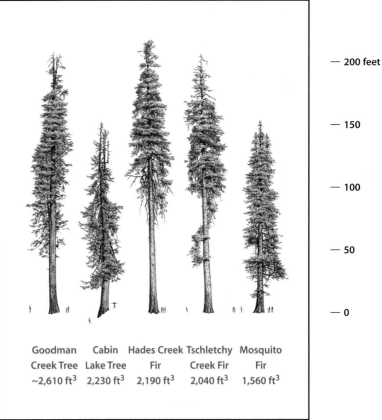

Goodman Creek Tree	Cabin Lake Tree	Hades Creek Fir	Tschletchy Creek Fir	Mosquito Fir
~2,610 ft³	2,230 ft³	2,190 ft³	2,040 ft³	1,560 ft³

— 200 feet

— 150

— 100

— 50

— 0

Goodman Creek Tree

The national champion since 1983, this giant was located on state land south of Forks, Washington, on the Olympic Peninsula. The state is under pressure to raise money for schools from its land, and so has had the habit of systematically clearcutting its lands to meet this goal. Many record or near-record trees have been logged by the Department of Natural Resources because of this situation. Both this tree and the Nolan Creek Cedar were discovered while planning timber sales, and in both cases the trees were saved because of their champion status. Other giant trees of these and other species were sacrificed because they were not *the* champion. In addition, no buffers were left around these two giants—the surrounding forest was clearcut. "This shortsighted policy will probably end up killing both trees in the long run," I wrote only a few years ago. As it turned out, these words were prophetic, as the Goodman Creek Tree blew over in 1997.

The tree itself was spectacular, and its location shattered all of my previous preconceptions about this species. First, the tree was enormous. At nearly 8 feet in diameter and 208 feet tall, it easily ranked among the largest known species of *Abies* in North America. Second, the tree was growing only a few miles from the ocean at an elevation of 120 feet—and all this from a tree that typically gets 2 to 3 feet thick at 3,000 to 5,000 feet in the Cascades and Olympic Mountains. While I never got to measure the tree's volume with the laser, I have several photos of the unobscured tree, and these, when combined with the existing measurements, allowed me to get a reasonable estimate as to its size. ▲

Volume	~2,610 ft³	~74 m³
DBH	7.8 ft	237 cm
Height	208 ft	63.4 m
AF Points	509	

The moderate environment of the western Olympics allows Pacific silver firs to grow down to near sea level. The Goodman Creek Tree, a giant fir towering over Goodman Creek, was discovered when the surrounding forest was clearcut. Separated from the forest, it stood for 15 years after that (longer than I thought it would) before falling in 1997.

Cabin Lake Tree

Volume	2,230 ft³	63m³
DBH	7.6 ft	233 cm
Height	154 ft	46.9 m
AF Points	453	

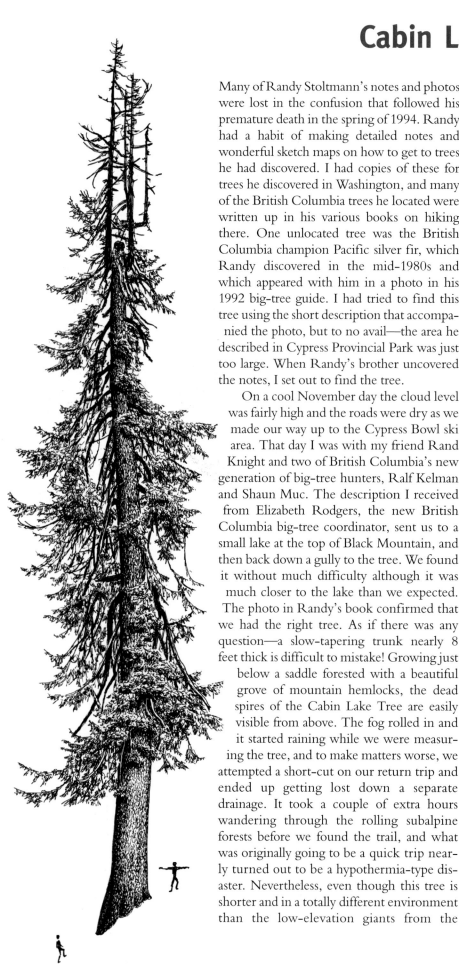

Many of Randy Stoltmann's notes and photos were lost in the confusion that followed his premature death in the spring of 1994. Randy had a habit of making detailed notes and wonderful sketch maps on how to get to trees he had discovered. I had copies of these for trees he discovered in Washington, and many of the British Columbia trees he located were written up in his various books on hiking there. One unlocated tree was the British Columbia champion Pacific silver fir, which Randy discovered in the mid-1980s and which appeared with him in a photo in his 1992 big-tree guide. I had tried to find this tree using the short description that accompanied the photo, but to no avail—the area he described in Cypress Provincial Park was just too large. When Randy's brother uncovered the notes, I set out to find the tree.

On a cool November day the cloud level was fairly high and the roads were dry as we made our way up to the Cypress Bowl ski area. That day I was with my friend Rand Knight and two of British Columbia's new generation of big-tree hunters, Ralf Kelman and Shaun Muc. The description I received from Elizabeth Rodgers, the new British Columbia big-tree coordinator, sent us to a small lake at the top of Black Mountain, and then back down a gully to the tree. We found it without much difficulty although it was much closer to the lake than we expected. The photo in Randy's book confirmed that we had the right tree. As if there was any question—a slow-tapering trunk nearly 8 feet thick is difficult to mistake! Growing just below a saddle forested with a beautiful grove of mountain hemlocks, the dead spires of the Cabin Lake Tree are easily visible from above. The fog rolled in and it started raining while we were measuring the tree, and to make matters worse, we attempted a short-cut on our return trip and ended up getting lost down a separate drainage. It took a couple of extra hours wandering through the rolling subalpine forests before we found the trail, and what was originally going to be a quick trip nearly turned out to be a hypothermia-type disaster. Nevertheless, even though this tree is shorter and in a totally different environment than the low-elevation giants from the

While Pacific silver firs are common at higher elevations, the giants listed here are all from low elevations—save one. The Cabin Lake Tree was an early Randy Stoltmann find that I was not able to visit until late 1999. It is now the largest known living specimen of this species.

Olympics, at 2,230 cubic feet the Cabin Lake Tree is now the largest known living Pacific silver fir. ▲

Hades Creek Fir

Volume	2,190 ft³	62 m³
DBH	6.9 ft	210 cm
Height	218 ft	66.4 m
AF Points	487	

The Bogachiel Valley in Olympic National Park contains the finest examples of Pacific silver fir forest I have ever seen. The upper terraces are covered with extremely old (climax) forest patches, covering sometimes only a few acres. In this environment, a grove of small stature may be adjacent to a section with many blown-over trees, which may be next to a wet grove, which in turn could be adjacent to a very productive grove of towering trees. The Hades Creek Fir is found in one of these small groves (about 5 acres) in the company of very large and tall western hemlocks and Pacific silver firs. This grove sits high above the Bogachiel River on a large terrace between Cultus and Hades Creeks. In August of 1998, Steve Sillett and I were exploring this flat, searching (unsuccessfully) for an elusive Douglas fir remnant when we encountered this grove and its largest inhabitant.

The Hades Creek Fir instantly became the new national champ, since I had learned of the Goodman Creek Tree's demise earlier that summer. While smaller than its predecessor and now superceded as champion by the Cabin Lake Tree, this tree is nonetheless the second-largest Pacific silver fir that I have seen in the United States, and a suitable replacement for the former champion. The 7-foot DBH measurement is impressive, and the slow-tapering trunk keeps a greater than 5-foot diameter to over 22 feet, which accounts for its substantial volume. The tree is in a very remote spot and had probably never had a human visitor before we showed up. It may never have one again! ▲

The rain-forest valley of the Bogachiel River in the Olympics has had an unusual history. With no known fires, the climax forest here has a disproportionately large amount of low-elevation Pacific silver fir forest. The Hades Creek Fir, the largest discovered so far, and also the largest in the country, stands near Hades Creek.

Tschletchy Creek Fir

The Tschletchy Creek Fir is yet another giant Pacific silver fir that might never have been witnessed by humans before we discovered it. Steve Sillett and I encountered it on a very long bushwhack up Tschletchy Creek in the southwest Olympics, seeking a giant Douglas fir that had been spotted by Randy Stoltmann years earlier. While the Douglas fir had recently died (a tough loss—it would have been close to the largest known), our return trip took us over a large glacial terrace above the creek and through some very old forest. We did encounter groves of giant Douglas fir on this epic bushwhack, but one large section was completely devoid of them. Instead, we found climax stands of western hemlock and Pacific silver fir, complete with the dense, thorny, huckleberry-salmonberry understory that makes hiking off-trail so memorable. In one particular grove of these somewhat lesser giants, we found the Tschletchy Creek Fir.

We could tell that this tree was smaller than the Hades Creek Fir discovered earlier in the week, yet its slow taper indicated that its volume would compare favorably to that of the Hades. Indeed, the tree's diameter does not drop below 4 feet until over 70 feet up the stem, at which point it is slightly larger than the Hades Creek Fir. This slow taper allows it to amass over 2,000 cubic feet, which is within 7 percent of the volume for the Hades tree. ▲

Volume	2,040 ft³	58 m³
DBH	5.8 ft	176 cm
Height	207 ft	63.1 m
AF Points	434	

The very remote backcountry in the upper Queets Valley has some wonderful and very wild forest. On a return trip after measuring one of the largest recorded Douglas firs (which had recently fallen) we found the Tschletchy Creek Fir, a near-record tree for the species.

Mosquito Fir

Volume	1,560 ft³	44 m³
DBH	6.9 ft	211 cm
Height	150 ft	45.7 m
AF Points	421	

Tofino is an interesting little fishing and tourist town set in the center of Clayoquot Sound on the west coast of Vancouver Island. The town itself is replete with modern conveniences, yet it is totally surrounded by primeval coastal rain forest. Just across the bay on Meares Island stands some of the most intense coastal rain forest I have ever seen. Below the massive, ancient cedars are dense, impenetrable thickets of salal, huckleberries, ferns, and salmonberry. Two of the largest

The Mosquito is a giant Pacific silver fir that stands adjacent to the even larger Big Mother Cedar near the beach on Meares Island in Clayoquot Sound. Its unexpected appearance here is made stranger by its smooth bark, typical of a very young tree.

known cedars are found in the Clayoquot Sound area. On one of my visits to my friend Adrian Dorst in Tofino, he mentioned a Pacific silver fir (in British Columbia they call them "Amabilis fir") near the Big Mother Cedar along the Mosquito Harbour Trail that was the largest he had seen. This was a surprise to me, for such a tree would be within a few feet of sea level—not a common location for Pacific silver fir down in the states, although not unheard of in British Columbia. When we went out to the cedar, we also checked out the fir.

The Mosquito Fir was not what I had expected. From the description and estimated dimensions that Adrian had given me, the vision I had in mind was based on other Pacific silver firs I had seen. It would be a grand old forest giant, a pillar of craggy-barked wood piercing the forest canopy above. But no—the tree has smooth bark like a very young tree. The trunk also has the remnants of the branch scars that covered the lower trunk, marks also indicative of a young tree. The base is heavily buttressed, suggesting that the tree began its life atop the stump or log of a fallen giant. Most incongruous of all, though, was the fact that it was utterly dwarfed by the gigantic cedar growing 30 feet away, beside which this mighty fir seemed no more than a sapling (or mosquito). However, the laser does not receive such subjective impressions, and it clearly told us that we had found a whopping big fir. The trunk DBH measurement of 6.9 feet is one of the largest known, certainly not an indication of youth. I concluded that this tree may indeed be a young tree, just a very large young tree. And while decidedly smaller than the other trees listed here, it is nonetheless the fourth-largest known living Pacific silver fir. Other giants of this species may come to light in the future, for this species is one of the most common trees in the old-growth forests of the Pacific Northwest. ▲

ENGELMANN SPRUCE *Picea engelmannii*

In its specific name this tree, the fairest of its race, braving the fiercest mountain blasts, the fiery rays of the southern sun and the arctic cold of the northern winter, with tall and massive shafts brilliant in color, and graceful spire-like crowns of soft foliage of tenderest hue, keeps green on a thousand mountain-tops the memory of a good and wise man.
—Charles Sprague Sargent, 1901

Engelmann spruce is a subalpine tree throughout much of the West. Commonly found at many of our western timberlines as stunted, dwarfed trees, the species can obtain impressive dimensions under favorable conditions. It is primarily found in the Rocky Mountains from British Columbia to New Mexico, but also occurs in the eastern Cascades of Washington and Oregon. In fact, Engelmanns grow in every major mountain range in western North America except the Sierra Nevada in California.

Cold, upper-mountain slopes provide the conditions that this species prefers. In the stands within which they are found, Engelmanns are often the tallest trees. Their shade tolerance allows them to persist in forest understories until a disturbance allows them to replace the canopy species. As a result, the component of spruce tends to increase with stand age until fire, the ax, avalanches, or some other catastrophe befalls the stand. The Engelmann spruce's ability to withstand cold temperatures provides opportunities for it to grow at lower elevations along stream courses that descend from high mountains. These are not warm areas; cold air draining out of high mountain regions following these channels often limits the ability of the local species to grow in valley bottoms, explaining a localized flipping of vegetation zones that favors the high-elevation species in the valley bottoms of high mountain forests. Conditions like these are where most of the giants of this species are located—at elevations below what would normally be their main range, surviving in cold valley bottoms in wetland or riparian conditions.

Although Engelmann spruce is the smallest tree featured in this book, several individuals are very large, including the tallest specimen ever recorded for this species. Unfortunately, two of our largest specimens have died in recent years, including the Payette Lake Tree in Idaho, the largest Engelmann ever measured. ▲

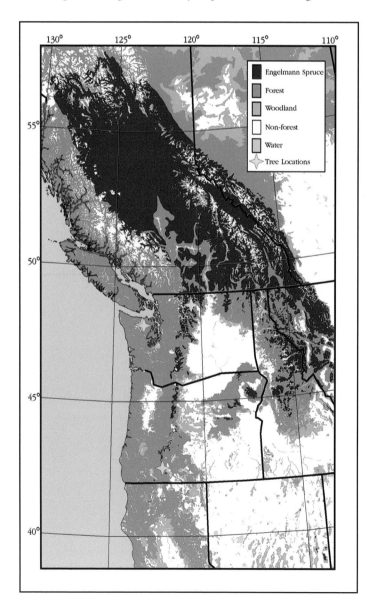

Engelmann spruce is the tree that frames many mountain views in the Rocky Mountains, all the way from Canada to Mexico. Many people do not realize that this smallish tree can become a giant in soggy mountain valleys much closer to the ocean.

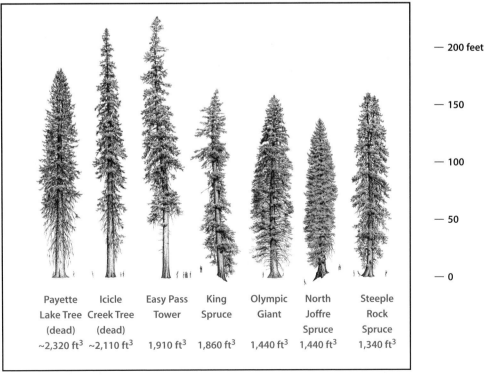

Payette Lake Tree (dead)	Icicle Creek Tree (dead)	Easy Pass Tower	King Spruce	Olympic Giant	North Joffre Spruce	Steeple Rock Spruce
~2,320 ft^3	~2,110 ft^3	1,910 ft^3	1,860 ft^3	1,440 ft^3	1,440 ft^3	1,340 ft^3

— 200 feet

— 150

— 100

— 50

— 0

Easy Pass Tower

Volume	1,910 ft³	54 m³
DBH	5.5 ft	169 cm
Height	223 ft	67.7 m
AF Points	440	

The North Cascades Highway is a scenic wonder. I always see something new along this diverse road. From the west, it starts in the Skagit Valley near Puget Sound and goes over the North Cascades right through the heart of the tallest and widest section of the mountain range. East of the crest, the road drops down to the ponderosa pine forests ringing the glorious Methow Valley. My favorite section is near the crest, at Washington and Rainy Passes, where one can gaze upslope and see the alpine larches cling to the rock cliffs above. The creeks near these passes are lined with an array of conifers that includes some very impressive Engelmann spruces. I first noticed the Tower while driving back to Seattle after a camping trip in the Lake Chelan area. As I gawked at the passing trees, one trunk caught my eye through the forest. I had to stop and check it out. The tree towered above the surrounding trees, many of which were spruces, and my laser measurement of its height was 223 feet, easily making it the tallest Engelmann spruce ever recorded. Later I returned on a cool November day to get more detailed and accurate measurements. It was just starting to snow, always a wonderful sight in the conifer forests of the Pacific Northwest.

The trunk of the Easy Pass Tower is a modest 17'5" around at breast height, making it nearly the smallest of the spruces mentioned here. Unlike most spruces, it lacked the usual bell-bottomed base. However, the trunk does not lose this modest diameter, and by 26 feet up only the King Spruce is larger. From the 73-foot point to its 223-foot top, this tree reigns supreme. The large upper trunk makes this tree the largest known living Engelmann spruce, even though two recently killed trees were probably larger. I have discovered or measured lots of trees that are the tallest of their species, even a few that are the tallest ever recorded, but most of these are not in this book. This tree is unusual in being both the tallest and largest known Engelmann Spruce. ▲

Accidentally discovered on a weekend drive through the Cascades, the Easy Pass Tower instantly became the tallest Engelmann spruce ever recorded. This fact blew me away, for once again this is a tree easily seen by thousands of people on a busy mountain highway.

King Spruce

Volume	1,860 ft³	53 m³
DBH	5.6 ft	170 cm
Height	161 ft	49.1 m
AF Points	380	

Down in the Sky Lakes Wilderness in southern Oregon, at the southern limit of the species' range, stands a giant Engelmann spruce. Frank Callahan first mentioned the area to me when I was questioning him on some big trees in his area. A place called King Spruce Camp is also shown on the old topographic maps, as well as the national forest map. Frank described the area as a series of wet meadows below a slope covered with springs—the perfect environment for Engelmann spruce. We set up a day when we could go out there together, and I brought along my friend Arthur Lee Jacobson. After parking, Frank showed us some tall trees not far from the road. Since the spruces are in the valley bottom along the creek and wet meadows, we forsook the trail in favor of hiking straight up the drainage. As we walked up the basin, we began shooting heights on some of the taller trees. We quickly found trees over 180 feet, and by the end of the day had measured four trees over 190 feet, making this the tallest known "grove" of Engelmann spruce. The largest trees were in the upper meadow, where we re-intersected the trail as it crossed the valley to the other side of the creek. Several of these were in the 6-foot DBH range, but were moderately sized trees on heavily buttressed bases. Farther up the slope, we traversed an area where several springs seep out of the hillside, and where there were more large spruces. The last of these seeps has the King Spruce, a tree not so much remarkable for its base as for its main trunk, which seemed to get larger as it went up.

With a 5.6-foot DBH, King Spruce is nearly the thinnest tree in this book. Above the modest base, however, this tree becomes much more impressive. It actually does have a section of negative taper. At 12.5 feet up, the tree has a "waist" where it is only 5.38 feet thick. The tree then swells out to 5.44 feet at 25 feet up before resuming a more typical taper. While at the high point of ground on the uphill side of the tree it is 6 feet thick, the trunk does not drop below 5 feet thick until 50 feet up, and from 7 to 70 feet, the King Spruce is thicker than any other known for this species. ▲

King Spruce Camp is located in the Sky Lakes Wilderness of southern Oregon, very close to the limit of the southern range for Engelmann spruce. Yet this locale, with its abundant seeps and ideal topography, supports a very large and tall Engelmann spruce population around its wet meadows, including this tree, the King Spruce.

Olympic Giant

Cameron Creek in the eastern Olympics was the home of the national champion from 1969 through 1970, prior to the nomination of the great Payette Lake Tree, the largest ever recorded. While I was aware that a few small populations of Engelmann spruce existed in the Olympics, I did not know that some of the trees were very large. While looking through some old issues of *American Forests,* I came across the 1969 Big Tree Register, which listed a tree from the Olympics that was 22 feet around, or 7 feet in diameter—much larger than any I had measured in Washington at that time. So in 1995, Arthur Lee Jacobson and I hiked the 15 miles up Cameron Creek to see if we could find the tree. Engelmann spruce grow only in the upper valley in this drainage, and if we had known that ahead of time, we might have taken a quicker, shorter route. In the upper Cameron Basin, spruce are found near the creek between shrub-filled avalanche chutes. One particular grove of very large trees seemed to us the most likely location of the former champ, so we forded the creek to investigate. We were greeted almost immediately by an exceptionally large spruce snag, probably the former champ and the largest spruce trunk we saw on the entire trip. Although it was broken off at about 50 feet, we concluded from its measurements that this must have been the former champ.

We then wandered around in the grove and found the largest living spruce, which turned out to have nearly the same measurements as the former champ had in 1969, although it had more taper than the big snag. The Olympic Giant was growing out in the open, a common situation in these very wet meadow-forests, and the base was heavily armored with spiny gooseberries that took their toll on us before the measurements were completed. Once I learned of the demise of the Payette Lake Tree, and saw the fallen log of the Icicle Creek Tree, I nominated this tree as the new national champ. ▲

Volume	1,440 ft³	41 m³
DBH	7.0 ft	214 cm
Height	156 ft	47.6 m
AF Points	428	

The Olympic Giant is the largest tree in the largest grove of Engelmann spruce in the Olympics. It stands near the site of an even larger tree, the champion during part of the 1960s, that remained only as a large snag by the time we refound it in the mid-1990s.

North Joffre Spruce

Volume	1,440 ft³	41 m³
DBH	7.2 ft	220 cm
Height	135 ft	41.1 m
AF Points	416	

Deep in the British Columbian Coast Mountains beyond the Whistler ski resorts stands a giant Engelmann spruce whose location stretches the definition implied by the title of this book. The main reason why so many giant oaks, maples, and cottonwoods, all of which can be forest trees, were not included here is that the champions of many of these species are ancient hulks standing out in some farmer's field. Also, the main rival to Engelmann spruce as the twentieth species listed, mountain hemlock, was excluded because many of the giants of this species in Oregon and California grow in open timberline environments, even though this is a forest tree in Washington and British Columbia. The forest the North Joffre Spruce stands in consists of a 30-foot-tall canopy of Sitka alder with a devil's club understory, in an avalanche chute below an unnamed peak. Several more giant spruces, some nearly as big, ring the base of the chute at a point where several streams converge to form a large wetland. A number of small groves of spruce occur out in this diminutive forest, but the North Joffre Spruce stands alone, several hundred feet from its nearest conifer neighbor.

The North Joffre Spruce is easily visible from an abandoned logging road nearly a mile away; it's a perfectly formed sentinel, beckoning from afar. Randy Stoltmann had seen the tree from that road a decade earlier, when the road was still being used. Its perfect form demands a closer look, and a short walk through the forest and over a stream brings one to a near view of the tree, its sprawling roots clinging to a huge boulder in the path of winter snow slides. The base of the tree is as large as that of any Engelmann I have ever seen, swelling to over 8 feet thick before it dives into the boulder-strewn slope, and expanding still farther into massive, flaring roots on the downslope side. The main trunk tapers to 5 feet thick by 19 feet up, and from there to its 135-foot top the North Joffre Spruce is unremarkable, albeit perfectly formed. ▲

North Joffre Creek is in the Canadian Coast Mountains up past Whistler and Pemberton. A large spruce swamp may be found here along with the North Joffre Spruce, a tree that stands at the base of a fell field.

Steeple Rock Spruce

Volume	1,340 ft³	38 m³
DBH	6.4 ft	194 cm
Height	157 ft	47.9 m
AF Points	405	

The Steeple Rock Spruce was discovered during the summer of 1998 on an all-day bushwhack, as I was attempting to locate a former champion yellow cedar. It grows in Wells Valley, a small valley that drains the eastern half of Steeple Rock, one of the more prominent features along Hurricane Ridge in the Olympic Mountains. Wells itself is a short, north-facing cirque basin that drains into Cox Valley, the site of the cabin of A. E. Cox, a pioneer and early game warden for what was then called Olympic National Monument. While Wells Valley is small and very steep, the valley floor is flat and supports several small wetlands. A few of these are dry enough to grow trees, while others are too moist to grow anything but wetland plants. This drainage holds one of only three known populations of Engelmann spruce in the Olympics. The steep, north-facing basin with its adequately sized swamps has maintained Engelmann spruce habitat across the last 10,000 years, while the species has died out elsewhere on the Olympic Peninsula.

The Steeple Rock Spruce is by far the largest of the several dozen spruce with whom it shares the valley. The burl-covered base sweeps and twists as it emerges from the ground, giving it an added bit of character. While it is the smallest tree listed in this book at only 1,340 cubic feet, the tree is nonetheless wonderful. By volume, it is currently the fifth-largest known Engelmann spruce. ▲

The Steeple Rock Spruce is tucked away in a tiny, relict population of spruce near Hurricane Ridge in Olympic National Park. Survivors from glacial times, these small outlier populations persist only near wet meadows or high-elevation swamps.

Appendix 1

Tree Summaries—English Measures
(Values in feet and inches, volume in cubic feet)

	Circ.	Diameter	Height	AF Spread	Points	Volume	State/ Province	Location
GIANT SEQUOIA								
General Sherman	85'0"	27.06'	274'	107'	1,321	55,040	CA	Sequoia National Park, Giant Forest
Washington	87'8"	27.91'	254'	85'	1,327	49,220	CA	Sequoia National Park, Giant Forest
General Grant	91'2"	29.02'	266'	80'	1,380	47,930	CA	Kings Canyon National Park, Grant Grove
President	80'3"	25.54'	245'	103'	1,234	47,440	CA	Sequoia National Park, Giant Forest
Lincoln	82'6"	26.26'	250'	88'	1,262	45,030	CA	Sequoia National Park, Giant Forest
Stagg	80'1"★	25.49'★	242'	80'	1,223	44,100	CA	Camp Nelson, Alder Creek Grove
Boole	92'7"★	29.47'★	267'	101'	1,403	44,080	CA	Sequoia National Forest, Converse Basin Grove
Franklin	76'6"	24.35'	223'	85'	1,162	43,440	CA	Sequoia National Park, Giant Forest
Genesis	74'0"	23.55'	253'	80'	1,161	40,530	CA	Mountain Home State Forest, Dogwood Meadow
Ishi Giant	88'6"	28.17'	255'	85'	1,338	39,210	CA	Sequoia National Forest, Kennedy Grove
COAST REDWOOD								
Del Norte Titan	74'6"	23.71'	307'	83'	1,222	36,890	CA	Jedediah Smith Redwoods State Park
Iluvatar	63'3"	20.13'	300'	101'	1,084	36,470	CA	Prairie Creek Redwoods State Park
Lost Monarch	79'2"	25.20'	321'	75'	1,290	34,910	CA	Jedediah Smith Redwoods State Park
Howland Hill Giant	62'1"	19.76'	329'	71'	1,092	33,580	CA	Jedediah Smith Redwoods State Park
Sir Isaac Newton	72'3"	23.00'	311'	101'	1,203	33,190	CA	Prairie Creek Redwoods State Park
El Viejo del Norte	69'6"	22.12'	324'	75'	1,177	32,640	CA	Jedediah Smith Redwoods State Park
Terex Titan	66'11"	21.30'	262'	87'	1,087	32,380	CA	Prairie Creek Redwoods State Park
Adventure	51'0"★	16.23'★	334'	85'	967	31,170	CA	Prairie Creek Redwoods State Park
Bull Creek Giant	70'0"	22.28'	332'	71'	1,190	31,140	CA	Humboldt Redwoods State Park, Bull Creek Trail
Arco Giant	76'9"	24.43'	265'	99'	1,211	30,700	CA	Redwood National Park, along Prairie Creek

	Circ.	Diameter	Height	Spread	AF Points	Volume	State/ Province	Location
WESTERN RED CEDAR								
Quinault Lake Cedar	61'3"	19.50'	174'	45'	920	17,650	WA	Olympic National Park, N shore of Quinault Lake
Cheewhat Lake Cedar	60'2"	19.15'	182'	51'	917	15,870	BC	Pacific Rim National Park, E shore of Cheewhat Lake
Nolan Creek Cedar	58'3"	18.54'	171'	54'	884	15,330	WA	Forks, Nolan Creek Road, S of Hoh River
Willaby Creek Tree	56'8"	18.04'	195'	51'	888	12,410	WA	Olympic National Forest, S of Quinault Lake
Kalaloch Cedar	61'9"	19.65'	123'	51'	877	12,370	WA	Olympic National Park, N of Kalaloch at 5th Beach
Big Mother Cedar	58'2"	18.52'	154'	50'	865	10,350	BC	Meares Island, Mosquito Harbour Trail
Stoltmann Cedar	60'11"	19.39'	146'	50'	890	10,320	BC	Kennedy Lake, Clayoquot Arm Recreation Site
Niawiakum Giant	54'4"	17.29'	154'	55'	820	10,310	WA	Bay Center, South Bend–Pallix Road
Seal Slough Cedar	58'1"	18.49'	150'	55'	861	9,810	WA	Willapa Bay, Seal Slough
DOUGLAS FIR								
Red Creek Tree	43'7"	13.87'	242'	75'	784	12,320	BC	Vancouver Island, Port Renfrew
Queets Fir	50'0"	15.92'	200'	37'	809	11,710	WA	Olympic National Park, Queets River Trail
Tichipawa	42'1"	13.40'	281'	71'	804	10,870	WA	Olympic National Forest, Quinault Lake
Rex	40'10"	13.00'	302'	59'	807	10,200	WA	Olympic National Forest, Quinault Lake
Ol' Jed	42'8"	13.58'	301'	65'	829	10,040	CA	Jedediah Smith Redwood State Park
Cedar Flats Sentinel	37'2"	11.83'	264'	65'	726	9,350	WA	Gifford Pinchot National Forest, Cedar Flats RNA
Quamal	39'7"	12.60'	276'	61'	766	9,350	WA	Olympic National Forest, Quinault Lake
Gatton Goliath	40'11"	13.02'	295'	48'	798	9,080	WA	Olympic National Forest, Quinault Lake
Indian Pass Tree	36'4"	11.57'	198'	63'	650	9,060	WA	Olympic National Park, Indian Pass Trail
Mauksa	37'5"	11.91'	290'	61'	754	8,740	WA	Olympic National Forest, Quinault Lake
SITKA SPRUCE								
Queets Spruce	46'11"	14.94'	248'	83'	832	11,920	WA	Olympic National Park, Queets Campground
San Juan Spruce	38'3"	12.18'	205'	75'	683	11,780	BC	San Juan River, San Juan Bridge Picnic Area

	Circ.	Diameter	Height	Spread	AF Points	Volume	State/ Province	Location
Quinault Lake Spruce	55'7"	17.68'	191'	96'	882	10,540	WA	Olympic National Forest, SE shore of Quinault Lake
Klootchy Creek Giant	52'4"	16.66'	204'	93'	855	10,450	OR	Seaside, Klootchy Creek Recreation Site
Rector Ridge Spruce	44'6"	14.16'	185'	83'	740	9,870	OR	Nehalem, above Gods Valley
Preston Macy Tree	41'2"	13.10'	257'	67'	768	9,600	WA	Olympic National Park, Hoh River Road
Maxine's Tree	41'6"	13.21'	265'	60'	778	9,410	BC	Carmanah Walbran Provincial Park
Cougar Flat Sentinel	42'9"	13.61'	202'	65'	731	9,150	WA	Olympic National Park, Hoh River Trail
Big Flat Tree	42'1"	13.48'	189'	56'	708	9,080	WA	Olympic National Park, South Fork Hoh Trail
Cape Meares Giant	48'5"	15.42'	182'	73'	781	9,030	OR	Cape Meares State Park

SUGAR PINE

	Circ.	Diameter	Height	Spread	AF Points	Volume	State/ Province	Location
Whelan Tree	34'5"	10.95'	206'	68'	636	8,990	CA	Dorrington, Camp Connell
Pickering Pine	36'3"	11.54'	209'	59'	659	7,230	CA	Dorrington, North Fork Stanislaus River canyon
Calaveras Colossus	30'11"	9.84'	202'	57'	587	6,600	CA	Calaveras Big Trees State Park, ridge above Beaver Creek
One-Armed Bandit	28'8"	9.13'	209'	59'	568	5,540	CA	Dorrington, North Fork Stanislaus River canyon
Yosemite Giant	29'0"	9.23'	268'	68'	633	5,390	CA	Yosemite National Park, Hodgdon Meadow

INCENSE CEDAR

	Circ.	Diameter	Height	Spread	AF Points	Volume	State/ Province	Location
Devil's Canyon Colossus	39'0"	12.41'	165'	49'	645	7,860	CA	Marble Mountains Wilderness, Devil's Canyon
Tannen Lakes Titan	40'7"	12.92'	137'	37'	633	4,350	OR	Red Buttes Wilderness, East Tannen Lake
Big Bear Cedar	28'7"	9.10'	141'	45'	495	2,890	CA	Trinity Alps Wilderness, Big Bear Lake Trail
Lonesome Meadow Monarch	29'3"	9.31'	143'	39'	504	2,640	OR	Umpqua National Forest, Incense Cedar Botanical Area

YELLOW CEDAR

	Circ.	Diameter	Height	Spread	AF Points	Volume	State/ Province	Location
Admiral Broeren	34'1"	10.85'	154'	47'	575	6,650	BC	Kelsey Bay, Memekay River Valley
Sergeant RandAlly	42'11"	13.66'	200'	53'	728	6,200	BC	Kelsey Bay, Memekay River Valley
Big Creek Cedar	37'7"	11.96'	129'	27'	587	4,530	WA	Olympic National Park, Big Creek Trail
General Buxton	34'3"★	10.90'★	148'	50'	572	4,520	BC	Kelsey Bay, Bigtree Creek
Cypress Park Cedar	23'6"★	7.48'★	130'	35'	421	3,650	BC	Cypress Provincial Park, entrance road

NOBLE FIR

	Circ.	Diameter	Height	Spread	AF Points	Volume	State/ Province	Location
Yellowjacket Creek Champion	29'11"	9.52'	278'★★	41'	647	5,700	WA	Gifford Pinchot National Forest, Yellowjacket Creek

	Circ.	Diameter	Height	Spread	AF Points	Volume	State/ Province	Location
Goat Marsh Giant	26'1"	8.30'	272'	49'	597	4,430	WA	Mount St. Helens National Volcanic Monument, Goat Marsh RNA
Ipsut Creek Colossus	28'1"	8.94'	217'	41'	564	4,140	WA	Mount Rainier National Park, Ipsut Creek Trail
Riker!	22'11"	7.29'	253'	43'	539	3,810	WA	Mount St. Helens National Volcanic Monument, Goat Marsh RNA

PORT ORFORD CEDAR

	Circ.	Diameter	Height	Spread	AF Points	Volume	State/ Province	Location
Elk Creek Champion	37'7"	11.96'	229'	39'	690	5,020	OR	Siskiyou National Forest, S of Powers on Elk Creek Road
Coquille Falls Tree	28'4"	9.02'	206'	39'	556	3,610	OR	Siskiyou National Forest, Coquille Falls RNA
Survivor	26'9"	8.51'	235'	33'	564	3,020	OR	Siskiyou National Forest, Coquille Falls RNA
Neighbor	26'5"	8.41'	228'	32'	553	2,970	OR	Siskiyou National Forest, S of Powers on Elk Creek Road

JEFFREY PINE

	Circ.	Diameter	Height	Spread	AF Points	Volume	State/ Province	Location
Eureka Valley Giant	25'6"	8.12'	192'	90'	521	4,560	CA	Stanislaus National Forest, near Dardanelle
Smoky Jack	23'5"	7.45'	186'	73'	485	4,100	CA	Yosemite National Park, Tioga Pass Road
Huntington Lake Giant	23'10"	7.59'	173'	67'	476	3,830	CA	Sierra National Forest, Huntington Lake
Lost Bear Survivor	22'10"	7.27'	173'	59'	462	3,660	CA	Yosemite National Park, Glacier Point Road
Brush Meadow Giant	21'8"	6.90'	200'	53'	473	3,200	CA	Sierra National Forest, near McKinley Grove

PONDEROSA PINE

	Circ.	Diameter	Height	Spread	AF Points	Volume	State/ Province	Location
Grizzly Meadow Monarch	22'10"	7.27'	223'	55'	511	4,460	CA	Sierra National Forest, West Fork Chiquito Creek
Hartman's Bar Tree	24'5"	7.77'	227'	68'	537	4,130	CA	Plumas National Forest, Hartman's Bar Trail
Bear Creek Twin	24'6"	7.80'	223'	59'	532	4,080	CA	Trinity Alps Wilderness, Bear Creek Trail
La Pine Giant	28'6"	9.07'	166'	45'	519	4,020	OR	La Pine State Recreation Area
Fish Camp Pine	23'4"	7.43'	223'	44'	514	3,790	CA	Sierra National Forest, Fish Camp

WESTERN HEMLOCK

	Circ.	Diameter	Height	Spread	AF Points	Volume	State/ Province	Location
Enchanted Valley Hemlock	27'11"	8.89'	172'	65'	523	4,270	WA	Olympic National Park, Enchanted Valley Trail
Mammoth of Milk Creek	27'11"★	8.89'★	167'	57'	516	3,480	WA	Glacier Peak Wilderness, Milk Creek Trail
Wynoochee Giant	28'6"★	9.07'★	195'	47'	549	3,060	WA	Olympic National Park, Wynoochee Trail

	Circ.	Diameter	Height	Spread	AF Points	Volume	State/Province	Location
Norvan's Castle	29'11"	9.52'	149'	66'	525	2,930	BC	Lynn Headwaters Regional Park, Norvan Creek
Gandalf	22'2"	7.06'	168'	53'	447	2,840	WA	Olympic National Park, Wynoochee Trail

CALIFORNIA RED FIR

	Circ.	Diameter	Height	Spread	AF Points	Volume	State/Province	Location
Leaning Tower	30'5"	9.68'	172'	41'	547	3,880	CA	Yosemite National Park, near White Wolf Road
Seven Sisters	25'4"	8.06'	148'	41'	462	2,930	CA	Yosemite National Park, near White Wolf Road
Big Red	23'3"	7.40'	203'	37'	491	2,840	CA	Yosemite National Park, South Fork Tuolumne River
Porcupine Flats Tree	22'8"	7.22'	159'	44'	442	2,390	CA	Yosemite National Park, W of Porcupine Flats

CALIFORNIA WHITE FIR

	Circ.	Diameter	Height	Spread	AF Points	Volume	State/Province	Location
Merced Lake Giant	23'0"	7.32'	217'	39'	503	3,510	CA	Yosemite National Park, Merced Lake
Tioga Road Fir	22'6"	7.16'	176'	39'	456	2,990	CA	Yosemite National Park, Tioga Pass Road
Badger Pass Tree	23'0"	7.32'	207'	35'	492	2,970	CA	Yosemite National Park, Glacier Point Road
Sinuosity	20'0"	6.37'	202'	35'	451	2,540	CA	Yosemite National Park, Little Yosemite Valley

WESTERN WHITE PINE

	Circ.	Diameter	Height	Spread	AF Points	Volume	State/Province	Location
Fish Lake Pine	21'1"	6.71'	222'	35'	484	3,210	OR	Rogue River National Forest, near Fish Lake
Idaho Giant	21'3"	6.76'	210'	39'	475	2,530	ID	Clearwater National Forest, White Pine Drive
Floodwood Giant	20'8"	6.58'	227'	25'	481	1,850	ID	Floodwood State Forest

WESTERN LARCH

	Circ.	Diameter	Height	Spread	AF Points	Volume	State/Province	Location
Seeley Lake Giant	22'9"	7.24'	162'	34'	444	2,940	MT	Lolo National Forest, Seeley Lake near Paxton Camp
Burnt Corral Larch	21'7"	6.87'	130'	30'	397	2,750	OR	Near Starkey Experimental Forest
McGinnis Meadow Giant	19'9"	6.29'	177'	37'	423	1,970	MT	Near Libby, McGinnis Meadows
Limber Jim Larch	20'0"	6.37'	159'	37'	408	1,870	OR	Wallowa-Whitman National Forest, Limber Jim Ridge
Pleasant Valley Larch	19'2"	6.10'	189'	35'	428	1,730	WA	Wenatchee National Forest, Pleasant Valley Campground

GRAND FIR

	Circ.	Diameter	Height	Spread	AF Points	Volume	State/Province	Location
Chilliwack Giant	22'3"	7.08'	246'	36'	522	2,770	BC	Ecological Reserve 98, Chilliwack River Trail
Bald Hills Champion	20'5"	6.50'	257'	36'	511	2,640	CA	Redwood National Park, Bald Hills Road

	Circ.	Diameter	Height	Spread	AF Points	Volume	State/ Province	Location
Barnes Creek Survivor	20'4"	6.47'	218'	47'	474	2,370	WA	Olympic National Park, Barnes Creek
Duckabush Champion	19'1"	6.07'	246'	43'	486	2,280	WA	Olympic National Park, Duckabush River Trail
Joyce Kilmer Tree	17'4"	5.57'	219'	47'	439	2,000	WA	Olympic National Park, Barnes Point

PACIFIC SILVER FIR

	Circ.	Diameter	Height	Spread	AF Points	Volume	State/ Province	Location
Goodman Creek Tree	24'5"	7.77'	208'	31'	509	~2,610	WA	Forks, Goodman Creek
Cabin Lake Tree	24'0"	7.64'	154'	43'	453	2,230	BC	Cypress Provincial Park, N side of Black Mountain
Hades Creek Fir	21'8"	6.90'	218'	37'	487	2,190	WA	Olympic National Park, Hades Creek
Tschletchy Creek Fir	18'2"	5.78'	207'	35'	434	2,040	WA	Olympic National Park, Tschletchy Creek
Mosquito Fir	21'9"	6.92'	150'	41'	421	1,560	BC	Meares Island, Mosquito Harbour Trail

ENGELMANN SPRUCE

	Circ.	Diameter	Height	Spread	AF Points	Volume	State/ Province	Location
Easy Pass Tower	17'5"	5.54'	223'	33'	440	1,910	WA	Mount Baker National Forest, N of Rainy Pass on Hwy 20
King Spruce	17'6"	5.56'	161'	35'	380	1,860	OR	Sky Lakes Wilderness, King Spruce Camp
Olympic Giant	22'1"	7.03'	156'	27'	428	1,440	WA	Olympic National Park, Cameron Creek Trail
North Joffre Spruce	22'8"	7.22'	135'	35'	416	1,440	BC	Squamish Forest District, North Joffre Creek
Steeple Rock Spruce	20'0"	6.37'	157'	33'	405	1,340	WA	Olympic National Park, Wells Valley

★ Diameter not measured at 4.5', but at lowest practical point
★★ Currently measures 227'

Appendix 2

Tree Summaries—Metric Measures
(Values in meters, diameter in centimeters, volume in cubic meters)

	Circ.	Diameter	Height	Spread	AF Points	Volume	State/ Province	Location
GIANT SEQUOIA								
General Sherman	25.9	825	83.5	33	1,321	1,489	CA	Sequoia National Park, Giant Forest
Washington	26.7	851	77.4	26	1,327	1,394	CA	Sequoia National Park, Giant Forest
General Grant	27.8	885	81.1	24	1,380	1,357	CA	Kings Canyon National Park, Grant Grove
President	24.5	779	74.7	31	1,234	1,318	CA	Sequoia National Park, Giant Forest
Lincoln	25.1	800	76.2	27	1,262	1,275	CA	Sequoia National Park, Giant Forest
Stagg	24.4★	777★	73.8	24	1,223	1,249	CA	Camp Nelson, Alder Creek Grove
Boole	28.2★	898★	81.4	31	1,403	1,244	CA	Sequoia National Forest, Converse Basin Grove
Franklin	23.3	742	68.0	26	1,162	1,223	CA	Sequoia National Park, Giant Forest
Genesis	22.6	718	77.1	24	1,161	1,148	CA	Mountain Home State Forest, Dogwood Meadow
Ishi Giant	27.0	859	77.7	26	1,338	1,110	CA	Sequoia National Forest, Kennedy Grove
COAST REDWOOD								
Del Norte Titan	22.7	723	93.6	25	1,222	1,045	CA	Jedediah Smith Redwoods State Park, Mill Creek
Iluvatar	19.3	614	91.4	31	1,084	1,033	CA	Prairie Creek Redwoods State Park
Lost Monarch	24.1	768	97.8	23	1,290	989	CA	Jedediah Smith Redwoods State Park, Mill Creek Trail
Howland Hill Giant	18.9	602	100.3	22	1,092	951	CA	Jedediah Smith Redwoods State Park
Sir Isaac Newton	22.0	701	94.8	31	1,203	940	CA	Prairie Creek Redwoods State Park, Prairie Creek Trail
El Viejo del Norte	21.2	674	98.8	23	1,177	924	CA	Jedediah Smith Redwoods State Park, Mill Creek Trail
Terex Titan	20.4	649	79.9	27	1,087	917	CA	Prairie Creek Redwoods State Park
Adventure	15.5★	495★	101.8	26	967	883	CA	Prairie Creek Redwoods State Park

	Circ.	Diameter	Height	Spread	AF Points	Volume	State/ Province	Location
Bull Creek Giant	21.3	679	101.2	22	1,190	882	CA	Humboldt Redwoods State Park, Bull Creek Trail
Arco Giant	23.4	745	80.8	30	1,211	869	CA	Redwood National Park, along Prairie Creek

WESTERN RED CEDAR

	Circ.	Diameter	Height	Spread	AF Points	Volume	State/ Province	Location
Quinault Lake Cedar	18.7	594	53.0	14	920	500	WA	Olympic National Park, N shore of Quinault Lake
Cheewhat Lake Cedar	18.3	584	55.5	16	917	449	BC	Pacific Rim National Park, E shore of Cheewhat Lake
Nolan Creek Cedar	17.8	565	52.1	16	884	434	WA	Forks, Nolan Creek Road S of Hoh River
Willaby Creek Tree	17.3	550	59.4	16	888	351	WA	Olympic National Forest, S of Quinault Lake
Kalaloch Cedar	18.8	599	37.5	16	877	350	WA	Olympic National Park, N of Kalaloch at 5th Beach
Big Mother Cedar	17.7	564	46.9	15	865	293	BC	Meares Island, Mosquito Harbour Trail
Stoltmann Cedar	18.6	591	44.5	15	890	292	BC	Kennedy Lake, Clayoquot Arm Recreation Site
Niawiakum Giant	16.6	527	46.9	17	820	292	WA	Bay Center, South Bend–Pallix Road
Seal Slough Cedar	17.7	564	45.7	17	861	278	WA	Willapa Bay, Seal Slough

DOUGLAS FIR

	Circ.	Diameter	Height	Spread	AF Points	Volume	State/ Province	Location
Red Creek Tree	13.3	423	73.8	23	784	349	BC	Vancouver Island, Port Renfrew
Queets Fir	15.2	485	61.0	11	809	332	WA	Olympic National Park, Queets River Trail
Tichipawa	12.8	408	85.6	22	804	308	WA	Olympic National Forest, Quinault Lake
Rex	12.4	396	92.1	18	807	289	WA	Olympic National Forest, Quinault Lake
Ol' Jed	13.0	414	91.7	20	829	284	CA	Jedediah Smith Redwood State Park
Cedar Flats Sentinel	11.3	361	80.5	20	726	265	WA	Gifford Pinchot National Forest, Cedar Flats RNA
Quamal	12.1	384	84.1	19	766	265	WA	Olympic National Forest, Quinault Lake
Gatton Goliath	12.5	397	89.9	15	798	257	WA	Olympic National Forest, Quinault Lake
Indian Pass Tree	11.1	353	60.4	19	650	257	WA	Olympic National Park, Indian Pass Trail
Mauksa	11.4	363	88.4	19	754	247	WA	Olympic National Forest, Quinault Lake

	Circ.	Diameter	Height	Spread	AF Points	Volume	State/ Province	Location
SITKA SPRUCE								
Queets Spruce	14.3	455	75.6	25	832	337	WA	Olympic National Park, Queets Campground
San Juan Spruce	11.7	371	62.5	23	683	333	BC	San Juan River, San Juan Bridge Picnic Area
Quinault Lake Spruce	16.9	539	58.2	29	882	298	WA	Olympic National Forest, SE shore of Quinault Lake
Klootchy Creek Giant	16.0	508	62.1	28	855	296	OR	Seaside, Klootchy Creek Recreation Site
Rector Ridge Spruce	13.6	432	56.4	25	740	280	OR	Nehalem, above Gods Valley
Preston Macy Tree	12.5	399	78.3	20	768	272	WA	Olympic National Park, Hoh River Road
Maxine's Tree	12.7	403	80.8	18	778	266	BC	Carmanah Walbran Provincial Park
Cougar Flat Sentinel	13.1	416	61.6	20	731	259	WA	Olympic National Park, Hoh River Trail
Big Flat Tree	12.9	410	57.6	17	708	257	WA	Olympic National Park, South Fork Hoh Trail
Cape Meares Giant	14.8	470	55.5	22	781	256	OR	Cape Meares State Park
SUGAR PINE								
Whelan Tree	10.0	334	62.8	21	636	255	CA	Dorrington, Camp Connell
Pickering Pine	11.0	352	63.7	18	659	205	CA	Dorrington, North Fork Stanislaus River canyon
Calaveras Colossus	9.4	300	61.6	17	587	187	CA	Calaveras Big Trees State Park, ridge above Beaver Creek
One-Armed Bandit	8.7	278	63.7	18	568	157	CA	Dorrington, North Fork Stanislaus River canyon
Yosemite Giant	8.8	281	81.7	21	633	153	CA	Yosemite National Park, Hodgdon Meadow
INCENSE CEDAR								
Devil's Canyon Colossus	11.9	378	50.3	15	645	223	CA	Marble Mountains Wilderness, Devil's Canyon
Tannen Lakes Titan	12.4	394	41.8	11	633	123	OR	Red Buttes Wilderness, East Tannen Lake
Big Bear Cedar	8.7	277	43.0	14	495	82	CA	Trinity Alps Wilderness, Big Bear Lake Trail
Lonesome Meadow Monarch	8.9	284	43.6	12	504	75	OR	Umpqua National Forest, Incense Cedar Botanical Area
YELLOW CEDAR								
Admiral Broeren	10.4	331	46.9	14	575	188	BC	Kelsey Bay, Memekay River Valley
Sergeant RandAlly	13.1	416	61.0	16	728	175	BC	Kelsey Bay, Memekay River Valley

	Circ.	Diameter	Height	Spread	AF Points	Volume	State/ Province	Location
Big Creek Cedar	11.5	365	39.3	8	587	128	WA	Olympic National Park, Big Creek Trail
General Buxton	10.4★	332★	45.1	15	572	128	BC	Kelsey Bay, Bigtree Creek
Cypress Park Cedar	7.2★	228★	39.6	11	421	103	BC	Cypress Provincial Park, entrance road

NOBLE FIR

	Circ.	Diameter	Height	Spread	AF Points	Volume	State/ Province	Location
Yellowjacket Creek Champion	9.1	290	84.7★★	12	647	161	WA	Gifford Pinchot National Forest, Yellowjacket Creek
Goat Marsh Giant	8.0	253	82.9	15	597	126	WA	Mount St. Helens National Volcanic Monument, Goat Marsh RNA
Ipsut Creek Colossus	8.6	272	66.1	12	564	117	WA	Mount Rainier National Park, Ipsut Creek Trail
Riker!	7.0	222	77.1	13	539	108	WA	Mount St. Helens National Volcanic Monument, Goat Marsh RNA

PORT ORFORD CEDAR

	Circ.	Diameter	Height	Spread	AF Points	Volume	State/ Province	Location
Elk Creek Champion	11.5	365	69.8	12	690	142	OR	Siskiyou National Forest, S of Powers on Elk Creek Road
Coquille Falls Tree	8.6	275	62.8	12	556	102	OR	Siskiyou National Forest, Coquille Falls RNA
Survivor	8.2	260	71.6	10	564	86	OR	Siskiyou National Forest, Coquille Falls RNA
Neighbor	8.1	256	69.5	10	553	84	OR	Siskiyou National Forest, S of Powers on Elk Creek Road

JEFFREY PINE

	Circ.	Diameter	Height	Spread	AF Points	Volume	State/ Province	Location
Eureka Valley Giant	7.8	247	58.5	27	521	129	CA	Stanislaus National Forest, near Dardanelle
Smoky Jack	7.1	227	56.7	22	485	116	CA	Yosemite National Park, Tioga Pass Road
Huntington Lake Giant	7.3	231	52.7	20	476	109	CA	Sierra National Forest, Huntington Lake
Lost Bear Survivor	7.0	222	52.7	18	462	104	CA	Yosemite National Park, Glacier Point Road
Brush Meadow Giant	6.6	210	61.0	16	473	91	CA	Sierra National Forest, near McKinley Grove

PONDEROSA PINE

	Circ.	Diameter	Height	Spread	AF Points	Volume	State/ Province	Location
Grizzly Meadow Monarch	7.0	222	68.0	17	511	126	CA	Sierra National Forest, West Fork Chiquito Creek
Hartman's Bar Tree	7.4	237	69.2	21	537	117	CA	Plumas National Forest, Hartman's Bar Trail
Bear Creek Twin	7.5	238	68.0	18	532	115	CA	Trinity Alps Wilderness, Bear Creek Trail
La Pine Giant	8.7	277	50.6	14	519	114	OR	La Pine State Recreation Area
Fish Camp Pine	7.1	226	68.0	13	514	107	CA	Sierra National Forest, Fish Camp

	Circ.	Diameter	Height	Spread	AF Points	Volume	State/ Province	Location
WESTERN HEMLOCK								
Enchanted Valley Hemlock	8.5	271	52.4	20	523	121	WA	Olympic National Park, Enchanted Valley Trail
Mammoth of Milk Creek	8.5★	271★	50.9	17	516	99	WA	Glacier Peak Wilderness, Milk Creek Trail
Wynoochee Giant	9.1★	276★	59.4	14	549	87	WA	Olympic National Park, Wynoochee Trail
Norvan's Castle	9.1	290	45.3	20	525	83	BC	Lynn Headwaters Regional Park, Norvan Creek
Gandalf	6.8	215	51.2	16	447	81	WA	Olympic National Park, Wynoochee Trail
CALIFORNIA RED FIR								
Leaning Tower	9.3	295	52.4	12	547	110	CA	Yosemite National Park, near White Wolf Road
Seven Sisters	7.7	246	45.1	12	462	83	CA	Yosemite National Park, near White Wolf Road
Big Red	7.1	226	61.9	11	491	80	CA	Yosemite National Park, South Fork Tuolumne River
Porcupine Flats Tree	6.9	220	48.5	13	442	68	CA	Yosemite National Park, W of Porcupine Flats
CALIFORNIA WHITE FIR								
Merced Lake Giant	7.0	223	66.1	12	503	99	CA	Yosemite National Park, Merced Lake
Tioga Road Fir	6.9	218	53.6	12	456	85	CA	Yosemite National Park, Tioga Pass Road
Badger Pass Tree	7.0	223	63.1	11	492	84	CA	Yosemite National Park, Glacier Point Road
Sinuosity	6.1	194	61.6	11	451	72	CA	Yosemite National Park, Little Yosemite Valley
WESTERN WHITE PINE								
Fish Lake Pine	6.4	205	67.7	11	484	91	OR	Rogue River National Forest, near Fish Lake
Idaho Giant	6.5	206	64.0	12	475	72	ID	Clearwater National Forest, White Pine Drive
Floodwood Giant	6.3	201	69.2	8	481	52	ID	Floodwood State Forest
WESTERN LARCH								
Seeley Lake Giant	6.9	221	49.4	10	444	83	MT	Lolo National Forest, Seeley Lake near Paxton Camp
Burnt Corral Larch	6.6	209	39.6	9	397	78	OR	Near Starkey Experimental Forest
McGinnis Meadow Giant	6.0	192	54.0	11	423	56	MT	Near Libby, McGinnis Meadows
Limber Jim Larch	6.1	194	48.5	11	408	53	OR	Wallowa-Whitman National Forest, Limber Jim Ridge
Pleasant Valley Larch	5.8	186	57.6	11	428	49	WA	Wenatchee National Forest, Pleasant Valley Campground

	Circ.	Diameter	Height	Spread	AF Points	Volume	State/ Province	Location
GRAND FIR								
Chilliwack Giant	6.8	216	75.0	11	522	78	BC	Ecological Reserve 98, Chilliwack River Trail
Bald Hills Champion	6.2	198	78.3	11	511	75	CA	Redwood National Park, Bald Hills Road
Barnes Creek Survivor	6.2	197	66.4	14	474	67	WA	Olympic National Park, Barnes Creek
Duckabush Champion	5.8	185	75.0	13	486	65	WA	Olympic National Park, Duckabush River Trail
Joyce Kilmer Tree	5.3	170	66.8	14	439	57	WA	Olympic National Park, Barnes Point
PACIFIC SILVER FIR								
Goodman Creek Tree	7.4	237	63.4	9	509	~74	WA	Forks, Goodman Creek
Cabin Lake Tree	7.3	233	46.9	13	453	63	BC	Cypress Provincial Park, N side of Black Mountain
Hades Creek Fir	6.6	210	66.4	11	487	62	WA	Olympic National Park, Hades Creek
Tschletchy Creek Fir	5.5	176	63.1	11	434	58	WA	Olympic National Park, Tschletchy Creek
Mosquito Fir	6.6	211	45.7	12	421	44	BC	Meares Island, Mosquito Harbour Trail
ENGELMANN SPRUCE								
Easy Pass Tower	5.3	169	67.7	10	440	54	WA	Mount Baker National Forest, N of Rainy Pass on Hwy 20
King Spruce	5.3	170	49.1	11	380	53	OR	Sky Lakes Wilderness, King Spruce Camp
Olympic Giant	6.7	214	47.6	8	428	41	WA	Olympic National Park, Cameron Creek Trail
North Joffre Spruce	6.9	220	41.1	11	416	41	BC	Squamish Forest District, North Joffre Creek
Steeple Rock Spruce	6.1	194	47.9	10	405	38	WA	Olympic National Park, Wells Valley

★ Diameter not measured at 1.37 m, but at lowest practical point

★★ Currently measures 69.2 m

Appendix 3

Predicting Volume from Diameter

As I hope this book makes clear, DBH is a poor predictor of tree size with large trees. Various forms of buttressing influence this measurement to such an extent that the volume of the tree does not correlate well with its lower diameters. With the few species of trees that I have enough data for, I have developed calculations for regressions that predict volume using the diameter of the tree at various heights. In general, the best single measurement to take to predict volume is much higher up on the stem. Remember that these specific regression estimators are based only on the largest trees known. For more typical trees, DBH is often a fairly good predictor. All regressions take the form of $Vol = A_0 + A_1(\text{diameter}^2)$.

Species	r^2 at DBH	best r^2	Height of best r^2	N	A_0	A_1
Giant sequoia	0.071	0.703	150'	27	−113.43	0.0072
Coast redwood	0.173	0.893	50'	33	4.16	0.0062
Douglas fir	0.424	0.928	140'	14	−14.42	0.0053
Sitka spruce	0.082	0.740	30'	12	6.48	0.0088
Ponderosa pine	0.074	0.884	100'	9	−7.21	0.0082
Grand fir	0.787	0.960	100'	7	−2.83	0.0069

Appendix 4

Big-Tree Nomination Form

COMMON NAME OF TREE _____

SCIENTIFIC NAME OF TREE _____

CIRCUMFERENCE OF TRUNK (in feet and inches) _____

TREE HEIGHT (feet) _____

AVERAGE CROWN SPREAD (feet) _____

CONDITION OF TREE _____

EXACT LOCATION OF TREE (photocopy of map/street atlas helpful) _____

_____

_____

_____

NAME AND ADDRESS OF NOMINATOR _____

_____

_____

_____

NAME AND ADDRESS OF OWNER _____

_____

_____

_____

DATE AND METHODS OF MEASUREMENT _____

_____

_____

_____

PHOTOGRAPH ENCLOSED? _____ YES _____ NO

SEND NOMINATIONS TO:

Forest Giants of the Pacific Coast
Robert Van Pelt
2400 NW 80th Street, Box 133
Seattle, WA 98117-4449

Glossary

architecture

In addition to its more familiar uses, *architecture* can refer to the structure of trees—the spatial arrangement of trunks and branches within a tree, and their size and distribution. The juvenile architecture of most conifers resembles that of a Christmas tree—a small cone. The adult architecture, however, is unique for every species, giving each its own distinctive look at maturity.

biomass

Biomass literally means "the weight of all life." This term is often broken up into parts based on whatever aspect is being studied. The term *ecosystem biomass* refers to the entire ecosystem and includes not only the trees, but also the shrubs and other plants, and often the insects, birds, mammals, and other creatures as well. *Plant biomass* refers to all of the trees, shrubs, and herbs, the total of which can be related to primary productivity or the amount of photosynthesis generated by a forest. Foresters are often interested in *stem biomass,* which relates to the amount of wood in a forest. The stem biomass is the stem volume multiplied by the density of the wood. This is probably the most common use of the term because stem biomass is relatively easy to measure when compared to trying to measure leaf, or branch, or soil insect biomass, for example. Stem biomass, when combined with age, is also related to the productivity of a site. Since much of the activity initiated by photosynthesis is converted into wood, stem biomass can be used to estimate the tree-growing potential of an area. In the massive forests of the Pacific Northwest and the Sierras, the stem biomass can be over 90 percent of the total biomass.

bole

The *bole* is simply the trunk of the tree, which is also known as the *stem.* I use *trunk* or stem when referring to all the vertical parts of a tree I measure in order to compute volumes, whereas I usually use *bole* to refer to the lower trunk, that part below the crown.

bushwhacking

Bushwhacking refers to any off-trail hiking. In the forests of the Pacific Northwest this is often a major challenge. Dense and often spiny brush, steep slopes, huge logs, unexpected cliffs, swamps, route-finding problems, enraged yellowjackets, and biting flies all combine to make bushwhacking a slow, arduous, often painful and sometimes dangerous pastime. I love it, but most people wisely keep to the trails, hence most of our champion trees are found on or near them. While I know many big-tree hunters, I know only a handful who like and are willing to go this extra mile to find the elusive giants.

character

Character describes the general appearance or gestalt of a tree. Trees that conform to the regular model of branching and are predictable in growth form have simple architecture, and, like Christmas trees, have little character. Ancient trees, particularly western red cedars, giant sequoias, or coast redwoods, are so old that individual features develop in each tree. The eccentricities that these trees develop make them different from the rest, and the quality that makes them unique is what I call character (see *gnarl*).

climax

While *climax* is a scientific buzzword probably best avoided, I use this term to imply ancient forests of Pacific silver fir, western hemlock, and western red cedar that have grown without major disturbance for thousands of years. These forests probably once contained Douglas fir, but it has been so long since they have died that no trace of even their stumps or logs is detectable. Climax implies some sort of steady state has been reached; although that is probably not the case, the word is nonetheless familiar enough to convey the idea of very old forests.

cubic feet

A measure of *cubic feet* is the main measure I use to compare trees. It is a unit of volume consisting of a cube 12 inches on each side. Foresters have used this term for a century or more in computing how much wood is in a log or tree. The term is used in many specific ways, leading to the development of additional terms such as board feet. *Board feet* more specifically refers to how much lumber can be made out of a log. Technically, there are 12 board feet in a cubic foot because one board foot is a 1-inch-thick board that is 12 inches square. In practice, 12 board feet cannot be obtained from a cubic foot of tree. Waste products such as the amount of bark, the amount of sawdust produced, the pieces left over between boards, rotten wood, or the smaller part at the top of a tree are often taken into account when computing board feet. In reality only 5 to 9 board feet are ever really obtained from a cubic foot. Because I am not interested in converting these giant trees into boards, I simply measure the volume of the trunk (including bark) that exists in the standing tree. I include the entire aboveground portion of the stem, and all major trunks (reiterations), but no branches. I do not, however, subtract for rotten cavities, burns, and similar variables. This is the simplest and most accurate measure and, for nearly all of our trees, the trunks include well over 90 percent of the total amount of wood.

DBH

Diameter at breast height or DBH is a forestry standard used to compare trees. Specifically, breast height is 4.5 feet (4'6" or 1.37 m) above the *average ground level* of the tree. On flat ground, this means the height above the ground. On sloping ground (the usual case), it is the average between the high point of ground and the low point of ground. In many ecological or forestry studies, DBH refers to 4.5 feet above the high point of ground, in order to avoid problems associated with distinguishing the tree from its roots. However, the big-tree programs have always used average ground level, which is adopted here. (For more about measuring DBH, see the Introduction of this book.)

double tree

Double trees are two separate trees that have fused together at the base. From the standpoint of making a measurement of diameter, this is essentially one tree. Double trees often start as two separate trees, but as they grow larger their stems come in contact. If they are the same species, they can merge so completely that they appear to be a single tree. Many trees can send up root sprouts that can become trees themselves. Root sprouts can form a double tree with their parents and can graft together at the fusion because they are the same genetic individual. However, even if they are from the same tree, I consider these as separate individuals and do not count them as a single tree.

epiphytes

Epiphytes are plants that grow on other plants, usually on the branches of trees. In humid climates such as the Pacific Northwest, horizontal surfaces do not remain free of plants for long. Large branches on old trees usually have at least a covering of mosses and lichens on them. Given enough time, a soil layer will develop under the epiphytes on these branches that is often sufficient to support vascular plants such as ferns, shrubs, and even small trees. Most epiphytes do not harm the tree but are simply using it as a growing site. Mistletoe is a parasitic epiphyte; its fibers, which are technically not roots, enter the tree through the bark and actively use sugars produced by the tree.

fire regime

Fire regime refers to the frequency and intensity of fires on a site. Generally speaking, the coastal forests described in this book have very infrequent fires (centuries between fires) that are very intense (nearly all trees killed in a fire). Conversely, the interior forests usually have fires at a much higher frequency (years or decades between fires) and of lower intensity (most large trees survive a fire). In most forests, the fire regime is a major factor determining which conifers will grow on a given site. The term *fire cycle* refers to the time between fire events. Some trees, such as Douglas fir or noble fir, are pioneer species, and are found only in forests up to a certain age. Because pioneer trees do not often regenerate in closed forest conditions, once the original trees have died, they are out of the forest mix until the next major disturbance. Many larger Douglas fir trees, for example, are located in forests that are between 500 and 1,000 years old. Much younger than this and they are too small to be giants. Much older than this and they are dead. Knowing the fire history of an area is helpful when big-tree hunting.

fire scar

Fire scars are basal wounds on trees caused by fire. In most cases, a small portion of the tree was killed, but the remaining circumference of the tree was not. Fire scars often become the sites of future wounding, as the tree has less protection in these areas. The result is that fire scars are often the result of multiple fires, each of which adds to the wound. Fire scars are most common in areas where there are frequent, low-intensity fires, such as those in the Sierras or Interior Montane Forests. Coastal forests are often completely consumed by fires, so most coastal trees do not have fire scars. Fire scars are very common on aged giant sequoia, sugar pine, and ponderosa pines.

floodplain

The *floodplain* of a river is formed from alluvium (silt, sand, or gravel deposited by moving water). Alluvial soils tend to be moist, because the water table is close to the surface. Due to their being deposited from floodwaters, they tend to be very rich soils, consisting of fine-grain sediments. In the Pacific Northwest, the main limitation to growth for most trees is the summer drought, so floodplains are one of the few habitats that are free from this limitation. Floodplain ecosystems are where the majority of our tallest trees may be found.

frustum

A *frustum* is a section of a conic shape that is bounded by two parallel planes. A fez-shaped hat, for example, is a frustum of a cone—in this case a cone in which the top has been cut off parallel to the bottom. Sections of logs often approach the shape of a conic or parabolic frustum. I use frustum formulas to calculate the volumes of trees from many separate diameter measurements.

fusion

A *fusion* is a place at which two separate parts of a tree, through continued close contact, graft together. Branches in the crown of a tree are where fusions are most commonly found. Most trees are capable of developing fusions, but coast redwoods are supremely adept at this. In our analysis of redwood crowns, fusions are common, and every type imaginable has been seen in this gigantic tree. The most mysterious examples of fusion are found in the gigantic fused sections on the side of El Viejo del Norte. We are still speculating about the process that causes these strange formations.

glacial terrace

Glacial terraces are flat areas formed by alpine glaciers that once occupied our major river valleys. They are similar to the alluvial terraces that rivers have formed in the 15,000 years or so since the last glaciers receded. Glacial terraces may often lack the moist and rich soils of the alluvial terraces but can nonetheless support large, and often very old, forests.

gnarl

Gnarl describes some characteristics of a tree that separate it from its associates. Deformities, irregularities, snapped tops, unusually large branches, twisted trunks, and reiterations are all features that give the tree gnarl. Gnarl goes hand-in-hand with *character,* as it is gnarl that gives the tree character.

gnarl factor

Gnarl factor describes an arbitrary scale used to compare the gnarliness of trees. For example, high gnarl-factor trees would be the Kalaloch Cedar or the Arco Giant. Low gnarl-factor trees are those that conform to the general architectural model of that species. In this book, trees with low gnarl factors would include the North Joffre Spruce or the Floodwood Giant.

lean

Nearly all trees *lean*. While the lean is often not apparent, perfectly vertical trees are quite rare, a circumstance that makes measuring heights more difficult. Most of the famous height errors reported for our western giants have probably resulted from assuming that the trees are vertical. Modern lasers allow us to accurately determine the distance from the top of the tree (the slope-corrected horizontal distance), which avoids this problem. While a pronounced lean often adds to the character of a tree, it usually shortens the tree's life.

old growth

Old growth is a structural term that has to do with the physical makeup of the forest. Words that are nearly synonymous include ancient, virgin, primeval, overmature, climax, and pristine. Individual forests may be any of these. Old-growth forests must have a wide variety of tree sizes (both in diameter and height), and must contain dead wood in the form of logs and *snags* (standing, dead trees). In our Douglas fir/western hemlock forests, for example, this usually happens after about 200 years. Some forests may require less time to become old growth, others more.

pioneer species

Pioneer species are the first species to establish after a disturbance to the forest. Their particular strengths usually include fast early-growth rates, a tolerance of high light and heat levels, and the ability to grow in nutrient-poor soils. Pioneer species will often moderate the site by their presence, making it more suitable for other species. These other species are in turn often capable of eventually replacing the pioneer species by overtopping them and shading them out. Some short-lived pioneers include willows and alders. An anomalous species is the long-lived pioneer Douglas fir, which as a pioneer species can survive for 1,000 years or more. Even though the establishment period for Douglas fir is similar to other pioneer species, its longevity allows it to persist, usually until the next disturbance.

rain forest

Rain forest is often a poorly defined term. In tropical regions it usually describes a region that receives at least 80 inches (250 cm) of annual precipitation. The original use, in P. W. Richards's *The Tropical Rain Forest,* also stipulates that no month can receive less than 4 inches (10 cm) of precipitation during the year. Exceptions are allowed, however, in certain monsoonal regions; some places in India and Africa, for example, receive 400 inches (1,000 cm) annually, yet have stretches for three months or more where the monthly average drops below 4 inches (10 cm). For this book, I have adopted the 80-inch (250 cm) definition, with no monthly limit, as the entire Pacific Coast experiences summer drought.

reiteration

A *reiteration* is a secondary trunk. Most conifers have single stems, yet nearly every species is capable of developing secondary trunks. If this occurs near the top of the tree, the tree is often referred to as having *multiple tops*. If it occurs lower down, we will often refer to a *double-trunked tree*. In any case, these are not branches but independent vertical stems. Sometimes it is impossible to tell which is the main stem and which are secondary trunks, particularly in western red cedar or coast redwood. In this book, if the tree has more than one vertical stem, each additional stem is a reiteration.

spike top

A tree with a *spike top* has a dead top sticking up above the live part of the tree. Once the top dies, the dead branches usually fall off, leaving a spike of wood sticking up above the tree. Some trees are capable of regrowing a new top after the original one has died. Cedars and redwoods are particularly adept at doing this. Cedars are generally poor at dealing with drought, and will often die back during a bad year. They are, however, very difficult to kill, and their decay-resistant wood allows these tops to persist long after they have died. Over the centuries, multiple tops can develop, many of which will be dead.

taper

Taper describes how quickly a stem goes from the maximum diameter (at the base of the tree) to the minimum diameter (the tree top). For conifers, this shape ranges from a cone (a smooth, linear taper), to a paraboloid (a gradually curving taper, with highest curvature near the top of the tree). The volume of a cone is one-third that of a cylinder with a given base diameter, while a paraboloid has half the volume of a cylinder. Of course the base of the tree does not conform to any of these formulas, since its sides generally tend to be concave, and moreover it is frequently very irregularly shaped, as influenced by its roots. Therefore a tree's base section is measured separately and is generally not considered when discussing taper. Sections of the main trunk can approach a cylinder in shape—with no taper, or even with a slight negative taper, as when a diameter slightly increases as one moves up the stem.

volume

Volume is the amount of wood in the stem of a tree. To measure this, I use *cubic feet*. For many of the large conifers in this book, the stem is usually a single, erect trunk. On many of the trees, however, there is more than one erect trunk. Vertical stems are fairly straightforward to measure with lasers. Any object that is not vertical is much more difficult to measure, because this requires mapping out, in three dimensions, the branch or object of interest. For this reason (among many others) I do not include branches in the volume calculations. For most trees the branches do not add much volume, although including branch volume for the giant sequoias could add several thousand cubic feet of wood. In this case, branch volumes are left off largely due to the difficulty involved in accurate measurements, and to be consistent throughout the book. My friends in eastern North America are currently struggling with the task of measuring branch volume. To them I say good luck. ▲

Sources of Information

Books

Arno, S. F., and J. Gyer. 1973. *Discovering Sierra Trees.* Yosemite National Park, Calif.: Yosemite Association, 1973.

Arno, S. F., and R. P. Hammerly. *Northwest Trees.* Seattle, Wash.: The Mountaineers, 1977.

Carder, A. C. *Forest Giants of the World, Past and Present.* Markham, Ontario: Fitzhenry & Whiteside, 1995.

Dorst, A., and C. Young. *Clayoquot: On the Wild Side.* Vancouver, B.C.: Western Canada Wilderness Committee, 1990.

Flint, W. D. *To Find the Biggest Tree.* Three Rivers, Calif.: Sequoia Natural History Association, 1987.

Franklin, J. F., and C. T. Dyrness. *Natural Vegetation of Oregon and Washington.* Portland, Ore.: Forest Service, U.S. Dept. of Agriculture, Pacific Northwest Forest and Range Experiment Station, 1973.

Franklin, J. F., and R. H. Waring. Distinctive features of the northwestern coniferous forest: development, structure, and function. In *Forests: Fresh Perspectives from Ecosystem Analysis,* 40th Biology Colloquium, R. H. Waring, ed., pp. 59–86. Corvallis, Ore.: Oregon State University Press, 1980.

Kirk, R., and J. F. Franklin. *The Olympic Rain Forest: An Ecological Web.* Seattle, Wash.: University of Washington Press, 1992.

Norse, E. A. *Ancient Forests of the Pacific Northwest.* Washington, D.C.: Island Press and the Wilderness Society, 1990.

Peattie, D. C. *A Natural History of Western Trees.* Boston, MA: Houghton Mifflin, 1950.

Richards, P. W. *The Tropical Rain Forest: An Ecological Study.* Cambridge, England: Cambridge University Press, 1952.

Stoltmann, R. *Hiking Guide to the Big Trees of Southwestern British Columbia,* 2nd ed. Vancouver, B.C.: Western Canada Wilderness Committee, 1991.

———. *Guide to the Record Trees of British Columbia.* Vancouver, B.C.: Western Canada Wilderness Committee and Lynn Canyon Ecology Center, 1992.

———. *Hiking the Ancient Forests of British Columbia and Washington.* Vancouver, B.C.: Lone Pine, 1996.

Van Pelt, R. *Champion Trees of Washington State.* Seattle, Wash.: University of Washington Press, 1996.

Willard, D. *Giant Sequoia Groves of the Sierra Nevada: A Reference Guide.* Berkeley, Calif.: Dwight Willard, 1995.

Wood, R. L. *Olympic Mountains Trail Guide.* Seattle, Wash.: The Mountaineers, 1991.

Wood, W. *A Walking Guide to Oregon's Ancient Forests.* Portland, Ore.: Oregon Natural Resources Council; Seattle, WA: The Mountaineers, 1991.

Websites

American Forests
http://www.americanforests.org

Big Trees of British Columbia
http://www.elp.gov.bc.ca/rib/wis/cdc/trees.htm

California Register of Big Trees
A listing of the largest native and introduced trees.
http://urbanfor.cagr.calpoly.edu/data/bigtrees/index.html

Gymnosperm Database
Interesting facts about the trees featured in this book.
http://www.conifers.org

Idaho's Champion Big Trees
http://www.ets.uidaho.edu/extforest/bigtree.htm

National Register of Big Trees
http://www.davey.com/cgi-bin/texis/vortex/bigtrees

Oregon Register of Big Trees
http://www.odf.state.or.us/bigtrees/btreg.htm

Index

Abies amabilis. See Pacific silver fir
Abies concolor. See California white fir
Abies grandis. See grand fir
Abies lowiana. See California white fir
Abies magnifica. See California red fir
Abies magnifica var. *shastensis. See* Shasta red fir
Abies procera. See noble fir
Admiral Broeren, 87–88, 182, 188
Adventure, 17, 27, 180, 186
AFA (American Forestry Association). *See* American Forests
AF points, xvi–xvii; problems with, 4, 24, 60, 64, 150
Agathis australis. See kauri
age. *See* tree age
Alaska cedar. *See* yellow cedar
Alder Creek Grove, 11
Alex Hole Cedar, 81
amabilis fir. *See* Pacific silver fir
American Forestry Association. *See* American Forests
American Forests (association), ix, 111, 116
American Forests (periodical), xiii, 74, 111, 114, 136, 150, 162, 176
American River, 155
architecture, of trees, 194
Arco Giant, 17, 29, 180, 187

Badger Pass Tree, 137, 140, 184, 190
Bald Hills Champion, 157, 160, 184, 191
Barnes Creek Survivor, 157, 161, 185, 191
Bear Creek Twin, 84, 115, 117–19, 183, 189
Beese, Bill, 88–89, 92
Big Bear Cedar, 81, 84, 182, 188
Big Creek Cedar, 87, 90–91, 182, 189
Big Flat Tree, 59, 70, 182, 188
Big Mother Cedar, 31, 38, 171, 181, 187
Big Red, 131, 134, 184, 190
big tree. *See* giant sequoia
biomass, 194
board feet, 194
Bogachiel Valley, 56, 164, 169
boles, 194
Boole, 3, 12, 180, 186
branch fusions, 20–21, 25
Brightman, Ron, 147
British Columbia, trees in, 34, 38–39, 46–47, 62–63, 68, 88–89, 92–93, 128, 158–59, 168, 171, 177
Brummitt Fir, xvi, 45

Brush Meadow Giant, 107, 113, 183, 189
Bull Creek Giant, 17, 28, 180, 187
Burnt Corral Larch, 149, 152, 184, 190
bushwhacking, 194

Cabin Lake Tree, x, 165, 168, 185, 191
Calaveras Big Trees State Park, 2, 72, 74, 77
Calaveras Colossus, 73, 77, 182, 188
California, trees in, 2–29, 52, 72–79, 82, 84, 106–13, 116–19, 121, 130–41, 160
California red fir, 130–35, 184, 190
California white fir, 136–41, 184, 190
Callahan, Frank, 71, 81, 83, 152, 175
Calocedrus decurrens. See incense cedar
Canadian Coast Mountains, trees in, 93, 128, 168, 177
canoe cedar. *See* western red cedar
Cape Meares Giant, 59, 71, 182, 188
Carder, Al, 16, 46
Carmannah-Walbran Provincial Park, 34, 68
Cascade Mountains, xxii; trees in, 53, 85, 96–99, 120, 125, 144–45, 155, 158–59, 174–75
cedar. *See* incense cedar; Port Orford cedar; western red cedar; yellow cedar
Cedar Flats Sentinel, 43, 53, 181, 187
Chamaecyparis lawsoniana. See Port Orford cedar
Chamaecyparis nootkatensis. See yellow cedar
character, of trees, 194
Cheewhat Lake Cedar, 30, 34, 181, 187
Chilliwack Giant, 157–59, 184, 191
Clatsop Fir, 44–45
Clayoquot Sound, 31, 38–39, 71
climate, xx–xxiii
climax, of forests, 194
climbing. *See* tree climbing
coast redwood, xxi, 16–29, 160, 180, 186–87, 192
Converse Basin Grove, 3, 12
Coquille Falls Tree, 101, 103, 183, 189
Coquille Valley, 102–5
Cougar Flat Sentinel, 59, 69, 182, 188
Cronartium ribicola. See white pine blister rust
crown spread, xvi, xviii
cubic feet, in tree measurement, 194

Cypress Park Cedar, 87, 93, 182, 189
Cypress Provincial Park, x, 93, 168

Day of Discovery, 18, 22, 25, 52
DBH (diameter at breast height), xiii–xv, 194; problems with: 24, 48
Del Norte Titan, 16–19, 180, 186
Dendroctonus ponderosae. See mountain pine beetle
Deschutes River, 120
Devil's Canyon Colossus, 81–82, 182, 188
diameter of trees. *See* DBH; tree measuring
Dorst, Adrian, 38, 171
double trees, 194
Douglas fir, 36, 42–57, 170, 181, 187, 192
Drawson, Maynard, 64–65
Duckabush Champion, 157, 162, 185, 191
Dutton, Morgan, 75, 79, 121
Dyerville Giant, 16

Earle, Chris, 47, 51, 63, 103–4
eastern white pine, 142
Easy Pass Tower, 173–74, 185, 191
Elk Creek Champion, 101–2, 183, 189
Elkhorn Mountains, 154
El Viejo del Norte, 17, 25, 180, 186
Enchanted Valley Hemlock, 90, 123–24, 183, 190
Engelmann spruce, 158, 172–79, 185, 191
epiphytes, 195
Erben, Peter, 51, 54–55
Eureka Valley Giant, 107–9, 183, 189

Finnegan Fir, 44–45
fire regimes and cycles, 195
fire scars, 195
Fish Camp Pine, 115, 121, 183, 189
Fish Lake Pine, 143–46, 184, 190
Flint, Wendell, xvii–xix, 2, 6, 11, 13–14
floodplains, 195
Floodwood Giant, 143, 147, 184, 190
forests, Pacific Coast, xx–xxiii; zone map, xx
forest zones, xx
Franklin, 3, 13, 180, 186
Franklin, Jerry, 45, 97, 103
frustum, used in measurement, 195
fusion, within trees, 195

Gandalf, 123, 126, 129, 184, 190
Gatton Goliath, 43, 55, 181, 187

General Buxton, 87–88, 92, 182, 189
General Grant, 2–3, 8, 180, 186
General Sherman, xiii, 2–5, 180, 186
Genesis, 3, 14, 180, 186
giant arborvitae. *See* western red cedar
Giant Forest, 3; trees in, 4–7, 9–10, 13
giant sequoia, 2–15, 180, 186, 192
glacial terraces, 195
Glacier Peak Wilderness, 125
Glacier Point Road, 112, 140
gnarl, 195
Goat Marsh, 97, 99
Goat Marsh Giant, 95–97, 99, 183, 189
Gods Valley Spruce, 66
Goodman Creek Tree, 165–67, 185, 191
grand fir, ix, 156–63, 184–85, 191–92
Gronki, Al, 82, 84, 118
Grant Grove, 3, 8
Grizzly Meadow Monarch, 115–17, 183, 189
Grove of Titans, 17–18, 22, 25

Hades Creek Fir, 165, 169, 185, 191
Hartman's Bar Tree, 115, 117–18, 183, 189
height. *See* tree height
Hoh Valley, 45, 67, 69–70
Howland Hill Giant, 17, 23, 180, 186
Humboldt Redwoods State Park, xxi–xxii, 25
Humboldt State University, 18, 160
Huntington Lake Giant, 107, 111–12, 183, 189

Icicle Creek Tree, 173
Idaho, trees in, 146–47
Idaho Giant, 143–44, 146, 184, 190
Iluvatar, 16–17, 20–21, 180, 186
incense cedar, 80–85, 182, 188
Indian Pass Tree, 43, 56, 181, 187
Inland Empire, xxii–xxiii, 142–43, 146–48, 150–54
Ipsut Creek Colossus, 95, 98, 183, 189
Ishi Giant, 3, 15, 180, 186

Jacobson, Arthur Lee, 64, 90–91, 124–25, 147, 161, 175–76
Jedediah Smith Redwoods State Park, xxi–xxii, 18, 22–23, 52
Jeffrey pine, 106–13, 183, 189
Joyce Kilmer Tree, 157, 163, 185, 191

Kalaloch Cedar, xix, 31–32, 37, 181, 187
kauri, xvii, xxiv, 32
Kelman, Ralf, 128, 168
Kenworthy, Bart, 40
Kings Canyon National Park, 2, 3, 8
King Spruce, 173, 175, 185, 191
Klamath Mountains, xxiii, 80, 82–84, 118
Klootchy Creek Giant, 64–65, 182, 188
Knight, Rand, 79, 108–9, 121, 132, 151, 168

Lake Crescent, ix, 161–63
La Pine Giant, xiii, 114–15, 117, 120, 183, 189
Larix occidentalis. See western larch
lasers, x, xv, xvii–xix
lean, and measurement, 196
Leaning Tower, 131–33, 184, 190
Limber Jim Larch, 149, 154, 184, 190
Lincoln, 3, 10, 180, 186
Lonesome Meadow Monarch, 81, 85, 182, 188
Lost Bear Survivor, 107, 112, 140, 183, 189
Lost Monarch, 17, 22, 180, 186
Lynn Headwaters Regional Park, 128

Macy, Preston, 44, 67, 122, 124
Mammoth of Milk Creek, 123, 125, 183, 190
maps, explanation of, xix
Marble Mountains Wilderness, xxiii, 82
Mattos, Brian, 79, 110, 112
Mauksa, 43, 57, 181, 187
Maxine's Tree, 59, 68, 182, 188
McGinnis Meadow Giant, 149, 153, 184, 190
measuring. *See* tree measuring
Merced Lake Giant, 137–38, 140, 184, 190
Mineral Tree, 44–45
Montana, trees in, 150–51, 153
Montezuma cypress, 12, 20
Mosquito Fir, 165, 171, 185, 191
mountain hemlock, xxiv, 124
Mountain Home Grove, 2, 14
mountain pine beetle, 142, 146
Mount Rainier National Park, 98
Mount St. Helens National Volcanic Monument, 53, 94, 97, 99
Muc, Shaun, 168
Muir, John, xxiii, 72

National Geographic, 16, 29, 38
Neighbor, 101, 105, 183, 189
New Zealand, xvii, xxiv, 32
Niawiakum Giant, 31, 40, 181, 187
noble fir, 94–99, 182–83, 189
Nolan Creek Cedar, 30, 32, 35, 37, 166, 181, 187
nominating big trees, 193
Nootka cypress. *See* yellow cedar
North Cascades Highway, 174
North Joffre Spruce, 173, 177, 185, 191
Norvan's Castle, x, 123, 128, 184, 190
nurse logs, 59, 64

O'Brian, Brian, 66, 71, 85
Octopus Tree, 71
Ol' Jed, 43, 52, 181, 187
old-growth forests, 196
Olympic Giant, 173, 176, 185, 191
Olympic National Forest, trees in, 36, 50–51, 54–55, 57
Olympic National Park, 37, 44–45; trees in, 32–33, 37, 48–49, 56, 60–61, 67, 69–70, 90, 124, 126, 129, 161–63, 169–70, 176, 178
Olympic Peninsula, xxi–xxii, 31, 35, 166
One-Armed Bandit, 73, 76, 78, 182, 188
Oregon, trees in, 65–66, 71, 83, 85, 100–105, 120, 144–45, 152, 154, 175
Oregon Coast Range, xxi, 65–66, 71

Pacific Rim National Park, 34
Pacific silver fir, x, 164–71, 185, 191
Payette Lake Tree, 172–73, 176
pencil cedar. *See* incense cedar
Phytophthora lateralis, 100–104
Picea engelmannii. See Engelmann spruce
Picea sitchensis. See Sitka spruce
Pickering Pine, 73–74, 76, 78, 182, 188
Pinus jeffreyi. See Jeffrey pine
Pinus lambertiana. See sugar pine
Pinus monticola. See western white pine
Pinus ponderosa. See ponderosa pine
Pinus strobus. See eastern white pine
pioneer species, 196
Pleasant Valley Larch, 149, 155, 184, 190
Plumas National Forest, 117
ponderosa pine, 114–21, 183, 189, 192

Porcupine Flats Tree, 131, 135, 184, 190
Port Orford cedar, 100–105, 183, 189
Prairie Creek Redwoods State Park, xxi–xxii, 17, 20, 24, 26–27, 29, 58
President (tree), 3–4, 9, 180, 186
Preston Macy Tree, 59, 67–68, 182, 188
Pseudotsuga menziesii. See Douglas fir

Quamal, 43, 54, 181, 187
Queets Fir, xiii, 42, 44–49, 61, 181, 187
Queets Spruce, 46, 58–61, 181, 188
Queets Valley, 48–49, 60–61, 170
Quinault Lake, 32–33, 36, 50–51, 54–55, 57, 64, 90–91
Quinault Lake Cedar, xiii, 30, 32–34, 181, 187
Quinault Lake Spruce, 58–60, 64–65, 182, 188

rain forests, xxi, 196
Rector Ridge Spruce, 59, 66, 182, 188
Red Buttes Wilderness, 83
Red Creek Tree, 42, 45–48, 61–62, 181, 187
redwood. *See* coast redwood
Redwood National Park, 17, 29
reiterations (secondary trunks), 196; examples of, 5–6, 18, 20–22, 25, 27, 29, 30–41, 50, 60, 62–63, 69, 71, 82, 98, 110, 128–29, 133, 140
Research Natural Areas, 53, 97, 99, 103–5
Rex, 43, 51, 181, 187
Riker!, 95, 99, 183, 189
Roosevelt, Franklin Delano, 163

sacrificial trees: defined, 65; examples of, 4–5, 8, 35, 37, 64–65, 67, 120
San Juan Spruce, 58, 62–63, 181, 188
Save-the-Redwoods League, 16, 25
Seal Slough Cedar, 31, 41, 181, 187
Seeley Lake Giant, 149–52, 184, 190
Sequoiadendron giganteum. See giant sequoia
Sequoia National Park, 2; trees in, 4–7, 9–10, 13
Sequoia sempervirens. See coast redwood
Sergeant RandAlly, 87–89, 182, 188
Seven Sisters, 131–33, 184, 190
Shasta red fir, 94, 130

Shaw, Dave, 50
Sierra National Forest, 111, 113, 116, 121
Sierra Nevada, xxiii; trees in, 2–15, 72–79, 106–13, 116–17, 121, 130–41
Sierra redwood. *See* giant sequoia
Sierras. *See* Sierra Nevada
Sillett, Steve, 6–7, 15, 17–18, 20, 22, 25, 50, 52–53, 56, 129, 140, 169–70
Sinuosity, 137, 141, 184, 190
Sir Issac Newton, 17, 24, 180, 186
Siskiyou Mountains, xxiii, 80, 83–84, 100–105, 118–19
Sitka spruce, 58–71, 158, 181–82, 188, 192
Sky Lakes Wilderness, 175
Smoky Jack, 107, 110, 183, 189
South Fork Hoh Tree, 45
specimen trees, 134
spike tops, of trees, 196
Stagg, 3, 11, 180, 186
Steeple Rock Spruce, 173, 178–79, 185, 191
Stoltmann Cedar, 31, 39, 181, 187
Stoltmann, Randy, ix–x, 39, 56, 61, 68–69, 93, 125, 128, 158, 168, 170, 177
Stratosphere Giant, 17
sugar pine, 72–79, 182, 188
Survivor, 101, 104, 183, 189

Tannen Lakes Titan, 81, 83, 182, 188
taper, and measurement, 196
Taxodium mucronatum. See Montezuma Cypress
Taylor, Michael, 17–18, 23, 25–27, 29, 52
Terex Titan, 17, 26, 180, 186
Thornburgh, Dale, 160
Thuja plicata. See western red cedar
Tichipawa, 42, 45, 50, 181, 187
tideland spruce. *See* Sitka spruce
Tioga Pass Road, 110, 132–35, 139
Tioga Road Fir, 137, 139, 184, 190
tree age, xxi–xxii, 86, 98
tree climbing, 6–7, 11, 18, 20, 22
tree height, measuring, xiv–xvi
tree hunting, x, 15, 18, 34, 38, 50–52, 56, 66, 72, 77, 79, 103, 132, 140, 170, 175
tree measuring, xiii–xix, 9, 12, 18–19, 32, 39, 44–45, 48, 64, 192, 194–97
Trinity Alps Wilderness, xxiii, 118–19
Tschletchy Creek Fir, 165, 170, 185, 191

Tsuga dumosa, 122
Tsuga heterophylla. See western hemlock
Tsuga mertensiana. See mountain hemlock

Unmpqua National Forest, 85

Vancouver Island, xxi–xxii, 68; trees on, 34, 38–39, 46–47, 62–63, 68, 88–89, 92, 171
volume. *See* wood volume

Wallowa-Whitman National Forest, 152, 154
Washington (state), trees in, 32–33, 35–37, 40–41, 48–51, 53–57, 60–61, 64, 67, 69–70, 90–91, 94–99, 124–27, 129, 155, 161–63, 166–67, 169–70, 174, 176, 178–79
Washington (tree), 2–3, 6–7, 180, 186
western hemlock, x, 122–29, 183–84, 190
western larch, 148–55, 184, 190
western red cedar, 30–41, 181, 187
western white pine, 142, 147, 184, 190
Whelan Tree, 72–76, 182, 188
white pine blister rust, 142, 146
Willaby Creek Tree, 31, 36, 181, 187
Willapa Hills, xxi, 40–41
Willard, Dwight, 15
Wolf Valley Tree, 148–49, 153
Wood, Bob, 45, 56, 60, 69, 90, 124, 126
wood volume, xvii–xix, 196. *See also* tree measuring
Wynoochee Giant, 123, 126–27, 183, 190
Wynoochee Valley, 126, 129

yellow cedar, 86–93, 182, 188–89
Yellowjacket Creek Champion, 95–96, 182, 189
Yosemite Giant, 73, 79, 182, 188
Yosemite National Park, 2, 72, 116; trees in, 79, 110, 112, 130–41